BOUND BY HONOR

Fostering a Great Relationship With Your Teen

FOCUS ON THE FAMILY®

BOUND BY HONOR

Fostering a Great Relationship With Your Teen

GARY & DR. GREG SMALLEY

TYNDALE

Tyndale House Publishers, Wheaton, Illinois

BOUND BY HONOR

Library of Congress Cataloging-in-Publication Data
Smalley, Gary.
    Bound by honor / Gary Smalley and Greg Smalley.
        p.   cm.
    At head of title: A Focus on the Family book.
    Includes bibliographical references.
    ISBN 1-56179-875-4
    1. Parent and teenager. 2. Honor. 3. Anger. I. Smalley, Greg. II. Focus on the
Family (Organization) III. Title.
HQ799.15.S63 1998   98-6299
649'.125—DC21   CIP

A Focus on the Family book published by
Tyndale House Publishers, Wheaton, Illinois.

People's names and certain details of the case studies in this book have been changed to
protect the privacy of the individuals involved. However, the facts of what happened and the
underlying principles have been conveyed as accurately as possible.

Editor: Larry K. Weeden
Front cover design: Brad Lind
Cover photos: Jim Lersch

Printed in the United States of America

00 01 02/10 9 8 7 6 5 4 3 2

To our other children, Kari and Michael
During their teen years, they were raised in a "fishbowl," in full view
of thousands, while developing their skills for adulthood. They're
both happily married now and parents themselves.

To their mother, my beloved Norma
She paid continual attention to all her children's needs and gave them
wise guidance through their teen years. Simply put, she's the best.

Gary Smalley

To my wife, Erin
Many years ago, you saw my potential and believed in me.
Through your love, support, and encouragement, you have helped
me to become a more godly man, husband, and father.
Thank you for your example, sacrifice, and friendship.

To my girls, Taylor and Madalyn
You have shown me that being a father is the greatest privilege in life.
Thank you for teaching me humility and the value of play.

To my parents, Gary and Norma
Thank you for giving me a wonderful foundation
characterized by honor, believing in my dreams,
admitting your mistakes, and creating lasting memories.

To my siblings, Kari and Michael
Thank you for our lifelong friendship.

Greg Smalley

Contents

Acknowledgments

I (Greg) would like to express deep gratitude to all the mentors who have influenced and molded my life: Terry Brown; Gary Oliver; Jim Brawner; Jim Shaughnessy; John Trent; John Michael; Bill Root; Jim Justus; Kris Cooper; Michael Brashears; Jim Stewart; Rod Cooper; Chris Grace; Charles Dickens; Keith Edwards; Marcia Stroup; Dan Trathen; Joan Winfrey; Coaches Dean, Neillie, and Jamison; Paul and Nicole Johnson; and the staff at Kanakuk Kamp.

To our editors, Larry Weeden and Al Janssen, and the wonderful staff at Focus on the Family and Tyndale House Publishers, thank you for all your hard work.

A special thank you to all the individuals who helped review and critique the manuscript: Joy and Johnny Walters; Mike and Donna Leidecker; Todd and Angela Ellett; Susan and Randy Warner; Allen and Janet Ritchie; Edd and Karen Akers; Charlie and Mary Engram; Susan and Dave Cornett; Jim and Jennifer Freeman; Peg Herschend and Todd Welte; Jack and Sherry Herschend; Rick and Trish Tallon; Jay and Kay Scribner; Jim and Suzette Brawner; Terry and Jana Brown; Steve and Lisa Fisher; Charles and Rebecca Dickens; Patrick and Rosalie Murphy; Rich and Penny D'Ortenzio; Janet and Bob Yarbrough; and Chris and Alisa Grace.

MAKING THE TEEN YEARS YOUR BEST YEARS

Any adult who behaved the way that teenagers behave would be judged as certifiably insane.
Ana Freud, daughter of Sigmund Freud

One time when Greg was a teenager and our family was driving from Arizona to Missouri, we saw a clear example of why it's so dangerous to allow anger to take root in a home. But we also saw how honor can erase anger in a matter of minutes.

Near the New Mexico state line, Greg and I (Gary) started arguing about an unresolved conflict. Norma, my wife, was in the back of the camper with our other two kids, so she couldn't hear us. Greg had taken some money from Norma's purse to buy a video game. She had given him permission to take $20, but he'd taken $30. What he called an "advance" on his allowance, I was calling stealing. We had argued about the details but had gotten nowhere. I didn't like the fact that Greg wanted to keep this a secret. But he was upset because he'd returned the extra money and didn't feel his mother needed to know about it. He was also afraid she'd get angry.

The other problem was that I'd been pretty harsh with my tongue. I'd blown up during the original discussion at home and called Greg a liar and a thief. I could tell his feelings were hurt, but I had no idea that anger had infiltrated his heart. At least I didn't know until we approached New Mexico. Then, like a volcano, his anger erupted in my face.

As Greg and I argued once again about telling Mom, the discussion quickly escalated to the point that I had to pull the camper off to the side of the road. Suddenly, Greg jumped out of the vehicle, hopped a fence, and disappeared over a hill. As he ran, I could hear him screaming, "I want out of this family!" Then he was gone.

Teenagers! I thought as I rolled my eyes. Watching all the cars and trucks that I'd passed earlier roar by, I wondered how long this was going to take. "This will certainly put us behind schedule!" I yelled to no one in particular.

Since this was my first runaway situation, I didn't know what to do. Should I wait until he came back? Should I run after him? It was so hot outside that I was leaning toward staying in the air-conditioned camper. However, the rest of the family made my decision when they collectively screamed, "Go get him!"

Now I was really frustrated. Greg was pretty fast. Who knew how far he'd run by this time?

As I approached the fence Greg had jumped over, I noticed a sign that read: NO TRESPASSING! DANGER!

Danger? I thought. *What could possibly be dangerous out here in the middle of nowhere?* So I climbed over the fence and walked to the top of the hill behind which Greg had disappeared. Then I quickly realized what made the sign necessary. Danger was everywhere.

The scene was like something out of the movie *Dances with Wolves.* An entire herd of huge buffalo was grazing down below. The thought passed through my mind that instead of driving to this area in our camper, we should have traveled in a covered wagon. I had been instantly transported back into the Old West.

As I scanned the area for Greg, I discovered that he had descended the far side of the hill and walked about 20 yards into the herd, then suddenly stopped. I smiled as I thought about how his stubbornness had carried him far into the herd but not all the way through. His strong will had given way to fear. Greg now stood face to face with a large male buffalo. As they stared at each other, the buffalo started snorting and stamping his foot, inching toward Greg. I knew very little about buffalo, but that didn't look good.

Greg was searching for an escape route when his eyes found me. His expression turned to one of great relief. We still had no idea how to solve his dilemma, however. I slowly walked down to where he was standing, thinking the buffalo might charge at any moment. Instead, though, he simply snorted a few more times and then walked away. Thankfully, my presence must have confused the great beast.

We later found out just how dangerous buffalo can be. We heard that if they're frightened, they can run through a wagon load of people in seconds, scattering their remains. Hearing this disturbing news caused the hair on our arms to stand straight up!

When we were out of harm's way, Greg and I stood on the other side of the fence and resolved our conflict. I asked him to explain why he'd run.

"It really hurt when you called me a liar and a thief," Greg choked out, not looking at me. "I know what I did was wrong, but it really killed me to hear you say those things. Having them brought up again today only made it worse. I just wanted to forget the whole thing happened."

Hearing his pain, I realized my sarcasm had deeply hurt my son. I wanted to say I had just been kidding, but he needed to hear me say I was sorry. So I asked him to forgive me for attacking him as a person. Then I put my arms around him and held him for a few seconds. When I could tell he'd forgiven me, I said, "Watch out—the buffalo is right behind us!" He jumped about three feet into the air, and then we laughed about our adventure.

Although Greg had been in the wrong for taking the money, I had been equally wrong for flippantly calling him names. The anger that had developed in his heart had started to cause serious damage. But once I asked him to forgive me, the bitterness melted in his heart, and he was able to seek forgiveness as well. When we got back to the camper, Greg and Norma had a long talk. Our other two children, Kari and Michael, asked what had happened, and I simply said, "It's a long story. Greg will tell you later. In the meantime, let's just say that it will be a while before Greg wants to visit the buffalo exhibit at the zoo!"

As Norma and I were reminded through that experience with Greg, it's so important to *increase honor* and *decrease anger* in the hearts of our teenagers. (Seeking forgiveness for the wrong we've done is one of the most honoring things we can do for one another.) In fact, doing those two things is the key to making our kids' teen years our best parenting years.

Increasing Honor and Decreasing Anger

We (Gary and Greg) feel so strongly about this subject that we decided years ago to write this book together. It wasn't long ago, at the time we're writing this, that I (Greg) was a teenager myself, so many of the changes and challenges are still fresh in my mind. And in the hope of helping you to be a better parent to your own teen, I'm willing to discuss in these pages some of my problems and victories during those turbulent years.

In addition to recounting our family's experiences, to help provide the best information possible, we're going to offer what we've learned from surveying more than 5,000 former teenagers at our monthly seminar. We asked those adults to tell us two primary things:

1. *What were the best things your parents did for you during your adolescence?*

2. *What do you wish your parents had done differently?*

We have been stunned by the answers we got to these two questions, and we'll sprinkle the results throughout the book.

For now, we'll tell you that both our experience and our research indicate that increasing honor and decreasing anger in the home are *the two main principles* in raising healthy teenagers. Talk about simplifying the struggles of adolescence! We're convinced that if these two things are dealt with daily, parents and their teens will find a much more satisfying life together, and teens will be much more open to their parents' advice. Also, a lot of the pain and heartache often associated with the teen years will be avoided.

In fact, increasing honor and decreasing anger make up the foundation of all healthy homes and relationships. Honor fortifies love; anger kills it—if left unresolved for weeks, months, or even years, anger becomes an acid that eats away love and maturity in teens as well as adults.[1] That's why everything we discuss throughout this book will run through these two themes. And that's why we want parents, teachers, coaches, doctors, youth ministers—anyone touching the lives of teenagers—to know about the great importance of honor and anger.

The Times Are Changing!

Adolescence. The word alone sends chills up the backs of many parents. It may seem like just yesterday that you and your teenager had a great relationship, one that didn't seem so confusing or frustrating. We're not suggesting that everything will become terrible as your son or daughter moves into adolescence. Every child is unique and will respond to the teenage years differently. What we can guarantee, however, is that things *will* change.

One reason adolescence can be so difficult for parents is that for the past 12 years you have been accustomed to a certain type of relationship with your son or daughter. Then, sometimes even overnight, so many things can change. Unfortunately, we often resist change by either ignoring what's taking place or trying to continue using the same old habits. But failure to adapt to change usually leads to disaster, as the following story illustrates.

For many years, up into the late 1960s, Switzerland dominated the world of watchmaking. Most people who wanted a high-quality watch bought a Swiss watch. Over the next decade, however, the Swiss dominance eroded steadily. By the early 1980s, Switzerland's market share had collapsed to less than 10 percent. In an instant (historically speaking), it was no longer the market leader.

What caused this huge turnaround? The Swiss ran into a change in the way watches were made. In the past, all watches had used mechanical components like gears, bearings, and mainsprings. But then the industry turned to electronics. Suddenly, high-quality, dependable, and less-expensive watches could be bought from the Japanese and others. In less than 10 years, the "secure" Swiss watchmaking future was greatly diminished.

Both our experience and our research indicate that increasing honor and decreasing anger in the home are the two main principles in raising healthy teenagers.

The irony was that the situation could have been avoided if only the Swiss had realized the kind of change they were facing. The Swiss themselves had invented the electronic quartz movement. Yet when their researchers presented this revolutionary technology to the Swiss manufacturers, it was rejected. In no way could this battery-powered, electronic device be the watch of the future, the watchmakers concluded. So they allowed their researchers to showcase this "inferior" invention at the World Watch Congress without a patent. A Japanese company took one look, and the rest, as they say, is history.[2]

For the past 12 years, you have become a "market leader" in the field of parenting. We hope you've become an expert at understanding the needs and desires of your child. But the times are changing as your child enters adolescence! Your teenager will face much transition, which we'll discuss throughout the book. As a parent, you need to keep from making the same mistake the Swiss made when faced with major changes. Instead of rejecting this new phase and trying to parent in the same manner you always have, you'll want to learn new ways to relate to your teen.

We're not suggesting you disregard what has worked in the past. But you can learn new methods that can meet the specific needs of your teenager. You may already be doing many of the things we'll advise. If so, great— keep doing those things. You might also have found methods that work that we will not discuss. That's great, too. We know there are countless ways to parent a teen effectively. What we'll offer are those things that worked for our family. Our main desire is to help you understand the changing needs of the adolescent and develop appropriate parenting skills.

Not only is this a time when your children are changing, but it's also a time when you're changing. This can be a traumatic period for everyone in the family. Below are some of these "quartzlike" changes that can affect both parents and teens during adolescence:

Parents:

- Marital dissatisfaction is greater when the kids are teens than when the kids are infants or adults.

- Many parents go through an identity or midlife crisis. Homemakers, after having spent years raising their families, may want something different, like a job or more education. Also, some fathers realize their careers have not brought happiness. They might want a career change, education, hobbies, cars, or a girlfriend.

- Economic burdens increase.

- Many parents at this stage feel that their physical attractiveness is in decline.

- Caring for aging parents becomes a major responsibility.

Teenagers:

- Friends become very important.

- Dating relationships develop.

- Acne may cover their faces.

- They get jobs.

- Rebellion is a possibility.

- They're more concerned about what they wear.

- They develop a taste for loud music.

- They want more independence.

- Peer pressure is a major influence.

- Premarital sex is a temptation.

- Drug or alcohol use is another temptation.

- They're becoming separate individuals.

- They tend to have an optimistic outlook on the future, seeing the time available to them as unlimited.

- They're reaching or have reached their peak of physical attractiveness.

- Identity crises are common.

As you can see, these can be dramatic changes for both adolescents and parents. Some of the changes parents experience, such as a decline in physical looks, are going in the opposite direction for teens, who are as lean as they'll ever be as adults. This is just one of the many reasons why conflict with parents increases when children first hit adolescence.[3] Also, parents' marital happiness hits its lowest level during the years when they have teen children.[4]

To deal with these changes, one of the best things parents can do is to work at keeping their marriage strong. The stress and tension of raising a teen can intensify any marital problems. When the couple feel unhappy in their relationship, the child is usually affected as well. Parents in conflict tend to express less concern and warmth toward their teenager and utilize stricter-than-usual discipline, creating increased emotional hardship for the child.[5]

When parents enjoy each other and are happy with their relationship, they're more likely to spend pleasurable time with their teenagers and to emphasize family teamwork.

Even when there's little conflict between parents, the overwhelming demands of providing such things as transportation and money, and of monitoring a teen's activities, can cause parents to neglect the marital relationship. This is why couples are more likely than usual to divorce when they have teenage children. But when parents enjoy each other and are happy with their relationship, they're more likely to spend pleasurable time with their teenagers and to emphasize family teamwork.[6]

It's also imperative for parents of teens to strengthen their personal relationship with God. This seems obvious, but the fact is that the same pressures that threaten the marital relationship tend to deprive parents of time with God as well. Regular time spent cultivating closeness with Him needs to be made and kept a high priority.

Your relationships with God and your spouse should form the foundation upon which you construct your parenting. In fact, we would go so far as to say that the building blocks we present in this book will not be effective if that foundation is not solid. Therefore, commit yourself to strengthening these two areas before attempting to enhance your adolescent-parenting skills.

Making the Teen Years
Your Best Parenting Years

As we discuss the things vital to raising a teenager, we will run our key principles of increasing honor and decreasing anger through the finest grid that has ever been designed. It's made up of the two great commandments Jesus gave, which He said cover all the commandments in the Bible. Here they are:

1. *"You shall love the Lord your God with all your heart, and with all your soul, and with all your mind. 'This is the great and foremost commandment.'*

2. *"The second is like it, 'You shall love your neighbor [as you value] yourself. On these two commandments depend the whole Law and the Prophets.'"*[7]

We believe that increasing honor and releasing anger daily is at the heart of following these commandments to love.

Love always implies value, worth, and honor. When *love* is used as a verb, it means to do something important for someone we consider valuable. When used as a noun, it denotes worth and great value placed on others and things. When we run our key principles through the grid of these two commandments, we arrive at these three specific goals in the area of increasing honor:

1. *Helping parents and teens to highly honor God*

2. *Helping parents and teens to highly honor others*

3. *Helping parents and teens to highly honor themselves*

By teaching our teens to honor God, others, and themselves, we're not just helping them and ourselves, but also hundreds of people in the future. Through our influence on any one teenager, we will affect more than 600 people in the next 100 years. Thus, the next several generations need for us to make wise decisions that will give them the best opportunity for successful lives. That's why we're looking for mothers and fathers, teachers, coaches, youth workers, and neighbors to join with us in breaking the past patterns that have brought much suffering to modern families. We're hoping you also desire a real awakening in the way we raise our teenagers. Wouldn't it be wonderful if people in the future could look back on this period as a time when adults became strongly committed to the principle of raising teenagers with greater honor and love?

For many reasons, we're optimistic about the "next generation." Various men's ministries, for example, are challenging and teaching millions of men to better love their wives and children. Dr. James Dobson's organization, Focus on the Family, is bringing parents and teens together at "Life on the Edge" conferences to teach them how to strengthen their relationships. Josh McDowell continues to be a front-runner in helping parents and teenagers pursue a life of moral purity. Nearly every ship in the U.S. Navy and virtually every American military base in the world has my (Gary's) videotape series *Keys to Loving and Lasting Relationships* to help the men and women learn how to be better mates and parents before they return home from active duty.

Furthermore, research experts like Dr. Howard Markman, Dr. Scott Stanley, and Dr. John Gottman are teaching people how to manage conflicts within their relationships at home, work, and at school. There's even a nationwide movement underway in which entire cities do not allow couples to marry until they study scientifically proven programs that prevent divorce.

People from all walks of life are getting serious about changing families for the better. Because so many individuals and organizations are dedicating themselves to strengthening the family, we're confident that, for the first time in decades, we are going to see the divorce rate decline.

But none of these large-scale efforts will mean anything unless we, as parents, take our children seriously. We need to dedicate ourselves anew to laying a solid foundation in our marriages and in our relationship with God, and then to building healthy, honoring relationships with our teens.

The same lesson the Swiss watchmakers learned is our biggest encouragement to parents of adolescents: *Don't be afraid to change.* (Mistrust of change is exactly what cost 50,000 watchmakers their jobs.)

The chance to help our teenagers through this difficult time is such a great opportunity! Now more than ever, they need our love, encouragement, support, understanding, and time. One of the greatest things my (Greg's) parents did during my adolescence was to never stop saying they loved me. Although many times I didn't respond to their encouragement, I still heard every word.

Let us restate an important point: We're not suggesting you give up your current parenting methods if they're working. Instead, we're encouraging you to think in new ways and try new things. We're talking about adapting to the changing circumstances and utilizing what works during this period. Most of all, we want you to have hope that your experience with your teenager doesn't have to be as depressing as it was for the man who, before he had children, conducted a seminar titled "Rules for Raising Children." After he became a father, he changed the title to "*Suggestions* for Raising Children." Finally, when his kids reached their teen years, he discontinued the seminar altogether.

Remember, in most families there will be difficult periods and many trials. This is normal any time we enter a new phase of life. As you focus on getting more honor into your home and more anger out, God will reward your faithfulness. The Bible says, "Consider it all joy, my brethren, when you encounter various trials, knowing that the testing of your faith produces endurance."[8]

We're excited you're joining us in the quest to build better relationships with our teens. Your efforts will benefit not only your own children but also generations to come. In the next chapter, we'll begin to see how to increase honor by discovering one of the greatest principles in life, the "I'm Third" principle.

2

HONOR:
THE GREATEST
PRINCIPLE OF LIFE

In no order of things is adolescence the simple time of life.
Jean Erskine Stewart

During several summers of the Smalley kids' high-school years, they attended an outstanding sports camp called Kanakuk Kamp in Branson, Missouri. Their time at camp transformed their lives. And the reason Kanakuk had such an impact is that the staff and counselors are prime examples of honor. Everything they did helped the Smalley teenagers to feel highly valued. All the children who attend camp win awards and ribbons, and the hugs and encouragement they receive are works of art.

In addition to demonstrating honor, the counselors teach lessons about things like spirituality, good sportsmanship, and the consequences of premarital sex. The Smalley teens' favorite lesson, however—the one that had the most profound impact on their lives—was about the "I'm Third" principle. The camp staff and counselors all strive to demonstrate this principle, which is exemplified by the heroic story they recount of an Air National Guard pilot named Johnny Ferrier.

The following is an account of a day Johnny Ferrier had been preparing for all his life. The story was originally featured in *The Denver Post* in the late 1950s.

Out of the sun, packed in a diamond formation and flying as one that day, the Minute Men dove at nearly the speed of sound toward a tiny emerald patch on Ohio's unwrinkled crazy quilt below. It was a little after nine on the morning of June 7, 1958, and the target of the Air National Guard's jet precision team was the famed Wright-Patterson Air Force Base, just outside Dayton.

On the ground, thousands of faces looked upward as Colonel Walt Williams, leader of the Denver-based Sabrejet team, gauged the high-speed pullout. For the Minute Men pilots—Colonel Walt Williams, Captain Bob Cherry, Lieutenant Bob Odle, Captain John Ferrier, and Major Win Coomer—the maneuver was routine, for they had given their show hundreds of times before millions of people.

Low across the fresh, green grass the jet team streaked, far ahead of the noise of the planes' own screaming engines. Judging his pull-up, Colonel Williams pressed the microphone button on top of his throttle: "Smoke on . . . now!" The diamond of planes pulled straight up into the turquoise sky, a bush tail of white smoke pluming out behind. The crowd gasped as the four ships suddenly split apart, rolling to the four points of the compass and leaving a beautiful, smoky fleur-de-lis inscribed on the heavens. This was the Minute Men's famed "flower burst" maneuver. For a minute the crowd relaxed, gazing at the tranquil beauty of the huge, white flower that had grown from the lush Ohio grasslands to fill the great bowl of sky.

Out on the end of his arm of the flower, Colonel Williams turned his Sabre hard, cut off the smoke trail, and dropped the nose of his F-86 to pick up speed for the low-altitude crossover maneuver. Then, glancing back over his shoulder, he froze in terror. Far across the sky to the east, John Ferrier's plane was rolling. He was in trouble. And his plane was headed right for the small town of Fairborn, on the edge of Patterson Field. In a moment, the lovely morning had turned to horror. Everyone saw; everyone understood. One of the planes was out of control.

Steering his jet in the direction of the crippled plane to race after it, Williams radioed urgently, "Bail out, John! Get out of there!" Johnny still had plenty of time and room to eject safely. Twice more Williams issued the command: "Bail out, Johnny! Bail out!"

Each time, Williams was answered only by a blip of smoke.

He understood immediately. John Ferrier couldn't reach the mike button on the throttle because both hands were tugging on a control stick locked in full-throw right. But the smoke button was on the stick, so he was answering the only way he could—squeezing it to tell Walt he thought he could keep his plane under enough control to avoid crashing into the houses of Fairborn.

Suddenly, a terrible explosion shook the earth. Then came a haunting silence. Walt Williams continued to call through the radio, "Johnny? Are you there? Captain? Answer me!"

No response.

Captain John T. Ferrier's Sabrejet had hit the ground midway between four houses, in a backyard garden. It was the only place where he could have crashed without killing people. The explosion had knocked a woman and several children to the ground, but no one had been hurt—with the exception of Johnny Ferrier. He had been killed instantly.

Major Win Coomer, who had flown with Ferrier for years, both in the Air National Guard and on United Airlines and had served a combat tour with him in Korea, was the first Minute Man to land. He raced to the crash scene, hoping to find his friend alive.

Instead, he found a neighborhood in shock from the awful thing that had happened. But then Coomer realized that the people felt no resentment as is ordinarily the case when a peaceful community is torn by a crash. A steady stream of people began coming to him as he stood in his flying suit beside the smoking, gaping hole in the ground where his best friend had just died.

"A bunch of us were standing together, watching the show," an elderly man with tears in his eyes told Coomer. "When the pilot started to roll, he was headed straight for us. For a second, we looked right at each other. Then he pulled up right over us and put it in there." And in deep humility, the old man whispered, "This man died for us."[1]

It had been a bold and courageous last act. But it was not an act alien to the nature of John Ferrier. He had been awarded one of the nation's highest medals for risking his life "beyond the call of duty" in Korea. And although he hadn't known it, he'd been preparing for this tragic day for years by practicing this most important principle:

> You shall love the Lord your God with all your heart, and with all your soul, and with all your mind. This is the great and foremost commandment. The second is like it, "You shall love your neighbor as yourself."[2]

A few days after Johnny's death, his wife, Tulie, wrote the founder of Kanakuk Kamp, Coach Bill Lantz, this letter:

> Coach,
> I went through my husband's billfold last night and found the old worn card which he always carried—"I'M THIRD." He told me once he got it from you. He said that you stressed it at one of your camp sermons. Johnny may have had faults, though they were few

and minor, but he followed that creed to the very end. *God is first, the other fellow second, and "I'm third."* Not just on June 7, 1958, but long before that—certainly as long as I've known him. I'm going to carry that same card with me from now on and see if it won't serve as a reminder. I shouldn't need it, but I'm sure I do as I have many more faults than Johnny.

The principle by which Johnny Ferrier lived and died is also the greatest lesson you can teach your teenager. *At the heart of making others feel valuable, loved, and accepted is a decision to honor them, even above ourselves.* To teach honor, however, we must have a clear, concrete understanding of what it means to honor someone.

What Is Honor?

When you think of honoring someone, you may envision attending your teen's award dinner, asking a famous celebrity for an autograph, or cheering for your favorite team. You may also think of honor as a feeling of respect that goes in only one direction—usually toward a superior or someone who has "earned" or "deserves" it. But honor can be passed on to loved ones regardless of whether they "deserve" it, because, like love, it's an act of the will.

Honor simply means *deciding to place high value, worth, and importance on another person by viewing him or her as a priceless gift and granting him or her a position in our lives worthy of great respect.*

In other words, honor is a gift we give to others. It isn't purchased by their actions or contingent on our emotions. It may carry strong emotional feelings, but it doesn't depend on them. Rather, it's a decision we make daily toward someone who is special and valuable to us.

As with genuine love, honor is one of the greatest gifts we can provide. In fact, honor is genuine love in action. To honor a person involves choosing to highly value him or her even before we put love into action. In many cases, love often begins to flow once we've decided to honor that person.

The opposite of honor is dishonor, which is almost certain to make anger develop in a teenager's heart. Since the goal of this book is to increase honor and decrease anger, we need to understand how we might dishonor a teen.

What Is Dishonor?

The Johnson family had been under tremendous pressure lately. Mr. Johnson had lost his job, and the oldest son had been arrested for shoplifting. Realizing the need for a vacation, the Johnsons decided to go camping. But the relaxing trip to Sequoia National Park in California turned out to be a nightmare for 15-year-old Amy.

Amy had been the one to suggest that the family go camping in the sequoias because she had wanted to see the petrified forest. And the towering stone trees were, indeed, the highlight of the trip for her. "This is the best vacation I've ever had," Amy exclaimed as the family sat around the campfire one evening. She was truly having the time of her life.

Honor is a gift we give to others. It isn't purchased by their actions or contingent on our emotions.

Before returning home, the Johnsons decided to go on one last hike through the petrified forest. Amy was ecstatic. She felt very honored that they would choose to revisit her favorite spot.

As a family, they wanted to remember the camping trip, so they each picked up a rock from a petrified tree as a souvenir. Walking back to the car, however, they passed a gift shop that had a sign hanging in the window. Amy read:

Petrified Wood Should Be Left Intact for All to Enjoy!

Being sensitive and thoughtful, Amy realized it wasn't right for her to keep the wood she had taken. After all, it would probably just end up on a shelf or in a drawer. As she set the stone down, she felt guilty that she couldn't return it to the spot where it had been for millennia.

When the Johnsons reached their camping site, the parents encouraged the children to show the "souvenirs" they had gathered. When her turn came, Amy explained, "I left mine back in the woods so that others will be able to enjoy it." She beamed with pride as she told about seeing the sign and making her decision.

To her dismay, the others broke into laughter. "That's the strangest thing we've ever heard!" her family howled.

"Maybe you'd better go clean up the entire forest so Smoky the Bear doesn't come looking for you," sneered her brother.

"No one is that gullible," her father said with a snicker.

Amy's younger sister even joined in the bashing: "Should I present Amy to the store owners as the only person who has ever obeyed their sign?"

The laughter seemed to last for an hour. Amy was devastated. What had been a wonderful family trip had suddenly turned into a humiliating experience. Amy didn't say a word during the ride home. *I was only trying to do the right thing,* she thought. *Why was I so stupid?* The more she thought about the rock, the more she questioned why she hadn't just held on to it. *None of this would have happened!* she berated herself. The dishonor was starting to invade her heart like a rising flood of self-condemnation.

Over the years that followed, each time Amy looked at the petrified wood sitting on her family's bookshelf, she was reminded of the way her family had laughed at her.

As Amy learned, when we dishonor others, we treat them (consciously or unknowingly) as if they have little value—as less important than a rock. Tragically, being dishonored in such a way can cause a lifetime of emotional damage.

When do we, in everyday family experience, tend to treat a teenager like that?

- When he has just asked the same question for the thousandth time

- When she leaves her "stuff" out at night, expecting us to clean up

- When he selectively forgets what he's been told

- When she brings home a boy who wears an earring and a leather jacket

- When he screams at us, claiming that "you just don't understand!"

- When she goes out on a date dressed in risqué clothes

Anger, unjust criticism, unhealthy comparisons, favoritism, inconsistency, jealousy, selfishness, envy, and a host of other weapons are "justified" as valid to use against people we consider to be of little value. When Amy decided to leave the rock behind, her family demonstrated how little they valued her through sarcasm. They invalidated her.

Here's something everyone ought to write on a card and read every day: *The lower the value we attach to people, the easier we can "justify" dishonoring them with our words or treating them with disrespect.* The 5,000 adults we surveyed reported that one of the least-popular things they received from their parents as teenagers was criticism.

Most parents, of course, do their best to genuinely love their teens, and most teens never have to face the degree of dishonor and hurt Amy endured. Nevertheless, we need to understand how our actions can affect our teens and lower their sense of self-worth.

You might be thinking, *But my teenager is doing great! Why do I need to learn to combat a problem he's not even facing today?*

The answer is that, as we've discovered in talking with people across the country, the results of dishonoring parental actions accumulate over time. On numerous occasions, we have counseled with well-meaning mothers and fathers who were shocked by their son or daughter's self-destructive behavior. Others were just as stunned when they discovered drug abuse, promiscuity, or other damaging patterns in their teenager's life.

As youngsters, many of these teens showed little or no evidence of the problems they face as adolescents today. And often, as we began to look into their history, we found that their parents had had no idea they were failing to honor their teens.

The great British statesman Edmund Burke once said with keen insight, "All that has to happen for evil to prevail in the world is for good men to do nothing." In today's distorted society, we parents need more than good intentions to raise secure, confident teenagers—we need to do something. We need a plan. Further, while things may be going well today, we need to take the initiative to understand how to honor our teens and raise their sense of self-worth, as well as what actions to avoid that can lower it.

"It could never happen to my teenager!" some might say. Let's look, however, at some of the problems young people often face because, in part, their parents never understood the tragic impact of their dishonoring actions. Some of the devastating things that can grow out of dishonor, either in the teen years or later in life, are:

- drug and alcohol abuse

- chronic lying

- procrastination

- extreme pride and self-centeredness (narcissism)

- workaholism and the need to achieve more and more

- vicious emotional ups and downs

- repeated absences from church and school

- extreme submission

- unhealthy legalism
- severe withdrawal from society
- sexual difficulties in marriage
- lower academic achievement
- feelings of loss of control
- stress-related heart problems
- homosexuality
- deep feelings of loneliness
- suicidal thinking and attempts
- poor marital mate selection
- clinical depression
- poor decision making
- lowered career achievement
- a pattern of outbursts of anger
- low energy in accomplishing school or work tasks
- extreme self-criticism
- gravitation toward cults and fringe religious groups
- unrealistic expectations of self and others
- eating disorders

Parents don't want to see their teenagers experience such problems. Yet without realizing it, some parents lead their children down these very paths.

As we've said, the key to avoiding such things in our teens' lives is to honor them. To make them (or anyone else, for that matter) feel valuable, loved, and accepted, we must *decide* to increase honor and help lower their anger. If you read these negative effects of dishonor and thought, *Great, another book that tells me what a bad parent I am!* we want to give you hope. Even if you've unknowingly been in the habit of dishonoring your teen, you can choose today to stop the devastating effects of dishonor—even reverse them—by giving your teen the gift of honor. And when you learn how to communicate in tangible ways to your adolescent that he or she is deeply loved and highly valued, it goes a long way toward combating future problems. With that in mind, let's look at three important ways to show honor.

Three Ways to Honor Teenagers

Each of the following three methods of communicating honor is part of the foundation on which the remainder of this book will rest. Each applies to how, like Johnny Ferrier, we can honor God, others, and, finally, ourselves.

One way to communicate honor is to grant each child a high place in our lives and the loving respect that accompanies it. A second is to look upon each teen as a priceless treasure. The third is to understand that to help teenagers develop honor, they must see us demonstrate it. Let's consider each of these methods in detail.

1. Place your teenager in a *highly respected position.*

One time when I (Greg) was in junior high, Mom and Dad made a simple decision that would have a far greater positive impact on me than they realized at the time. They decided that Dad would take me along to a conference of professional athletes at which he was speaking. At one point in our time there, while we were walking through the hotel, a football landed nearby. When I turned around, my jaw dropped and I almost fell over. Standing in front of me was my favorite football star, number 80 for the Seattle Seahawks, Steve Largent, who was later inducted into the NFL Hall of Fame.

It was like a fantasy come true. And as if that weren't exciting enough, Steve then talked and played catch with me for about an hour. Finally, to top off the perfect day, Steve gave me an autographed picture. Before I went to bed that night, I vowed to wear the number 80 if I ever got to play organized football.

Dad's taking me with him to the conference and introducing me to all the players was an act of honor. He was placing me—literally, in this case—in a highly respected position. Hearing my name coming from Dad's lips when meeting Steve Largent and others communicated that he thought enough of me to use my name with them and that I was worth their taking the time to meet me.

Early one summer morning a few years later, Mom woke me up at 5:30, just as I had begged her to do. The first day of freshman football practice had arrived, and it was terribly important for me to be first in line to get my equipment. I knew that I was about to be assigned the number that would identify me forever (or at least through my high-school football career). I had dreamed about this day for months, because only Steve Largent's number 80 would do. I had to get that number.

> *Even if you've unknowingly been in the habit of dishonoring your teen, you can choose today to stop the devastating effects of dishonor—even reverse them—by giving your teen the gift of honor.*

Practice started at 7:00 sharp, and I was standing in front of the equipment shed by 6:00. Fortunately, number 80 was still available, and my dream came true. Throughout my high-school days, I would be identified with the hero I had met years before because my mom and dad had chosen to put me in a position of high respect.

Coincidentally, this story also illustrates another fun way to communicate honor. When my jaw dropped and I gasped for air at the sight of Steve Largent that day in the hotel, I was greatly honoring Steve. Remember, honor is a decision to place high value, worth, and importance on another person. Dropping your jaw and gasping for air certainly expresses that.

To show honor to your teenager, then, the next time he walks into the room, drop your jaw and take a deep breath. Tell him how lucky you are to even be in the same room with such a valuable person. Or say something like, "I can't believe God entrusted me with someone as valuable as you." Your teen may tell you the same thing my kids said to me (Gary): "Dad, you are so weird!" But will he remember it and later appreciate it? Yes!

If you want to really "unnerve" your teen, hand her a piece of paper and beg for her autograph. Then, just as Greg hung the picture of Steve Largent on his wall, put your teenager's autograph next to her picture and display it in a prominent place in your home. This is another way of literally putting her in a highly respected position.

Be careful in following these last two suggestions, however, especially if you have not made a habit of honoring your child in the past. If these things aren't done right, with sincerity, your son or daugther might conclude you're being sarcastic, which is the opposite effect of what you want.

2. See your teenager as a *priceless treasure.*

A second way to communicate honor to our teens is to see and treat each of them as a priceless treasure. We honor God by recognizing that His worth is beyond any price; similarly, we honor our teenagers by considering them to be special gifts God has entrusted to us, as the Scriptures declare.[3]

A story called *Johnny Lingo's Eight-Cow Wife,* by Patricia McGerr, illustrates well the unlimited power of viewing and treating someone as a priceless treasure. Johnny Lingo was a young man who lived on the island of Nurabandi, not far from the island Kiniwata in the South Pacific. Johnny was one of the brightest, strongest, and richest men in the islands, but people shook their heads and smiled about a business deal he had made with a man on Kiniwata.

It was customary among the people of these islands for a man to buy his wife from her father, with the price being paid in cows. Two or three cows would buy an average wife, and four or five would fetch a highly satisfactory one. Yet for some reason, Johnny had paid the unheard-of price of *eight* cows for a wife, Sarita, who was unattractive by any standards. As one fellow explained, "It would be kindness to call her plain. She was skinny. She walked with her shoulders hunched and her head ducked. She was scared of her own shadow." Why did Johnny Lingo pay eight cows, especially for such a woman? Everyone figured Sarita's father, Sam Karoo, had taken young Johnny for a ride, and that's why the islanders smiled whenever they discussed the deal.

Patricia McGerr finally met Johnny for herself and got the chance to ask about his eight-cow purchase of Sarita. She had assumed he had done it for his own vanity and reputation—at least until she saw Sarita. "She was the most beautiful woman I have ever seen," McGerr wrote. "The lift of her shoulders, the tilt of her chin, the sparkle of her eyes all spelled a pride to which no one could deny her the right." Sarita was not the plain girl McGerr had expected, and the explanation lay with Johnny Lingo.

"Do you ever think," he said, "what it must mean to a woman to know that her husband settled on the lowest price for which she can be bought? And then later, when the women talk, they boast of what their husbands paid for them. One says four cows, another maybe six. How does she feel, the woman who was sold for one or two? This could not happen to my Sarita."

"Then you did this just to make your wife happy?" McGerr asked.

"I wanted Sarita to be happy, yes. But I wanted more than that. This is true. Many things can change a woman. Things that happen inside, things that happen outside. But the thing that matters most is what she thinks about herself. In Kiniwata, Sarita believed she was worth nothing. Now she knows she is worth more than any other woman in the islands."

"Then you wanted . . ."

"I wanted to marry Sarita. I loved her and no other woman."

"But . . ."

"But," he finished softly, "I wanted an eight-cow wife."

Because Johnny Lingo considered Sarita to be worth eight cows, she began to see and present herself as an eight-cow woman. Before Johnny entered her life, Sarita was a shy, plain island girl. After he placed incredible value upon her, she was transformed into a confident, attractive woman who knew she was worth far more than any other island woman.

Today, your teenager might be feeling the way Sarita did before she met Johnny. With all its physical changes, insecurities, and peer pressure, adolescence can be a cruel stage of life. During this awkward time, however, you can give your teen the same gift Sarita received: *incredible self-worth seen through the eyes of someone who considers her priceless.*

We encourage you to remind your teenagers daily how valuable they are. As you start to see them as priceless, they, like Sarita, are free to feel and present themselves as "worth many cows." If possible, give them a ring, a wall plaque, or something else that will remind them daily of their high value in your eyes.

> ### *When you treasure a person, you want to protect her. You'll go out of your way to see that she succeeds.*

Why is it so important to view our teens as special treasures? Because "where your treasure is, there your heart will be also."[4] Whatever we highly value naturally attracts our affections, desires, and enthusiasm. Likewise, when we learn to treasure our teenagers, our positive feelings for them go up as well.

To get a better handle on what we mean by treasuring someone, imagine that you owned a priceless painting. You would make it the center of attention in your home. You would protect it by making sure it was hung securely and away from direct exposure to the sun. You would highlight it with indirect lighting and a subtle yet elegant frame. You would certainly brag about it to your friends and family because it meant so much to you. You would constantly feel grateful for the opportunity to possess something so marvelous and valuable. Just coming home from work and looking at it would raise your spirits.

Parents who treasure their teenagers respond to them in many of the same ways. When you treasure a person, you want to protect her. You'll go out of your way to see that she succeeds. You'll highlight her best points, mentioning her frequently in conversations. The thought of coming home to see her after a long day at work will give you energy.

Isn't it interesting how inanimate objects such as paintings tend to keep their value over the years, whereas living objects like teenagers often see their value drop? The decision to treat teens as priceless treasures sometimes has to be made hourly! But it pays rich dividends.

We've looked at placing teens in a highly respected place and treating them as priceless treasure. Now let's turn our attention to a third way to communicate honor. We've saved the most important for last.

3. *Demonstrate* honor in your actions.

As we seek to communicate and teach honor to our teenagers, it's vital for us to understand that honor can't really be taught with words. Our kids must see it demonstrated in our actions. Thus, modeling is the best way to communicate honor.

One of the most powerful illustrations of the importance of modeling comes from the following poem by an unknown writer:

> *I'd rather see a sermon than hear one any day.*
> *I'd rather one should walk with me than merely show the way.*
> *The eye's a better pupil and more willing than the ear.*
> *Fine counsel is important, but example's always clear.*
> *The best of all the preachers are the men who live their creeds,*
> > *for to see the good in action is what everybody needs.*
> *I can soon learn how to do it if you'll let me see it done.*
> *I can watch your hands in action though your tongue too fast may run.*
> *And the lectures you deliver may be very wise and true,*
> > *but I'd rather learn my lesson by observing what you do.*
> *For I may misunderstand you and the fine advice you give,*
> > *but there's no misunderstanding how you act and how you live.*

Teenagers are incredibly perceptive about what we parents *do*. When it looks as if we value the house, job, car, or poodle more than them, our actions speak much louder than our words of love and honor.

I (Gary) had to continually remember the importance of modeling when my children were teenagers. They watched me all the time to see if my actions matched my words. One day while I was trying to take a nap, I learned a valuable lesson in this regard. I didn't want to be disturbed, so I had instructed my two boys to "leave me alone!" Looking back, that probably wasn't the best choice of words. It had the same effect as throwing fresh meat on the floor and instructing two puppies to "stay!" The problem was that my boys had seen me play plenty of practical jokes on others. I was in real trouble!

As I was sleeping comfortably in my chair, Greg and Michael determined this would be an excellent opportunity to give me a taste of my own medicine. They sneaked up behind me and poured warm water down my throat as I lay snoring. As I started to choke and gag, the boys ducked behind my chair. Dazed from being forced out of deep sleep, I was confused about what I had just swallowed. Then it hit me. I was hemorrhaging! I must be having a massive nosebleed!

To keep from dripping blood all over the floor, I cupped my hand over my face and ran toward the bathroom. After crashing into the coffee table and tripping over our dog on the way, I finally made it to the sink. Because I didn't want to faint at the sight of all my blood, I slowly removed my hands and exposed . . . *nothing*.

Where's all the blood? I thought as I carefully surveyed my body. I was sure I had felt a large amount of liquid gushing down my throat, so I had anticipated seeing quarts of blood flowing from my nose.

"What's going on?" I yelled.

Then it dawned on me: "Where are Michael and Greg?"

When I returned from the bathroom, I heard snickering coming from behind the chair. "Get out here!" I ordered. "Do you have any idea how dangerous that was?" I challenged after they had moved into the open.

My first instinct was to ground the boys for a year, yell at them for being so "irresponsible," and finally shame them with a few choice words. After all, they'd almost given me a heart attack! But as I stood there facing them, I suddenly remembered all the times I had played jokes on them. It was fair turnabout.

As I was reminded that day, *what we do as parents has a tremendous influence on our kids*. In areas both trivial and vitally important, they imitate our behavior. Thus, if we want to help our teens learn how to honor God, others, and themselves, we must first demonstrate it. Before I really started to learn the significance of honor, I had to ask for forgiveness so many times. Finally, I realized that honoring my kids right off kept me from constantly needing to ask for forgiveness.

If your teenagers are to develop a Johnny-Ferrier-like appreciation of honor, they first need to see it in you. We're not saying they shouldn't honor people unless they're honored first. But it's a fact of life that teens (or any children) rarely do something they haven't first seen done by their parents. Common sense tells us this as well as the research literature. For example, the aggression children observe in their families while growing up influences the amount and type of aggression in their own marriages.[5] Similarly, how people experience pain seems to be influenced by how important people in their lives have dealt with it.[6]

One of the most disturbing studies illustrating the seriousness of parental modeling was done by UCLA sociologist Nicholas Wolfinger, who conducted a national survey of 8,590 adults. His findings show that among adults whose parents had two or more failed marriages, 67 percent had been divorced themselves, 26 percent two or more times. Also, among adults whose parents divorced and remarried only once, 58 percent were divorced, 19 percent at least twice. Finally, among adults raised in intact homes, only 41 percent had been divorced, and only 9 percent two or more times.

"Cumulative stress as new parents move in and out of a child's life seems to be affecting his marital history as an adult," wrote Wolfinger. "Adults who take after their parents' divorce histories may have learned the best way to deal with problems in a relationship is to cut and run."[7]

Since what parents do has such an impact on their children, we encourage you to teach by example. Provide your teenager with a model of how others are to be honored.

But what if you have an angry teenager who is not receptive to the honor you show? Many parents experience this reality. If you find yourself in this position, we encourage you to do several things. First, continue to honor your teen. You can't control his heart, but you can choose to honor him no matter what. Even if you don't "feel" like it, remember that positive feelings flow from a decision to honor.

After the decision is made, you can try to deal with his anger. In the next chapter, we'll show how you can use four steps to open the closed spirit of an angry teenager. If your teen still does not respond to your honoring actions and chooses to remain angry, we encourage you to read chapter 12, which provides ways to deal with an angry teen who will not respond to you. But for now, we urge you to communicate honor to your teenager by placing her in a highly respected position, seeing her as a priceless treasure, and making sure she sees you modeling honor.

Deciding to increase honor and decrease anger in your teenager's heart begins by understanding how the "I'm Third" principle works in everyday life. In the next chapter, we present a plan to help you lower the anger level in your teen's life. And as singer Steve Green challenged all of us, "May the footsteps we leave help our children to believe" (our paraphrase).

3

KEEPING ANGER LEVELS LOW

Fathers, do not exasperate your children,
so that they will not lose heart.
The Bible

When my (Gary's) daughter, Kari, was 16, I once managed to close her spirit down tight in anger in just a few minutes.

We were on our way to a high-school basketball game to see her "heart-throb" boyfriend. In the past, we'd had fun together on outings when it was just the two of us. We sang, stopped for fast food, and talked about everything—and I mean that literally, because Kari can really talk. But this time, something very different happened.

"Dad," she said hesitantly as we were discussing her boyfriend, "I'm really starting to like Roger. I think I love him."

Love. I'd never had an adverse reaction to that word before. But coming out of my daughter's mouth in that context, it made me exhale so hard that pop squirted out my nose. Embarrassed and struggling to regain my composure, I said, "Pardon me, but did you say *love?* You think you're in love with Roger?"

"Yes," Kari said, looking at me as if I were strange. "You probably couldn't hear me with all that Pepsi blowing out your nose. Anyway, do you know what the best part is? We've even talked about the possibility of getting *married* some day."

Thank goodness I hadn't taken a bite of my hamburger or to this day it might still be lodged somewhere in my nasal cavity. "You've what?!" I demanded. "I can take the love thing, but if you guys are talking about marriage, that's where I draw the line! You're only 16 years old, for crying out loud!"

Our "discussion" quickly got so heated that I had to pull off the road. I couldn't believe what I was hearing. With tears filling her eyes, Kari finally fell silent and stared out the window, away from me.

I didn't know what to do next. Should we sit there? Should I keep driving? Should I go park in a convenience store lot and wait for things to cool down? (I needed a new Pepsi anyway.) One thing I quickly realized was that I had been wrong to react the way I had. Kari had trusted me with something special and secret. But instead of getting excited over her "puppy" love, I had sprayed pop at her. I didn't remember ever teaching that method at my seminar on loving relationships.

I was tempted to get defensive—to explain that, as a father, I was having trouble imagining any male "gorilla" taking my little girl away. But instead of saying something, I said nothing. We ended up going to the basketball game after all, but we didn't say another word to each other until we arrived back home around midnight.

The Importance of Arguing Well

Most of us dislike and try to avoid conflict, especially with our children. But, as you've no doubt already discovered, there are some things in adolescence that tend to provoke conflict. These include puberty; the child's expanded logical reasoning and increased idealistic thought; violated expectations; changes in schooling, peers, friendships, and dating; and the child's natural movement toward independence.[1] We'll expand on many of these changes in other chapters.

One mother already knew to expect conflict with her teenage son. When she arrived home from work one day, she met him at the door. "We're invited to the Stevens's for dinner," she said. "You've got 30 minutes to clean up and argue about it."

The good news is that you can both reduce your conflicts and use them to move into deeper friendship. That's right! Conflicts can either tear apart your relationship with your teenager or actually help you develop a more intimate friendship. The way you argue is the key. If you do it in an honoring way, a better relationship will result. Unfortunately, our human tendency is to argue in dishonoring ways, as Gary did that day in the car with Kari. The result, as it was in that case, is the biggest killer of love: *anger.*

The Three Faces of Anger

We'll say it again: *Unresolved anger is the number-one enemy of our teens' healthy development and spiritual growth.* But what does anger look like? What are its main ingredients?

Psychologist Gary Oliver, in a study of anger, found that it's made up of three primary emotions: hurt feelings, frustration, and fear or feeling unsafe.[2] Anger is really a secondary emotion that springs out of these other three.

Think of how many times each day we feel these primary emotions. For example, the traffic is frustrating, our boss hurts our feelings, and some of the places we drive through make us fearful. We need to find ways to reduce these emotions daily or we will suffer the negative consequences. It's true for both parents and teens.

What are the results of unresolved anger? For one thing, when anger is not dealt with for weeks, it can create a subtle distancing from others. The more anger we store inside, the more we tend to sabotage our closest relationships by saying and doing things that alienate others. It's almost as if we say, "Don't get too close to me; it's not safe for me or you."

Spiritually, unresolved anger causes us to "walk in the dark." We fail to understand how to love others or how to stay out of daily, self-inflicted "trials."

Emotionally, being loaded with anger tends to lower our sense of worth. We may feel like victims. We tend to be less sensitive to the feelings of others and can therefore appear to be less warm and caring than we would be otherwise. We might even become more prone to depression and thoughts of suicide.

Physically, we can experience greater stress and find ourselves more susceptible to all kinds of illnesses, because prolonged anger tends to weaken our immune system.

From just these few observations about the effects of anger, you can see why anger needs to be dealt with promptly and its level kept low in your home.

When Anger Hits Home

There's a verse in the Bible that summarizes the entire parenting process: "Fathers, do not provoke your children to anger; but bring them up in the discipline and instruction of the Lord."[3] When parents fail to follow that counsel and their teens get angry as a result, the effect is like something that happened to my (Greg's) daughter Taylor when she was 19 months old.

One day when Taylor was playing with me in our backyard, she discovered a bunch of sow bugs. She was so fascinated to see that every time she touched a bug, it rolled up into a little ball. Since she loves anything round, she kept flicking the bugs and squealing, "Ball! Ball!"

After being distracted for a few moments, I turned back toward Taylor and was horrified to see that she now had several sow bugs rolling around in her mouth. She pointed at the remaining bugs on the ground and shrieked, "Bawl! Bawl!"

Spiritually, unresolved anger causes us to "walk in the dark."

I quickly did a "finger sweep" and rushed her inside. I knew that when we reached Taylor's mother, I was going to be in big trouble. Unfortunately, the only thing I could think of saying was "At least she got plenty of protein!" No wonder most mothers get nervous when leaving the kids with their fathers!

What does this story have to with do with parenting teenagers? The sow bug is made up of three distinct parts: a protective shell, an outer body, and internal organs. When it feels threatened, it curls into a tight defensive ball so that only its hard shell is exposed to the danger. Human beings also consist of three parts: body, soul, and spirit. The body is our physical makeup. The soul includes our mind, will, and emotions. The spirit is our innermost being, like the conscience; it's at this level that we have our deepest friendships.

In healthy families, all the members relate to one another on all three levels. Everyone's body language expresses openness; everyone is free to speak, think, and feel—all of which communicates to the spirit. Over time, with many positive exchanges, relationships grow deeper on all three levels. However, if interfamily exchanges instead produce hurt feelings, frustration, and/or fear, a person's spirit can close in anger. He or she "curls up into a protective ball," figuratively speaking, offering only a "hard shell" to the cause of the anger.

That's what happened when Gary offended Kari on the way to the basketball game. Her spirit closed, as did her soul and body. Staring out the window in silence, she looked like a tightly closed sow bug who'd just been "flicked" by her thoughtless father.

What Happens When Your Teenager's Spirit Closes?

There are hundreds of ways to offend your teen and close her spirit, but we consistently see several that top the list. One was illustrated by a man named Chip who told us at our seminar about the lasting effects of a sarcastic comment made years before by his dad. When Chip was a teenager, a friend came over to his house one day, and Chip's father answered the door. This friend had not seen Chip's dad for several months, and the dad took one look at the boy and uttered in a bad attempt at humor, "You've grown so much! I didn't realize they stacked crap that high!"

The father's cutting remark left the young visitor hurt and embarrassed. As a result of that and similar comments, Chip's friend stopped coming over to his house. And Chip still remembered the deep hurt and pain from the experience.

Besides the making of sarcastic jokes or comments, here are the top five categories of teenage "spirit closers":

1. Don't let them think on their own.

- "That's the stupidest thing I've ever heard."

- "Try saying that at school and they'll laugh you out of the class."

- "You're too young to understand."

- "Who asked you?"

- "Please don't interrupt. Can't you see I'm trying to solve this problem?"

2. Inhibit their freedom to speak their mind.

- "That's enough talking. Go play and let us be alone for a while!"

- "No, I don't have time to listen to your drivel."

- "Is there an end to this?"

- "What you say is always so confusing!"

3. Regard their feelings as unimportant.

- "Son, you've got to get over those little things. Grow up!"

- "Come on, that's just the way your brother is. Stop taking everything so personally."

- "That shouldn't hurt your feelings. Why, when I was your age I got twice as much teasing as you get."

- "If you're going to get upset every time we go over there, I'm just not going to take you again."

- "Movies like that are just make-believe. Grow up! There's nothing to be afraid of."

4. Avoid spending time with them.

- "I've got only two days to finish this report, so no, I can't go see your play."

- "Do you think money grows on trees? I've got to work."

- "See if your mother will take you. I don't have time for this."

5. Disrespect their individuality.

- "I said, don't lock the bathroom. I may need in there to comb my hair."

- "I'm your father. I know what's best for you."

- "I don't care how many of your friends are going. You're not, and I don't want to know your reasons."

- "Don't be silly. They'll like your hairstyle."

Other parental actions likely to close a teen's spirit include the following:

- Speaking harsh words

- Telling your son that his opinions don't matter

- Being unwilling to admit mistakes

- Taking your daughter for granted

- Not trusting your son

- Forcing your teen to do something with which he's uncomfortable

- Being rude to him in front of others

- Dismissing her needs as unimportant[4]

How can you tell if these or other things have caused your child's spirit to close? It can be difficult to discern a closed spirit because the typical manifestations are usually present to some degree during normal adolescence—things like lengthy periods of silence, avoiding eye contact, and resisting touch. When a teenager's attitude or behavior changes drastically and seemingly overnight, however, or he begins to display some of the more rebellious kinds of actions, you need to look carefully for a closed spirit. Here are the most common signs of a closed spirit:

- Your teen develops an argumentative attitude.

- Your teen seeks friends who are the opposite of the kind you desire for him or her.

- Your teen swears or uses disrespectful language.

- Your teen's facial expressions begin to reflect anger or avoidance.

- Your teen is resistant to discussing or agreeing on almost anything.

- When touching your teen's hand, it's often cold and unresponsive.

- You sense your teen is avoiding you.

- Your teen often turns away in your presence.

- Your teen shows a lack of respect for your advice.

- Your teen becomes highly critical of you.

- Warm feelings that used to exist between you and your teen seem to have disappeared.

- Your teen begins to indulge in sex, alcohol, or drugs.

Our purpose in writing about a closed spirit is not to make parents feel guilty. Rather, we want to provide *hope*. We have closed the spirits of our own wives and children many times. But it's possible to reopen an angry, closed spirit, and next we'll show you how. We have found four essential steps in the process of doing it.

Four Steps in Opening a Teenager's Closed Spirit

1. Reflect Tenderness.

When we realize a teen's spirit is closed, the first step in opening it is to express a softness, or tenderness. The *opposite* of softness was demonstrated by a tough Marine drill sergeant when he got word that the grandmother of one of his men had died. At reveille the next day he barked, "Hey, Wilson, your grandmother died!" The young soldier fainted on the spot.

To reflect tenderness to your teen, we want you to . . .

- lower your voice
- become gentle in spirit
- get down on bended knee
- speak slowly
- relax your facial expressions
- become pleasant in your demeanor

All of these reflect honor and humility, and as the Bible suggests, "A gentle answer turns away wrath."[5] When we become tender, we communicate four important things. We're saying:

A. The teen is valuable and important. We express this in nonverbal ways: We're slow to move toward him. Our heads may be bowed, and we're obviously grieved that we have hurt him.

B. We don't want to see her spirit closed. We care about her.

C. We know something's wrong. We acknowledge by our softness that an offense has taken place, and we're going to slow down long enough to correct whatever has happened.

D. We're open to listening. It's safe for him to say how he feels about what has happened, and we're not going to get angry or hurt him.[6]

After I (Gary) offended Kari that day by reacting so negatively to her "love" news, I had to become soft with her. Although speaking face to face is the preferred method, you can utilize other means as well. For example, the next day after dishonoring Kari, I wrote her a note expressing, among other things, my love for her and my desire for another chance to talk with her. Saying things like "I love you" or "You're such an important person" are great ways to communicate softness.

Once we become soft, the next step is to better understand our teen's pain.

2. Increase our own understanding.

It's important to genuinely understand the pain a teenager feels and how she has interpreted our offensive behavior. We must ask for her perspective on what occurred so we can validate her feelings or needs. Taking the time to see someone as unique and very valuable is true friendship. We must resist the urge to defend ourselves, lecture, or question why she did or didn't do something.

When I (Gary) reacted to Kari that day in the car, I was tempted to defend why I had behaved in that manner. I wanted to say, "You just don't dump something like that on your father," "You were yelling at me, too," or "It's no big deal." But listening quietly to our teenagers is the way to make major progress toward opening their spirits. Later that same night, when Kari and I finally talked to each other again, I asked what it had felt like to have me react that way. As I listened to her describe her feelings, I simply validated them and empathized with what that must have felt like.

Empathy is identifying with and understanding the other person's situation, feelings, and motives. Empathy is easy to give. You start by taking a guess at what your son or daughter may be feeling. To empathize with Kari, I said, "You must have been angry at me. You also were probably hurt that I responded to your secret in that manner."

Listening and empathizing communicates that you believe your child has something valuable to say; consequently, she feels valuable. Listening shows that you respect her as a person; empathy communicates that you understand her. *Listen to understand rather than to respond;* desire to understand more than to defend yourself. In other words, listen with your heart—hear her pain and feel her needs.

When we're really listening, we don't need to tell anybody—it's evident. You can bet our teens know whether we're truly listening or faking it. We show we're listening by our body language, by nonverbal responses like facial expressions and eye contact, and by the follow-up questions we ask. Furthermore, we give cues that demonstrate we're paying attention. A good listener:

- is attentive, not distracted; does not look around or do something else at the same time

- does not rush the speaker
- is focused on the person speaking
- does not interrupt
- maintains good eye contact
- does not grunt responses

When we're really listening and empathizing, our attention is focused squarely on the other person. He will, therefore, feel like the most important person in our world at that moment. Listening does not require attempts at problem solving. Our teenagers merely want to know that we understand their point of view. They want to sense from us that it's okay to be upset and to show emotion.

Good listening takes time and work, which is why so few people practice it, much less master it. But know this: *If our teens don't feel they're being heard, it's unlikely that our relationships with them will improve.*

As a rule, to the same degree that they feel listened to, they will grant future opportunities for communication. After all, who wants to talk with someone who doesn't listen? For that matter, who wants to be in a relationship with someone who doesn't listen? To help you become a better listener, we will explore in the next chapter a communication method so powerful that it instantly allows you to completely hear and understand your son or daughter.

Now that we're becoming soft and tender, and we're listening and empathizing to understand our teenager's pain, the third step in opening a closed spirit is to admit our mistakes.

3. Admit the offense.

When someone who hurts us does not take responsibility for his actions, it can be discouraging. Perhaps your teenager feels like one of the monkeys at an unusual zoo. "That's incredible, having a monkey and a lion together in the same cage," said a zoo visitor. "How do they get along?"

"Pretty well, for the most part," answered the zookeeper. "But once in a while they have a disagreement, and then we have to get a new monkey."

Our teenagers may feel that each time they get into a disagreement with us, we come down on them like a strong lion. They may feel that their spirits have been "killed" like one of those monkeys—that we, instead of tending to their wounds by admitting our wrongdoing, have simply rejected their feelings as invalid the way I (Gary) did with Kari. As a parent, it can be hard to say "I was wrong," but it can work wonders.

The next day after that scene in the car with Kari, I was thinking more clearly and wrote the note we referred to earlier. She has held on to its few words ever since:

> Dear Kari,
>
> Last night I made another major mistake. I was wrong to react the way I did. I love you. I would really appreciate another opportunity to hear about your feelings for Roger. Maybe you could tell me tonight over a Pepsi.
>
> Love,
> Dad

Admitting we're wrong (when we obviously are) is like tending to our teenagers' wounds. Or, to change the analogy, it's like drilling a hole in their "anger bucket" and allowing that unhealthy emotion to drain away. Once they sense that we understand our mistake and they hear us admit it, the anger has a way of escaping from their lives.

Sometimes we may not be wrong about the facts or issues of a matter, but our *attitude* might be. Or perhaps the way we've done something is offensive. If our attitude is harsh and angry when telling our teens about legitimate problems, we're still wrong. The Bible affirms this: "The anger of man does not achieve the righteousness of God."[7] Stopping short of admitting we're wrong can leave a dangerous gap between us and our teens that may not mend quickly—or at all.

One time a 15-year-old named Chris stole money from his father's wallet. When the father confronted Chris, he first lied about his innocence. Guilt finally overcame Chris, however, and he admitted his mistake.

"Why did you steal the money?" his father demanded angrily.

Chris was afraid of the wrath he might have to endure. With his head lowered in embarrassment, he hesitantly replied, "I took the money to buy a birthday gift for Mom. Yesterday I overheard her telling someone that she has never received a present from her children or husband. I wanted her to have something nice, but I didn't have the money."

His son's words struck the man like a bolt of lightning. Although Chris's method had been wrong, his heart was in the right place. Instead of yelling at him for stealing the money, the father simply said, "Chris, I've been wrong. I had no idea how much I was hurting your mother."

Not only was Chris blown away to hear his father admit a mistake, but two days later, his mother also received her first surprise birthday party. As she tore open a small box from her husband, a new diamond ring fell out with this note attached: "For all the presents you never received!"

When parents don't admit their mistakes, they can delay the reopening of their teens' spirits indefinitely. On the other hand, teens feel valuable when they hear us admit our mistakes and see that we understand how they feel. Sometimes that's all it takes to open a closed spirit.

The last step in opening a teenager's closed spirit is one of the most honoring things we can do for someone. It's like giving a large bottle of cold water to someone dying of thirst in the desert.

4. Seek forgiveness.

The final part of opening a closed spirit is to seek forgiveness for whatever offense we've committed. If we don't do this, our teenagers will be left feeling violated and still angry, just like the man who discovered a gigantic dent in the back of his new car one morning. By the look of things, the damage would cost him thousands of dollars to repair. He was relieved, however, to find a note under the windshield wiper from the guilty party—until he actually read the note: "As I am writing this, your neighbors are watching me. They think I am giving you my name, address, license number, and insurance company. I'm not!"

Because we had a written family constitution in our home regarding anger (we'll explain the family constitution in chapter 6), I (Gary) knew that after closing Kari's spirit that night, I had to seek her forgiveness as well. Once I swallowed my pride, it wasn't difficult to do. And although it won't be this easy every time, Kari was able to instantly forgive me. I could tell by looking at her body language that her spirit was totally open once again. We could now go out for a Pepsi and enjoy our conversation.

As I did with Kari, it's important to give teenagers the opportunity to respond to our confession—to ask if they can find it in their hearts to forgive us. This is a wonderful opportunity to model seeking forgiveness. Our children need to see the importance of asking someone to forgive us when we make a mistake. Most young people are aware that the Bible says we're to seek forgiveness when we hurt someone. But unless they see us valuing it by doing it ourselves, they're not likely to ask forgiveness either.

When Bill was about 17, his father, Jerry, got a speeding ticket while in Florida on a business trip. Jerry decided to keep his mistake a secret. He had always taken great pride, after all, in his flawless driving record. He even went to great lengths to remind his family of it. Whenever a family member received a traffic ticket, Jerry was the first to give the "lawbreaker" a hard time.

Jerry's secret was safe until the state of Florida sent him a letter requesting his attendance at driving school. By mistake, Bill opened the letter and discovered his dad's misfortune. "Kelly, you'll never guess what I found!" Bill told his sister. "Dad was caught doing 75 on an on-ramp in Florida. Mr. 'I've never received a single speeding ticket' has to attend driving school!" The two laughed and couldn't wait until their dad got home.

When their parents walked through the door together that evening, Bill and Kelly asked them both to sit down. "Mom," the two stated while trying to remain serious, "we suspect that Dad has been hiding something from us.

If our teens don't feel they're being heard, it's unlikely that our relationships with them will improve.

"Dad," they questioned while holding up the letter, "do you have any idea why the state of Florida would be requesting your presence at *driving school?* Have you experienced any problems—no, make that 'delays'—while getting on the freeway?"

Jerry turned red as he realized he'd been caught.

"You should know you can't keep things from us," his children said while laughing. "We're very disappointed in you, young man."

The entire family had fun watching Jerry squirm. Much to their surprise, however, he didn't become defensive. Instead, he got down on his knees and made a remarkable statement: "I'm sorry for trying to deceive you guys about the ticket. Could you forgive me?"

His teenagers were taken aback. *Is Dad really apologizing for this?* they thought. It had been a long time since they had heard him seek forgiveness. He truly touched their lives with a valuable lesson.

For Christmas that year, one of Jerry's children gave him a special award in honor of his remarkable attitude, one that still sits on his desk. It's a small plaque that reads: "OUTSTANDING COMMITMENT TO CONTINUING DRIVER'S EDUCATION. THANKS FOR BEING A MAN, DAD!"

We strongly encourage you to begin modeling the seeking of forgiveness to your teenagers. It will encourage and inspire them, and most of the time it will open their closed spirits. You might be wondering, however, *What happens if I take all four steps and my child refuses to forgive me, keeping his or her spirit closed?*

What to Do if a Teenager Refuses to Forgive

If you follow these four steps and your teen still refuses to forgive you, there are several possible reasons:

- The offense was deeper than you realized.

- He wants to see your behavior change first.

- She may have been offended by someone outside the family as well.

- He may not have had time to think through what happened.

- She has a general resentment toward everyone around her.

- Simply asking forgiveness doesn't erase everything that has happened.

- You can't possibly understand how deeply he has been hurt.

Whatever the reason, the best thing to do is to be patient with your teenager. Don't feel that just because you have started doing some things differently and have sought forgiveness, your teen will be able to forgive you right away.

One way to picture what can happen is to imagine your offended teen as someone who has been out in cold weather too long. After the skin becomes numb, he or she can no longer feel the painful wind. In the same way, some teens seem indifferent or callous toward a parent because the relationship has gone on so long without the warmth of forgiveness for offenses committed. Once you seek forgiveness, however, it's like soaking that numb skin in warm water. Although the warm bath (forgiveness) is healthy, it doesn't bring instant relief. Instead, it initially causes a painful, tingling sensation. It first makes the skin feel worse before it begins to feel better. Likewise, it might take your hurting teenager some time to warm up to your forgiveness.

No matter how he responds, never drop the issue altogether simply because he isn't ready to forgive. Let the situation "warm up" for a while on its own; then come back and repeat the four steps.

Perhaps your act of tenderness was not what your teen needed. You may need to choose another way to demonstrate softness.

Maybe your teen did not feel you listened to her pain. We can't emphasize enough the importance of listening. Ask yourself, *Did I really listen to my offended child? Was I trying to defend my actions or justify why I behaved the way I did?* If you're not sure, go back and listen carefully to her pain or frustration.

It may also be that your teen did not feel you were sincere in taking ownership of your part of whatever conflict closed his spirit. Perhaps you came close to taking responsibility but didn't clearly acknowledge your fault. If that's the case, it will be difficult for your teen to forgive you. It's like trying to build something on sand; the foundation will always be shaky. But taking ownership of your mistakes is like laying four feet of reinforced concrete as the foundation of your relationship with your child.

If you continue to try these steps and your teen still refuses to forgive you, choosing to remain angry, you may need to try some additional things. In chapter 12, "When Teenagers Walk Away from the Light," we deal with this type of case. If this is your current situation, we encourage you to turn to that chapter immediately.

At the same time, we urge you *not* to adopt an attitude of, "Well, if she won't forgive me, that's her problem. I did my part." If you take up that mind-set, the problem may never be resolved.

But this also means not assuming all *the responsibility.* Just as you need to keep forgiving your teen for hurtful words and actions, so your teenager is responsible to forgive you as well.[8] You can be faithful to seek forgiveness and own your part of the problem. But you cannot take an inferior or guilt-ridden position if your teen consistently refuses to forgive you.

You may want to have someone hold you accountable for how you handle the situation—correcting your mistake and seeking forgiveness, yet not taking more than your share of the blame. It's possible to try too hard and get locked into feeling guilty and shameful. God does not want us to get stuck in shame if our children refuse to forgive. Do your part, but then allow God to work in your son or daughter's life.

Remember, opening a teenager's closed spirit involves reflecting tenderness, increasing your own understanding, admitting the offense, and seeking forgiveness. If this process doesn't work, repeat the steps, but make changes in the way you tried them the first time. If you keep doing things the same way, you're likely to keep getting the same results.

There's no set number of times to repeat the steps if your child won't forgive you. Each situation is different, and so is each teen. Turn the process over to God, find an accountability partner, and continue to love and forgive your teen.

Next, we'll look at how the right kinds of communication can increase honor and understanding and further strengthen your relationship with your teenager.

4

HOW TO ARGUE WITH TEENAGERS AND COME OUT AS CLOSER FRIENDS

But everyone must be quick to hear, slow to speak and
slow to anger; for the anger of man does not achieve the
righteousness of God.
The Bible

As we discussed in the preceding chapter, working to open a closed spirit is a great way to reduce anger in our teenagers. Another is a communication method called "drive-thru talking." It sounds like some secret McDonald's language, but we call it that because it mimics what takes place at the drive-thru of a fast-food restaurant.

Good communication is vital during conflict. When we asked 5,000 adults what they wished their parents had done differently during times of conflict, they gave these three responses most often:

1. They wished their parents would have listened more.

2. They wished they could have talked about feelings more.

3. They wished they would have talked to their parents more.

It's interesting that all three of those involve aspects of communication. And as this list suggests, good communication during conflict begins with *listening* and not with searching for solutions. Men especially tend to pay little attention to what their loved ones are saying, concentrating instead on trying to fix the problem. That's why we want to emphasize in this chapter that we need to listen first and *then* look for ways to resolve the conflict. It's also why we'll wait until the next chapter to discuss techniques for finding solutions.

Attempts at communication between parents and teens can be extremely frustrating for both parties. That's even more true when they have similar personalities, as is the case with me (Gary) and my son Michael. The stories of our conflicts and hurt feelings could fill a separate book! One such incident comes to mind that illustrates both my ability to blow it as a parent and the power of drive-thru talking to bring healing to the situation. See if you can't relate to what happened between us.

Michael was in high school at the time, and on this occasion he accompanied me to Boise, Idaho, where I was to give a seminar. The day before the seminar began, Michael had agreed to drive me to a special speaking engagement. I was suffering from the 24-hour flu and was not in the best of moods. Looking back now, it wasn't a good idea to put Michael and me together under those circumstances; it was like dumping gas on a massive bonfire.

Within five minutes of getting in the car, we were arguing about his choice of clothing for the day. He was not wearing a suit, as I wanted, because he'd been instructed by someone on my staff to wear khaki pants and a polo shirt with our seminar logo on the front. I strongly disagreed with this choice and took my frustration out on him. Just as your teenager might respond, Michael adamantly defended himself. "My clothes are fine," he snapped. "You're just not in touch with what's in style!"

"Right!" I shot back. "We'll see how 'in-style' you feel when everyone else has on a suit. You'll be embarrassed."

The argument continued to escalate until, frustrated and angry, we stopped talking altogether. Ironically, I was going to lecture about how to have healthy relationships!

To make matters worse, when we arrived at the place where I was to give the speech, I closed his spirit down completely. "By the way," I said sarcastically, "I'm not taking you in there to meet anyone—I'd be embarrassed. They would wonder why you don't at least have on a tie. Your casual clothes look dishonoring." Talk about dishonoring someone— what was I thinking?

"You're too concerned about your reputation," Michael informed me. "I guarantee that no one would mind if I'm not wearing a tie. Give me a break!"

"You *will* embarrass me," I shouted, "and you won't be coming in. That's final!"

Stuck in the car, Michael probably felt like the family pet instead of my son. He may have been tempted to "bark" as people walked past the car. Luckily, we weren't giving the lecture together or we might have been in even bigger trouble. I can picture the newspaper headline that might have resulted: "Family Speaker Verbally Abuses Son While on Stage!"

We drove back to our hotel that night in silence. As a matter of fact, we didn't talk for the rest of the weekend. When we finally got home, Michael returned to school with the conflict still simmering between us.

Later that week, I was feeling very guilty about being in disharmony. Then, while at a shopping mall, I ran into one of Michael's friends who is also close to our family. She had just been with him and mentioned that he was still upset.

As if I weren't feeling bad enough, I thought, *now I'm going to get a lecture from a high-school student.*

This high schooler, however, said something that changed my relationship with Michael from that day on. She told me that Michael was one of the most sensitive people she had ever met—more sensitive, even, than any of her girl friends. Hearing that struck me like being hit in the head with a huge board. Her words caused me to imagine what Michael must have gone through all those years with me. I started thinking, *What other things have I said or done that may have deeply hurt him?* When Michael got home after school, we set up a time to resolve our conflict and restore harmony.

Now, the amazing part of this story is that once we sat down to work things out, it took us only about 20 minutes to completely talk through the different issues. And it wasn't just me listening to him. Instead, we both walked away feeling heard and understood. It happened so fast that we both said, "This was way too easy. We must be missing something." But after closer review, we realized there wasn't anything we had failed to resolve.

Our quick success came because we used the drive-thru talking method taught (under a different name) by two of our favorite divorce-prevention experts, Dr. Howard Markman and Dr. Scott Stanley. It's amazing how quick and powerful this communication technique is.

Here is a brief summary of how Michael and I resolved our conflict; we'll go into more detail later in the chapter. I simply asked, "Would you be willing to describe your feelings about when I criticized your clothing?" As Michael began to speak, I slowly repeated back each feeling he expressed so he could hear whether I understood what he was saying. There were times when he said, "That's exactly right," and at other times I missed what he was trying to communicate. Michael would then say, "That's close, but it's not quite what I mean."

After he finished, I had a chance to describe my feelings about our conflict. Michael then repeated my message. This pattern of repeating back and forth enabled us to value each other's feelings. Just being able to express our deep feelings, and then having the other person validate and empathize with them, seemed to solve the problem.

Unfortunately, rather than using a mutually honoring approach like drive-thru talking to handle disputes, many families tend to use one or more of four common habits that bring further anger and destruction to the relationship. Drs. Markman and Stanley have discovered in their research that these negative approaches, when used in a marriage, often lead to divorce. They can also lead to strained relationships between parents and teenagers by contributing to the three primary causes of anger: *frustration, hurt feelings,* and *fear.*

In other words, these four common habits are what we *shouldn't* do when we have family disagreements. Before we get into a detailed explanation of drive-thru talking, then, let's examine these unhealthy ways of arguing so we know what to avoid.

Four Destructive Ways to Argue

1. Continually *withdrawing* from an argument

Conflict avoidance or withdrawal doesn't happen only in "dysfunctional" families; it's common in otherwise healthy families as well. In our seminar survey of more than 5,000 adults, when we asked "How did you and your parents deal with conflict?" the number-one response was avoiding or withdrawing from it.

How about your family? Do you find that you and your teenager continue to bring up the same areas of conflict without resolving them? If so, these discussions probably end in hurt, frustration, or fear because the issues have not been handled adequately.

2. Letting arguments *escalate* into hurtful, name-calling fights

If you and your teen find yourselves starting to shout and call each other degrading, dishonoring names during an argument, the anger level will usually skyrocket. Nothing can make a discussion escalate out of control faster. Yet when we asked our survey respondents how their families had handled conflict, "Yelling and screaming at each other" was the third-most-common answer.

What usually starts this kind of interaction is the accusatory word *you*. For example, "You never . . . You always . . . You make me . . ." As this happens, you're usually left with greater hurt and frustration. Furthermore, the fear level is now higher because you remember the increased pain of the argument. The result is more love-killing anger between those involved.

Usually following on the heels of an escalating argument is the third bad habit we need to avoid.

3. Belittling or *invalidating* each other during an argument

To invalidate someone is to make fun of him or attack his personhood. For example, during a conflict we might accuse our teenager of being stupid, uncaring, wild, immature, ugly, or something equally dishonoring. When this happens, it can cause emotional damage and sour the relationship.

A man named Hank understands invalidation all too well. At one of our seminars, he told us about an experience with his father that exemplifies invalidation. Hank's father always had to be "right" regardless of the facts. One day when Hank was about 15, he was watching his father prepare to cut some wood in the family garage. When his dad picked up the power saw, he received a strong electric shock. As his father screamed and threw the saw reflexively, Hank started coughing and choking in an effort to contain his laughter.

> *Invalidation takes place when we try to cut someone at the core of her being, like saying something about her age, personality, appearance, or intelligence.*

Hank's father decided to use this momentary setback to teach his son a valuable lesson about handling power equipment. He launched into a long and boring oratory about why he got shocked and what he should have done differently. Then he turned the plug around and demonstrated why this would solve the problem. The only thing that would have topped his lecture was if he'd been able to use a blackboard and four different colors of chalk.

Next, Hank's dad picked up the saw again and turned it on. "BZZZZ!" came the now familiar sound of his dad getting shocked.

Hank could no longer contain his laughter. As he doubled over, he was able to offer his frustrated father a few sympathetic words: "Obviously the saw wasn't paying attention to your lecture!" And with that, Hank fell off the table laughing.

Falling to the ground proved to be a good thing, because his father swung the 2x4 he was cutting at Hank. At that moment, Hank decided he'd better leave and come back later when his dad had calmed down.

Sadly, when Hank returned home, instead of the two of them enjoying a good laugh, his father shamed Hank for laughing. "You've done some pretty stupid things yourself, Hank," he said sarcastically, then laughed. "Getting a D in gym class—only a moron could almost flunk gym." Then he added, "See, it's not so funny when someone laughs at you, is it?" His dad was right—it wasn't funny anymore.

As Hank related this painful memory to us, he said, "I just needed for my dad to tell me that he had made a simple mistake. Then we could have laughed together. But his cutting remarks were typical of our relationship, and it's why we never were close."

Invalidation takes place when we try to cut someone at the core of her being, like saying something about her age, personality, appearance, or intelligence (such as when Hank's dad made fun of his low grade in gym class). To be invalidated can be extremely painful. Perhaps you remember a time when a parent, teacher, coach, or friend said something that hurt you deep inside, maybe not even realizing the depth of pain his comment caused.

Why do conflicts between parents and teenagers so often escalate into name calling, yelling, and invalidation? One reason we need to understand is the intensity and variability of teenage emotions.

The teenage emotional roller coaster. It's no secret that adolescence is a period of emotional highs and lows. Our teens may feel as if they're on an emotional roller coaster: loving one minute and hating the next; feeling a sense of pride and then suddenly feeling shame. One moment the future looks bright, and then in the blink of an eye it's hopeless.

Think of emotions as being on a continuum, with keeping rigid control of one's emotions on one end and being impulsive and highly reactive on the other.

Overcontrolled   **Impulsive and**
Emotions ——————————— + ——————————— **Highly Reactive**

Teenagers who tightly control their emotions are usually anxious about accepting or expressing them. Being out of balance on this end can cause teens to feel ashamed of their emotions and make them not want to be around others. They may even develop eating disorders.

On the other end of the continuum are those teenagers who are impulsive and highly emotional. These teens seem unable to adjust the intensity of their reactions. As a result, they can become involved in harmful activities like delinquency or premarital sex. Strong emotions can also cause poor judgment. When two people argue, many chemicals are released, such as adrenaline, which can interfere with one's ability to make a good decision.

One time when my mother and I (Greg) were arguing, we escalated out of control to the point where I stormed out of the room. I was so pumped full of adrenaline that I impulsively punched the hall wall on the way to my bedroom. The moment I hit the wall, an expensive picture fell. I tried to catch it, but my reflexes weren't fast enough. The picture crashed to the floor and smashed on top of my bare foot, and the glass over it broke into pieces. I was left with a severely bruised and lacerated foot and the obligation to pay for the broken glass.

The intensity and variability of emotions, especially in teenagers and especially during conflict, can cause a calm discussion to turn instantly into a raging war of words. It's no wonder that you can expect to experience occasional escalation and invalidation.

Time-out! One of the best ways to deal with escalation and invalidation during a conflict is to take a "time-out." In other words, when emotions start to heighten, body temperatures rise, and words start becoming dishonoring, it's time to take a break. Always agree to resume the discussion when everyone's emotions have settled. As you utilize the time-out with your teenager, you will be modeling a great conflict resolution skill that he or she will be able to use for a lifetime.

We've seen how destructive withdrawal, escalation, and invalidation can be. Let's now turn our attention to the final habit in arguing that can produce anger and become extremely toxic to the honor in your home.

4. Starting to *believe* that a family member is trying to hurt, frustrate, or cause fear on purpose

When we begin to develop a negative belief about someone, it can have permanent and ruinous consequences. Julie discovered just how damaging such beliefs can be when she was faced with one of the most challenging experiences of her life.

"You're so stupid!" her mother screamed. Mom was drunk again. How many times had Julie heard that same message? "You'll never amount to anything!" Her mother's words cut deep into her heart. "You'll end up pregnant just like me, you no-good tramp!"

What did she say? Julie thought. *Did she say* pregnant?

Julie had endured years of verbal abuse from her mother. By now she had heard pretty much everything. But tonight was different. Of all the things her mother could say, the statement about her getting pregnant was the worst.

You're so stupid, you'll never amount to anything. You'll end up pregnant!

It was hard not to dwell on all the things her mother said and believed about her. But she couldn't help it that her mother, at age 16, had gotten pregnant by some guy. It wasn't her fault. Or was it?

Over the years, Julie's mother had blamed her for many things, but especially for "destroying" her life. "If it wasn't for you, I would have gone to college!" her mother would scream. "I would have become something!"

Just once, Julie thought, *I would love to tell her that I, too, wish she had become something else. Then I wouldn't have been born!*

Julie's mind drifted back to her mother's comment "You'll end up pregnant!" There was no way in the world Julie would make the same mistake her mother had made. She hated everything about her mother, especially the way she had had a child when she was only 16. How could her mother have been so stupid? *That will never happen to me!* Julie had thought proudly over the years.

She soon realized she was wrong. "No!" Julie cried out now. "This can't be happening to me!" But there was no denying that the stick was pink. The pregnancy test was pink! Julie's worst nightmare had just come true.

You'll end up pregnant!

At 17, Julie was going to have a baby. How could this have happened? She had always been so careful. The worst part was that she couldn't even remember the guy's name.

You'll never amount to anything!

What was she going to do? She had to tell her mother, but that thought nauseated her. She hated thinking of how her mother would say, "I told you so."

You'll end up pregnant!

But she had to tell her. She was going to need help to raise this child. More importantly, however, Julie longed to have her mother tell her that everything would be okay, that she loved her. *Is it that hard?* Julie thought. *They're only three little words.* Julie made a vow to herself that day: If her mother said "I love you," Julie would stay. If not, she would leave forever.

In the following weeks, Julie tried to tell her mother so many different times, but it never seemed to be the right moment. Finally, one day Julie came home from school and found her mother sitting quietly in the living room. Everything appeared perfect. No drinking. No fighting. Just peacefulness!

Julie's heart started beating faster as she entered the living room. Her mother glanced up and said nothing. *This is going to work,* Julie thought.

Memories of all the times her mother had screamed at her raced through her mind. She had to push them back. She needed all the emotional strength she could find.

"Mother . . . I mean . . . Mom," she said in a soft voice. She didn't want to set her off. "Can we talk?"

As Julie knelt beside her mother, she accidentally knocked over Mom's glass of iced tea. "You idiot!" screamed her mother. "Now look what you've done! Can't you ever do anything right?"

"That was 33 years ago," Julie wrote in telling us her story. "I am now 50 years old. I've never seen my mother since that day . . . and I never will!"

What we believe about our children may come true, good or bad. Once we start developing a deep conviction that our teenager is stupid, clumsy, trying to drive us crazy, or going to get pregnant, we'll actually hear or see signs of it even if it isn't true. The power of belief is so great that we see what we expect to see. As Drs. Markman and Stanley explain,

> People tend to see what they expect to see in others and in situa-
> tions. In fact, we have a very strong tendency toward "confirmation
> bias," which consists of looking for evidence that confirms what we
> already think is true about a person or situation. We can be wrong
> in our assumptions, but we all have formed beliefs and expecta-
> tions about why those we know well do what they do.[1]

Confirmation bias is particularly destructive when it comes to parent-adolescent conflict. For example, Julie's mother believed all her problems were Julie's fault. No matter what Julie actually did, her mother always interpreted her actions in light of that belief. When Julie got pregnant, her mother (when she finally found out about it) interpreted the situation as just another attempt by Julie to destroy the mom's life.

As you can see, withdrawal, escalation, invalidation, and negative beliefs foster anger and destroy both the parent's and the teen's love if continued over time. That's why we need to be aware of these patterns and replace them with the *right* way—the best way we've found—to communicate during times of conflict. It's time, in other words, to look in detail at how drive-thru talking works and why it's so effective.

Using Drive-thru Talking to Resolve Family Conflicts

Remember the conflict Michael and I (Gary) had concerning his clothes and how, using drive-thru talking, we were able to resolve it in 20 minutes? It's as easy to use this communication method as it is to order a hamburger at McDonald's. Let me now give you the essence of how it works.

To resolve our conflict in honor that day, Michael and I first needed to agree to use drive-thru talking. I said to him, "How would you like to use a method of communication that guarantees I will hear and understand you?"

That got his attention. "What are you talking about?" he responded warily. "All you ever do is criticize me! You never listen, and you certainly don't understand me!"

"Michael," I said softly, "I know I've hurt you and that you don't trust I'll be able to hear and understand you." (Using a soft voice, as we saw in chapter 3, is vital in dealing with an angry teenager.) "But Michael," I continued honestly, "I want to hear how you're really feeling about what I did to you. This communication method I'm talking about will provide the structure for me to keep my focus exclusively on listening and understanding you."

Since that's what he, like all teens, ultimately wanted—to feel heard and understood—he agreed to use the drive-thru talking method.

The rules for drive-thru talking are simple, but they must be followed to keep the discussion honoring. One person agrees to start "*inside* the fast food restaurant" (the "employee"), and the other starts the discussion "*outside* in the car by the menu" (the "customer"). The employee says something like, "Welcome to the Smalley home. Can I take your order?"

The customer then expresses his feelings or his needs in the current conflict. He can't bring up anything from the past or start a new argument. (We can deal with only one argument at a time.) And the customer needs to offer only small amounts of information at a time. Making large statements or blending two ideas together can cause the employee to forget or miss something important.

The employee's job is to repeat what is said by the customer, making sure he understands the "order" clearly, and he isn't allowed to evaluate anything that's said. (Have you ever heard a McDonald's worker say after you order a super-sized meal, "Sir, I can see you in my mirror, and . . . well . . . are you sure you want the Big Mac? May I recommend the McLean?" Absolutely not! You'd drive away furious and never visit again.)

Drive-thru talking is successful because it helps your teenager feel safe to express his or her needs and feelings. Safety develops when your child trusts that your goal is to listen and understand, not to defend and challenge. That's why, in the employee role, we do not evaluate, edit, or defend ourselves. Instead, we simply *listen and repeat.*

How can you be sure drive-thru talking will really work with your teenager? If you enter into it with a spirit of honor by listening and repeating, you will provide your child with a tremendously safe environment in which to discuss feelings. Sit back and let God do the rest. Remember, we call this method drive-thru talking because fast-food chains have spent millions of dollars testing their ordering methods. If they can satisfy millions of drive-thru customers every day, why don't we use their knowledge to keep our "family customers" happy and satisfied? We can!

Drive-thru talking is successful because it helps your teenager feel safe to express his or her needs and feelings.

When Michael and I used it to resolve our conflict over his seminar outfit, I became the employee first and said, "Welcome to the Smalley home. May I take your order?"

Michael looked at me as if I were insane.

"Humor me," I told him. "This will work if you give it a chance."

Michael then said, "Dad, I felt stupid and humiliated when you told me I embarrassed you."

I repeated back what I had heard him say: "You're saying I humiliated you when I said your clothes would embarrass me." (It's better if you repeat using your own words.)

He agreed that I had heard and understood him by nodding his head.

I then said, "Would you like to 'order' anything else?"

Michael continued describing his feelings and needs, and I kept repeating each thing until he'd said everything he needed to say. Then we traded places. I became the customer, and he became the employee. I started stating my feelings and needs, and he repeated them.

I first said, "I was frustrated because I thought your casual clothes might communicate that the people were not worth your getting dressed up."

Michael answered, "That's stupid. No one would have thought that!"

That was an example of invalidating my feelings. It didn't matter at that point whether he agreed with me. His job was to validate me by repeating what he heard—not to edit my words or defend himself. After we clarified the rules, Michael repeated my original statement and the others I made until I felt he understood me.

The amazing part of this method is how fast anger is dissipated. When someone is listening to you with great concern and valuing who you are, the anger just seems to drain away.

Once each person feels heard, understood, and validated, you can begin to look for solutions to the problem if necessary. You'll be amazed, however, at how easily some arguments are solved after you both feel understood and valued.

Now that you've seen the drive-thru talking method in action, we suggest you start practicing it. If your teen is going to find value in this method, you need to demonstrate that it's worth using. Remember, the best lessons learned in life are caught, not taught. To help you, we offer the following summary of drive-thru talking guidelines:

Summary of Drive-thru Talking Rules

FAST-FOOD EMPLOYEE (listener)

- This person's job is to listen.

- When receiving an order, you can only repeat back what you've heard. No editing, evaluating, or defending yourself. You can ask to have the order repeated if you did not understand something. However, this is only for clarity—you don't have to agree.

CUSTOMER (speaker)

- This person's job is to express needs or feelings using "I" statements. No bringing up past issues, starting a new argument, or making blaming "You" statements (e.g., "You always . . .").

- Offer "bite-sized" thoughts or information so the other person can remember in order to repeat it back correctly and understand your feelings.

GENERAL RULES

- Repeating statements in the employee role does not mean you agree with what's being said. Instead, the goal is to listen and validate the other person's feelings and individuality.

• When the customer feels heard and validated, you switch roles.

• You are *not* looking for solutions at this time. Solutions can be sought after each person feels heard and validated.

• Agree to take a time-out if withdrawal, escalation, invalidation, or negative beliefs creep into the conversation.

• Above all else, strive to honor one another in all that is said and repeated!

WARNING...

As a word of caution, we highly encourage you *not* to begin drive-thru talking on a highly sensitive or controversial subject or a deeply hurtful area from your past. Start with less-volatile conflicts like being late for dinner or maybe wearing too much makeup. As your skills increase at using this life-changing method, you may feel safer to use it with more serious and sensitive matters. *Take your time.* It's not something you try and stop using because it didn't work immediately the way you wanted. Trust us, it works if you stay with it. It has been proved for years to be the most powerful communication method available, and it definitely lowers the anger level at home (as well as at the office or at school).[2]

Now it's time to consider how honoring, lasting solutions can be found for parent-teen conflicts. In the next chapter, we explain seven powerful steps any mom or dad can take to help resolve even the most difficult disagreements with adolescents.

5

FINDING THE BEST SOLUTION TO ANY CONFLICT

*Therefore, to one who knows the right thing
to do, and does not do it, to him it is sin.*
The Bible

Once you and your teen have heard and understood each other using drive-thru talking, it's time to pursue solutions to whatever conflict remains. The goal is for *both* of you to come away feeling like satisfied, honored winners.

I (Greg) vividly remember a heated conflict I had with my mother over a number of months when I was in my late teens. Throughout my entire senior year of high school, I had put off deciding which college I wanted to attend because I was having too much fun. I continually ignored Mom's encouragement to fill out applications. By the middle of August after my high-school graduation, I still had no idea where I was going to college.

"Why won't you fill out your applications?" Mom demanded. "Do you realize it might be too late now? I can't believe you're still procrastinating like this!"

"Get off my back!" I yelled at her. "I know what I'm doing!"

In fact, of course, I had *no* idea what I was doing. And when I finally started applying, I quickly discovered how foolish I had been. All the schools needed transcripts, letters of recommendation, and SAT scores. As crazy as this may seem, the thought had never crossed my mind before then that I couldn't simply "show up" and begin taking classes. After all, that's what I did in high school!

As the end of August approached, I reasoned that since my sister was attending Grand Canyon University in our hometown of Phoenix, that would be a logical place to apply. But on the day of registration, my high hopes quickly turned into panic. Because I had waited so long, the admissions department told me, they were already at full capacity for the incoming freshman class. "Sorry," the clerk said. "You can always go to a junior college and apply next semester." Mom had been right!

Hearing the news was like having someone slam a giant block of ice against my bare back. The reality sent shock waves through my entire body. I felt like going outside and beating myself up, but I figured the university staff would probably frown on that kind of behavior. Instead of a state college, they'd recommend a state hospital!

I felt about as low as a person could possibly get. As I was about to return home and face Mom with the terrible news, my sister came running up. After hearing about my admission trouble, she insisted I meet someone.

"Leave me alone, Kari," I said. "I'm not in the mood to socialize."

"Like anyone would want to socialize with you!" she snapped back. That made me feel even worse. I was just about to assault her verbally when she added, "Never mind all that. I know a professor who might be able to help."

Help. Help was good. Suddenly, I saw a glimpse of life in my dying college career. And fortunately, Kari introduced me to a person who was able to get my application approved. Although I started that week on academic probation, I was grateful just to be in college!

I learned a valuable lesson through that experience, and it wasn't about the importance of who you know. Instead, I realized that day that I needed to learn how to make wise decisions, especially during times of conflict, like the one with my mother over college preparations.

Our desire for this chapter is twofold: First, we want to give anyone dealing with teenagers a seven-step process for finding the best solution to any conflict. Second, we want to show how these seven steps can equip teenagers to make wise decisions at any time, not just during conflict.

It's vital that we teach teens how to make wise decisions, because there's no place to hide or shield them from life. Fortunately, we don't need to ship our kids to an island or lock them in their rooms until they turn 35. Helping them learn to make wise decisions is even better. What we mean by "make wise decisions" is *having the ability, through discretion and extensive knowledge, to sensibly discern and judge something before receiving or acting upon it.* This ability then becomes a skill that will benefit them for the rest of their lives. What a precious gift!

The Importance of Dealing with Conflict

Can helping our teens make wise decisions during conflict really make a difference in our relationship with them? Can it help us to increase honor and lower the anger level in our homes? Yes!

Researchers have consistently shown that healthy families have a coping ability during times of conflict. They can handle family problems without becoming divided or allowing anger to settle in. In a 1983 report, for example, Dolores Curran asked 551 professionals who work with families what specific factors contributed to a healthy family. One of the top 15 was "admits to and seeks help with problems."[1]

In contrast, when we asked the 5,000 adults in our survey, "How did you and your parents deal with conflict?" the number-one response was "We avoided it!" And one reason that's such a common response is that a crucial change occurs in adolescent kids, a change that tends to heighten conflict. But we can learn how to deal with it constructively.

The Change That Heightens Conflict

This significant change involves a teenager's mental abilities. Younger children tend to think their parents know everything. They focus on literal or concrete ideas and have trouble with abstractions. One Sunday school teacher discovered this when he tried to teach his primary-aged charges about miracles. "Boys and girls," he said, "suppose I stood on the roof of a 10-story building, lost my balance, and fell off. Then all of a sudden, in midair, a whirlwind swept me up and brought me safely to the ground. What word would you use to describe this?"

After a long silence, a boy raised his hand and said, "Luck?"

"True, true," replied the teacher, "it could be luck. But that's not the word I was looking for. I'll repeat the story. There I am on top of the 10-story building again, and I fall. A whirlwind catches me in midair and places me safely on the ground. Think now—what word would describe the situation?"

"Accident!" cried out one girl.

"No, no," answered the teacher. "Listen carefully for the third time. I'm on that same building, I fall and am swept to safety by a sudden whirlwind. What word could account for my safely reaching the ground?"

The boys and girls shouted in unison, "Practice!"

When adolescence hits, however, the child's reasoning process changes forever. The average teenager becomes highly logical and thinks *he* knows everything. Mom and Dad's word no longer automatically makes something so.

A father discovered how frustrating this change can be. Lecturing about the problems of staying out late and then sleeping away the morning, he reprimanded his teenage son. "You will never amount to anything unless you turn over a new leaf," he said. "Remember that the early bird gets the worm."

"But Dad," argued the son, "wasn't the worm stupid for getting up so early?"

Stunned by his son's question, the father stumbled for a reply. "Um . . . ah . . . hum . . . well . . . ah ha!" he finally shouted with confidence. "The worm hadn't been to bed—he was on his way home!"

It's vital that we understand our teenagers' mental changes because of how they can affect our approach to conflict resolution.

According to developmental expert Jean Piaget, the changes that take place in an adolescent's thinking are called formal operations. Formal operations appear between the ages of 11 and 15 and take children beyond the world of actual, concrete experiences to the realm of abstract and more logical thought.[2] They now have the mental capacity for problem solving and can detect the logical consistency or inconsistency in a set of statements—especially the ones their parents make! They also start thinking about the future and its endless possibilities. Some teens can't deal with all these new choices, and they lose hope. This is one reason suicide is a leading cause of death among adolescents.

It's vital that we understand our teenagers' mental changes because of how they can affect our approach to conflict resolution. Even if our teens seem to want to argue all the time, it may well be a direct result of these developmental changes. It doesn't necessarily mean they love terrorizing us or that we have a terrible relationship. Instead, we can try to picture their new mental abilities as a Christmas present they've just received. There's always great excitement and excessive usage when a present is first unwrapped. In the same way, teenagers need to experiment with their newfound abilities. There probably isn't a better "practice field" on which to do that than at home with us. But it needs to be done in a healthy and constructive manner.

We can guarantee that almost all families will experience conflict. It's a normal part of being in relationships. In fact, it's not only normal, but as we saw in chapter 4 and will see again in this chapter, conflict can be the doorway leading to intimacy. Intimacy is always achieved at the price of facing our differences and negative feelings and listening, understanding, and resolving them. But remember that conflict will lead to anger rather than intimacy if it's not handled properly, and anger may produce rebellion, promiscuity, drug or alcohol abuse, gang involvement, or running with the wrong crowd. So how can we resolve conflicts with our teenagers in honor? We start by establishing some ground rules.

Rules for Fair Fighting

Before the next conflict with your teenager arises, we encourage you to do something so valuable that it can save hours of pain: *With your family, establish rules for fair fighting.* Such specific rules concerning what's permitted and what's not will provide structure and safety and keep your discussion from getting out of control and slipping into one of the bad habits we explored in the last chapter (withdrawal, escalation, invalidation, negative beliefs). One rule, for example, could be that whenever you see one of those four things happening, you take a time-out.

At the beginning of the rule-setting discussion, the parent should provide a positive note by stating a desire to be fair.[3] That's the key word for creating rules: *fair.* Most teens have a heightened sense of fairness, so pointing out that these rules will promote fair play should motivate them to help set up some rules.

The best way to establish these rules is to begin by asking each family member, "What rules are needed when we argue in order to keep us from getting out of control or dishonoring each other?" Then, after everyone has spoken and you've reached agreement as a family, write down your rules and post them somewhere visible so you can see them during an argument. In the Smalley household, we kept our rules for fair fighting on the refrigerator because most of our conflict occurred in the kitchen (the family gathering place).

A good rule for every family is that both parents and children agree to treat each other with respect and listen to each other's point of view. In the Smalley home, we also agreed that we would not bring past mistakes into a current argument. Dredging up the past is never the way to solve a problem. This is exactly what one father realized when talking with his friend. "You know, Frank," he said, "whenever my daughter and I get into an argument, she gets historical."

"You mean hysterical, Pete, don't you?"

"No, I mean historical. She remembers everything I ever did wrong and the exact date and time when it happened."

The 5,000 adults we surveyed gave us these top 10 rules for fair fighting:

1. Listen for understanding.

2. Avoid yelling, verbal threats, or abuse.

3. Maintain an honoring, respectful, and loving atmosphere.

4. No name calling.

5. Use open communication.

6. Don't bring in past "garbage."

7. Keep the focus off the person's character.

8. No violence.

9. Avoid accusatory language (e.g., "You never . . . always . . .").

10. Make sure only one person talks at a time.

Select just a few key rules to start with, because most parents and teens can't remember too many in the heat of an argument. Having and using even four or five will usually calm down the emotions. And the calmer the argument, the better the chance of an honoring outcome. Make sure you follow the fairness rules from the start, too, as researchers have discovered that the first 30 seconds of a disagreement can determine whether the next two hours of arguing are carried out in honor or in anger.

Dads especially need the safety of rules and calmness to fight fairly. If the rules for fighting are not clear and a man feels overwhelmed by angry words, his tendency is to withdraw. As we have previously discussed, withdrawal does a great deal of damage. Anger flares. But using the drive-thru talking communication method and fair-fighting rules make it much more likely that Dad will remain and work things out.

Once your rules are established, you'll be ready to jump right into the seven steps for wisely resolving almost any conflict with your teenager.

Seven Steps Toward Making Wise
Decisions During Conflicts

When the Smalley kids were teens and large conflicts came up within our family, we tried to follow the next seven steps as closely as possible. They helped greatly to keep our anger levels low and our honor high.

1. *Clearly define* the problem issue.

To resolve a conflict, it's necessary to first clearly define what the conflict is about. It could just be the result of fatigue, miscommunication, unclear rules, or a low sugar level. Or perhaps someone has an unspoken desire.

When Michael was 16, he and his mother experienced a major conflict. He wanted to move from the private high school he was attending to a public school. When he first approached me (Gary) with the idea, I thought it sounded great. He could experience new challenges, meet new friends, and compete in a tougher sports division. "You're going to have so much fun," I said to Michael. "Why didn't we think of this before?"

"That's right," Michael agreed. "Plus, I already know some neat Christian guys and girls over there."

I was getting so excited that I wished I could go to school with him. Michael and I are just alike in loving new ideas—especially when we don't have to think about the details. Just as we were about to explode with enthusiasm, Mom walked by.

Mom! Michael and I exchanged knowing looks.

"Michael wants to tell you about an idea he has," I carefully told her. "And I want you to know that I had nothing to do with it. He came up with this one all by himself."

Norma rolled her eyes and gave us a look that means, "What impulsive scheme have you two concocted this time?"

"Mom," Michael confidently stated while winking at me, "I want to go to a public high school. I think it would be good for me. Besides, there are a lot of kids I could witness to."

"Gary, you put him up to this," Norma reacted. "Witnessing. Good one, Michael! You're not switching schools. Forget it."

Michael and I stared at each other in disbelief. "That went well," I said.

Norma is able to foresee the details of any idea. Although frustrating to my plans occasionally, this gift has proved extremely useful over the years. But in this case, I felt we should at least talk about Michael's desire. Even if it didn't seem wise, we needed to resolve this issue together.

Otherwise, Michael's spirit might close in anger—and I certainly didn't want another child running into a buffalo herd!

So we sat down and peaceably defined our disagreement. And as Michael explained why he wanted to switch schools, it became obvious that he had a hidden desire he wasn't expressing. After we repeated his needs and feelings, Norma had the opportunity to say gently, "Michael, I feel like you're not being 100 percent honest about your reasons for switching schools. Is there any other reason you haven't mentioned?"

"Well . . . Kevin just told me he's going to that school next year," Michael finally admitted. Michael wanted to stay in school with his best friend.

As that incident shows, a conflict may be fueled by family members' underlying, unspoken needs. Only when those needs or desires are brought into the open can we move toward resolution. It may help to ask questions like "What's really going on?" or "What change would be needed to satisfy you?"

2. Don't be impulsive—get the *facts*.

The next step in resolving a conflict is to consider all the important facts. Norma explained that switching schools wasn't as easy as Michael and I had assumed. For example, the city wouldn't let Michael attend that particular public school because we lived out of its district. Another important detail was that the sports program in the public school was about four times harder to get into than the program at the private school. Finally, Norma noted that Kevin and Michael attended the same youth group and could spend more "fun time" with each other away from school.

"I didn't realize that," Michael said while looking at me. "Dad, why didn't you tell me all this?"

"I was going to," I suggested with a straight face, "but your mother is so much better at explaining these things."

"Yeah, right!" Michael and Norma said in unison. And on that note, Michael decided that he was pretty satisfied at his old school.

Our family could give plenty of examples of when the kids and I acted impulsively and didn't check into the facts before making a decision. But one of the all-time craziest experiences was when Greg was just about to start his junior year of college.

During the summer before my junior year, I (Greg) worked as a camp counselor at Kanakuk Kamp in Branson, Missouri. And like thousands of other college kids, I fell in love. But this girl was from Oklahoma State University, and I lived in Arizona. When I returned home, I was heartbroken. My girlfriend and I tried to stay in touch, but the separation was straining our relationship.

One day while I was with my father, we had a long talk about my future. Looking for a way to be with my girlfriend, I told him about my desire to "venture away from home." Carefully, I explained how I had never lived away from the family. As the conversation progressed, my impulsive father started to get excited about my going to an out-of-state university. We laughed about how much fun it would be and how much I would learn. Finally, what had started out as a little idea had grown into serious plans for going away to college.

Of course, we needed to determine the best place for me to go. Feigning innocence, I asked Dad if he knew anything about the University of Oklahoma.

"I've got an old friend there who works at the Baptist Student Union," he said enthusiastically. "He would be a great person to disciple you!"

Realizing he had taken the bait, all I needed now was to set the hook and reel him in. "I wouldn't be lonely there," I said. "A bunch of camp friends attend the university, so I would be around Christian friends." More importantly, I knew my girlfriend lived only about an hour away!

It was too easy! I had set the hook, reeled him in, and mounted the "gullible fish" on the wall in a matter of minutes. But I realized that talking Dad into something was like fishing for perch in a barrel—it wasn't terribly difficult. The hard part was going deep-sea fishing for sailfish—trying to convince Mom.

Impulsive actions can be limited if we agree as a family to gather facts before making a decision, especially during the heat of a disagreement.

Over the years, my father and I have done some "strange" things together, and this was one of them. I wonder what my mother must have been thinking that night when I revealed that I was moving to Oklahoma. She put up a good fight, but she didn't have the kind of indisputable facts at hand that she had used in talking Michael out of changing high schools. So, ignoring her advice to seek additional input and check out a few facts, I was packed up and on my way to Oklahoma in less than two weeks.

In retrospect, I should have listened to Mom. My Oklahoma experience lasted one semester. Once I got there, my girlfriend and I broke up, and I learned it would take me an extra year to graduate.

King Solomon wrote about impulsive decisions, "It is not good for a person to be without knowledge, and he who hurries his footsteps errs."[4] Because I didn't check thoroughly into the move to Oklahoma, I lost a semester's work and the chance to live with my best friend in Phoenix. After returning to Arizona, I had to remain at my parents' house for another semester and commute to school.

Impulsive actions can be limited if we agree as a family to gather facts before making a decision, especially during the heat of a disagreement. But don't get overwhelmed thinking, *Great, we have to get all the facts before we can make any decision!* Sometimes the resolution to a conflict or the wise decision to make is so obvious that you don't need a major fact-finding mission. On the other hand, there will be times when a solution is not immediately apparent, or you and your teenager won't agree on the solution.

Sometimes, of course, we parents have to make tough decisions when we can't reach agreement with our teens, and they have to abide by them. But gathering the relevant facts often makes the right choice clear to everyone involved, and it also increases the honor and decreases the anger in our homes. Further, it teaches teenagers a valuable skill: logical discernment. It never hurts to consider facts, but ignorance of the facts can cause a lot of damage.

Fact finding can help resolve disagreements about what type of music to play at home, attending church together, what school to attend, appropriate dating behavior, dangerous-looking sports—in other words, the normal arguments that arise "out of the blue" and can blind-side parents or teens.

3. Seek *wise counsel.*

Sometimes simply considering the facts is not enough. So another way to help solve difficult problems or make wise decisions is to seek opinions from wise people. This doesn't mean just going to someone who you know already agrees with your position. We want to stress the word *wise.* It does no good to seek advice from those who may not know anything, are immature, or may be "darkened in their understanding" by sin.

I (Gary) clearly saw the value of getting wise counsel one summer when I was trying to lose weight. Right after I started on a diet with some friends, our now-married daughter, Kari, had us over for dinner. After a great, low-fat main course, the rest of the group sat in the living room to eat a low-fat dessert while I talked with Kari in the kitchen. As we spoke, I noticed another dessert that looked as if it belonged in a fancy restaurant.

The best part was that she claimed it was very low in fat. Before digging in, though, I asked Kari one more time if it was really low-fat. She assured me it was, so I took a mammoth portion. The satisfaction of being able to eat such a wonderful and low-fat cake was literally dripping off my face. I had so many different colors of icing on me that I looked like a circus clown.

In a matter of seconds, however, I was *feeling* like a clown. Some of my friends wandered into the kitchen and asked why I was eating such a high-fat dessert. "No, no, listen to this," I tried to explain. "Kari said it's healthy. Tell them what you told me, Kari."

As she began to list the cake's ingredients, my friends all realized there was no way in the world it was low in fat. The only thing low-fat about this dessert was that after eating it, the fat on my body would hang a little lower.

I dumped the remaining portion in the trash and glared at Kari. "How could you get so confused?" I growled at her. "That's a dirty trick to play on someone who's trying to lose weight!"

I should have asked my friends, who are well informed about nutritional issues, to inspect the cake before I ate it. It might have saved me a few pounds. Although I didn't lose any weight that week, I did learn a valuable lesson that we also need to teach our teenagers: Seek wise counsel before making a decision or you may bite off more than you can chew—or, in my case, swallow. Teens can also be attracted to things that look great on the surface, like that cake, but are really detrimental to their goals. Listening to good advice about such things can save them a lot of grief.

Whether the wise counsel comes from a parent, a teacher, a coach, a mentor, a youth pastor, civil servants, or other authority figures, help your teenager to actively pursue good advice when faced with a significant decision. King Solomon, in all his wisdom, talked about the value of receiving knowledgeable input: "Through insolence comes nothing but strife, but wisdom is with those who receive counsel."[5]

4. *Create solutions* by brainstorming a "pro versus con" list.

One of the best methods our family found for solving conflicts and making wise decisions was to brainstorm together a "pro versus con" list. It's simple, and it keeps peace in the midst of negotiation. It also helps guard against a major roadblock to honoring solutions: *manipulation.*

When parents put pressure on their teenager to make a particular choice (or vice versa), it can cause major conflict. But the pro versus con list enables us to look at the issues more objectively and factually, promoting harmony in the process.

Here's an example of how it works. One day when I (Greg) was a freshman in college, I wanted to go camping with my girlfriend and several other friends. The guys were going to sleep in one tent and the girls in another. I didn't foresee any problems. But when my mother heard about the plan, she erupted. "You're going camping all alone with who?" she asked irately.

I tried to explain the innocence of the trip, but she wasn't buying it. *Where's Dad when I need him?* I thought. *He'd fall for it.* Instead of arguing about the details, however, Mom suggested that we simply list the pros and cons of the idea.

First, we drew a line down the middle of a piece of paper, dividing it into a "pro" side and a "con" side. Next, we began on the con side and brainstormed why the trip might be a poor idea. Then we switched to the pro side and listed reasons why going camping might be a good choice. We avoided evaluating the reasons until we had recorded every idea. Here's what our finished list looked like:

Camping with Girlfriend

Pros:

- It would be fun and relaxing.

- Experience would bond us as closer friends.

- Spend large amount of time together away from school.

- Prove how responsible we really are by delaying gratification.

Cons:

- May not be strong enough to resist the sexual temptation.

- Look bad to others (hinder faith).

- Don't want to give even a hint of sexual immorality.

- People may spread rumors and thus affect our reputation.

Our next step was to evaluate each pro and con and identify the more relevant or important ones. We decided that on the pro side, the emotional bonding that could result and the responsibility we could exhibit were the most-important factors. The reality that we might look bad to others and people could spread rumors about us were the key factors on the con side.

The final step was to weigh the major factors to determine the best decision. Although I wasn't thrilled with the outcome, the obvious decision after working through this process was to not go camping. The good to be gained was not worth the price we might have to pay. My girlfriend and I did go to the lake for the day, though, and we had a great bonding experience. More important than the actual final decision, however, was that we all agreed that not going camping was the best choice.

If the best choice had not been obvious or Mom and I were still in disagreement at that point, we could have gone back and listed additional pros and cons. Those additional factors might have helped us reach a joint decision. We might also have needed to take a break or show the list to a neutral third party for advice.

The end result, however, was that using the pro versus con list allowed my mother and I to stay in harmony through a major disagreement. It can do the same for you and your teenager.

5. *Agree* on one or more of the solutions.

The goal in resolving a conflict is to find a workable and mutually satisfying answer. We call this a *win/win solution*. But suppose we've done a pro versus con list with a teen and we're still at odds. We, the parents, think wisdom calls for one course of action (solution A); our teen favors another (solution B). What do we do next?

One possibility, commonly used, is to agree to compromise (solution AB). But in that case, no one really wins. It's like a half-win because both parties give in some. Our recommendation is that the parent and teen brainstorm several additional potential solutions (e.g., solutions C-G). We've found that when parents and teens do this, a choice usually emerges that they both like; perhaps it's solution E. This is different from a compromise because instead of both parties giving in, they've identified a new solution that they both find acceptable.

Sometimes the win/win solution becomes apparent with amazing ease and quickness. There was, for example, the time when we asked a young couple to demonstrate conflict resolution at one of our live seminars. They had ongoing tension over the wife, Donna's, tendency to run late when they were going somewhere. Jeff, the husband, was growing more frustrated by the month. They were both storing up increasing amounts of anger. Jeff had resorted to sarcastic comments (escalation) if it looked as though Donna were running late again. This would result in Donna's not talking for long periods of time (withdrawal). As we've seen, if this pattern continued, their relationship would be in serious jeopardy.

They first clarified the conflict for the audience and then used the drive-thru talking method. Donna asked to be the "customer" first, and Jeff agreed to be the "employee." He began by saying, "Welcome to the Smith home. May I take your order?"

"I feel frustrated by the pressure you put on me when I'm going as fast as I can," Donna said.

Jeff repeated her statement in his own words. Then he asked if she wanted anything else with her order.

She continued, "I have so many things to do before we leave that I feel frustrated because I could use your help."

Jeff repeated her words again, and Donna explained that she felt understood and validated.

The couple then traded places, and Donna began with the same invitation: "Welcome to the Smith home. May I take your order?"

Jeff's first statement actually solved their problem: "I feel frustrated because I always get ready before you, and then I just sit around waiting for you. It's boring."

The audience laughed. Donna smiled and repeated his words slowly and lovingly. "If I hear you correctly," she said, "you get frustrated and bored just sitting around, waiting for me to finish getting ready."

"That's right," Jeff said, looking a little puzzled. Finally he put two and two together and realized why everyone was laughing. Donna needed help with several things before she was ready to leave the house. Jeff got bored just sitting around. There it was! After they agreed that he would help out and she would start getting ready earlier, the audience applauded and they sat down, holding hands. They had a win/win solution.

That's how quickly an answer can appear when two people get the opportunity to express their needs and feelings. But it must be done in honor. Donna could have shamed Jeff for not realizing sooner that she needed help. Likewise, as parents working through this process, we need to make sure we don't close our teen's spirit. Even after having a good drive-thru talking experience and doing a pro versus con list, anger can reemerge if a win/win solution isn't found right away. But if we remain persistent, most conflicts can be resolved.

6. *Write down* the agreement.

Because it's so easy to forget what decisions were made during an argument, it's good to develop the habit of putting agreed-upon solutions down on paper. That helps to assign responsibility for the future, as each person will then know exactly what's expected of him or her. It also holds those involved accountable for their future behaviors and choices.

7. Make sure *anger* is dealt with after the conflict has ended.

A 46-year-old mother of four, Cindy, wrote us the following story about one of the best experiences she ever had with her father. It happened when she was 13.

Cindy was helping her dad drive the family's cattle herd from the pasture to a corral, where he intended to wean the calves. One cow took her calf and ran off. Cindy's dad ordered her to bring the cow and calf back while he finished moving the rest of the herd into the corral.

Cindy was nervous because she didn't know what to expect when dealing with a cow and her calf. Plus, Cindy had to round them up on foot. If the cow charged or bucked, she'd be in big trouble.

As Cindy approached the cow quietly, it suddenly turned toward her and made a threatening advance. Cindy started to run for cover, but she was stopped dead in her tracks by her father's voice as he stood in the corral a short distance from her. "Get that cow!" he screamed. "Don't come back unless she's with you!" His sudden outburst nearly spooked the herd.

Scared, Cindy approached the cow again. This time the cow charged. Cindy barely made it under a fence to safety. Now she was not only frightened, but also bruised and bleeding. She realized she had no idea how to corral this cow, which had turned and was moving farther away by the second.

Cindy walked back to the corral, where her father was busily working. She was so nervous that she didn't think to close the gate completely after entering. When her father looked up and noticed she was alone, he screamed, "Cindy, where is that cow?" This time the loud noise was too much for the herd. In an instant, the cattle were out the open gate, running in all directions.

Cindy's dad came unglued. "Get to the house!" he yelled at her. "I don't need your kind of help around here!"

Cindy was devastated.

Hours later, her father found Cindy behind the house, weeping. In a soft tone he said, "I don't know what I was thinking. I got frustrated that the work wasn't getting done. I was wrong to say those things to you. I *do* need your help around the farm. Will you forgive me?"

Cindy was taken aback by her father's apology. She couldn't remember the last time he had admitted making a mistake. But because he humbled himself this time, what could have been a tragic, lifelong hurt in Cindy's heart actually brought the two closer together. And later that day, they went and found that stubborn cow and her calf.

When we parents admit our contribution to the problem and seek forgiveness, our words and actions go a long way toward promoting honor and decreasing anger in a teenager's life.

When All Else Fails, Call for Help!

"We need help!" screamed the frantic voice on the phone. "My wife just delivered my son in the toilet, and I can't get him to breathe. . . . Oh no! Another baby. . . . There's two of them. Twins!"

My (Greg's) mother-in-law, Rosalie Murphy, received this call one morning as a 911 operator. The first thing she had been taught is that you must remain calm and speak in a low tone. The worst thing a 911 operator can do is to sound scared. She must give the person in crisis hope that everything is going to be okay.

When the father called in a panic, Rosalie not only had to gather the necessary information so the fire department paramedics could respond, but she also had to calm him down so he could help his wife and twins.

In just a few minutes, Rosalie heard the paramedics enter the bathroom. She felt relieved because she knew everyone would now be all right. "Thank you, ma'am!" the grateful father said as he went to greet his rescuers.

To this day, I can't imagine how my mother-in-law does her job—and with such skill and compassion. I get an anxiety attack from the mere thought of trying to help someone on the phone who's in a life-or-death situation.

We encourage you as a family, however—much like being prepared to call 911 in a physical emergency—to establish a mutually agreed-upon person who, in the event of a major impasse, will listen to both sides and help solve the problem. This goes beyond seeking wise counsel, which we discussed earlier. Find someone acceptable to each member of the family—someone who can remain unbiased, whom everyone respects and feels safe with, and who will maintain confidentiality and privacy.

Having such a person available gives your family support and accountability. As the Bible says, "A friend loves at all times, and a brother is born for adversity."[6] When you're in trouble, you see who your friends are and how helpful a brother (or sister) can be. A genuine friend sticks with you and provides the accountability needed to resolve the problem.

Your family's 911 person can help in another way as well. When that mother was giving birth in her bathroom, Rosalie offered the resources and informed perspective needed to safely deliver the twins. She told the father how to position his wife, the supplies he should use, and how to help her with her breathing. Likewise, when you get an outside opinion to help solve a family conflict, you can tap into a source of new information or perspectives you hadn't considered before. That person might provide the fresh idea that helps you and your teen to find a win/win decision.

A Final Comment about Resolving Conflicts in Honor

Part of resolving conflicts with our teens in honor is to recognize that they need the freedom to make more and more of their own choices. Just how many and how soon depends on their age and maturity level (it will be different for every child). This is a normal and necessary part of growing into adulthood. As they demonstrate the ability to make wise choices, they earn further responsibility.

As parents, we help them not only by giving them this increasing freedom, but also by holding them accountable for their decisions. If they make poor choices, they need to face the logical and natural consequences that follow. This is called *discipline*, which is a clear parental responsibility: "Correct your son, and he will give you comfort; he will also delight your soul."[7] For our teens, discipline is a learning opportunity. Look at what the Bible says about receiving it:

> Whoever loves discipline loves knowledge, but he who hates reproof is stupid.[8]

> Poverty and shame will come to him who neglects discipline, but he who regards reproof will be honored.[9]

> He who neglects discipline despises himself, but he who listens to reproof acquires understanding.[10]

> No discipline seems pleasant at the time, but painful. Later on, however, it produces a harvest of righteousness and peace for those who have been trained by it.[11]

Agree ahead of time on what the consequences of poor choices will be. (In the next chapter, we'll show how to incorporate them into a family constitution.) The more our teens know in advance about what to expect, the easier it is to hold them accountable.

As we've said before, there will also still be times when parents have to make a decision their teenagers don't like. In that case, it's essential for both parents to be in agreement. If they're not, teens will use the conflict to their advantage. (Most teens seem to have a built-in radar that detects even the slightest marital discord.) King Solomon wisely said, "Two are better than one. . . . A cord of three strands is not quickly torn apart."[12] So, once you and your spouse agree on a decision, instead of simply "laying down the law," explain lovingly why you have made that particular choice.

> *We encourage you as a family to establish a mutually agreed-upon person who, in the event of a major impasse, will listen to both sides and help solve the problem.*

Conflict between parents and teenagers is inevitable, but it doesn't need to weaken their relationship or tear the family apart. Using drive-thru talking, establishing some basic rules for fair fighting, and utilizing the seven steps toward resolution described in this chapter will enable us to work out most disagreements in honor. If, after all that, a conflict has still not ended and a win/win solution hasn't yet been found, we can repeat the process or seek a third party to help bring about an honorable resolution.

Please understand that we're not saying we necessarily have to do all the things mentioned in this chapter to solve every problem. As we've seen, drive-thru talking alone can resolve many disputes. It's the starting point for working out differences in honor. Then beyond that, follow the other steps until you identify your win/win solution. It may come easily after just a few steps, or it may take more time to work further through the process. But keep honoring words and actions in the forefront of whatever you do.

6

HOW DEMOCRACY CAN BRING RESPONSIBILITY TO YOUR HOME

People do what you inspect, not what you expect!
Dr. Henry Brandt

Does it seem that as your child gets older, effective discipline becomes more and more difficult? That's exactly how one father felt about disciplining his teenage son. "When I was growing up," complained the frustrated father to a friend, "I was disciplined by being sent to my room without supper. That was punishment enough because I had nothing, so I was bored out of my mind. But my son has his own color TV, phone, computer with internet capabilities, and a stereo with a CD player."

"So what happens when your son gets into trouble?" his friend asked.

"I send him to *my* room!"

What's the best way for parents to deal with discipline issues during the teen years? Before we get to what we've found most effective, we want to encourage you *not* to do something my (Gary's) parents did.

I recently learned something I had never before known about my mother: When she was a teenager, she was sexually abused by a relative. That fact, combined with the way she was raised by an estranged uncle and aunt, rejected by my dad's parents, and suffered the death of her firstborn, helped me understand why she was so tolerant of those who mistreated her. I finally realized why my mother never disciplined any of her children—that is, none but Lorna.

When my oldest sister, Lorna, was five years old, she died from a combination of kidney failure and the effects of being given a spinal tap. Unfortunately, my mother was convinced that *she* was responsible for her daughter's death. She had spanked Lorna for misbehaving just before Lorna was admitted to the hospital. Realizing that Lorna's "bad" behavior was probably the result of her sickness, Mom was traumatized by the spanking memory and never again disciplined her children. She must have concluded that any "negative" behavior from her kids could be the beginning stages of some rare disease. She didn't allow my dad to do any disciplining, either.

One of the worst things we can do for our teenagers, however, is to stop holding them accountable for their mistakes and poor choices. Teens need independence and a decrease in parental control, but that doesn't mean we should take extreme stances like my parents' and stop all forms of discipline. The key is to develop a system that incorporates both the need for limits and accountability and the need for less control as adolescents mature.

How can we provide this balance for our teenagers? By emulating the centuries-old wisdom of America's Founding Fathers, who recognized the necessity of a constitution to govern the functioning of the young nation and regulate competing desires. Today, that constitution still provides limits and grants freedom in the United States. A family constitution, and a contract that grows out of it, can do the same within our homes.

Two Documents That Can Increase Honor and Decrease Anger in Our Homes

In the Smalley family and in other families with whom we've worked, we've found that two documents provide a great foundation for discipline, especially during the children's teenage years. One we call a "family constitution." It contains the foundational principles (e.g., the desire to increase honor and decrease anger) that guide the family and help to create a healthy home. These principles do not change over time (though their wording might). It's important to create this kind of document first because it governs the family decision-making process. For instance, when the Smalleys were deciding between several different options, we tried to determine which one would create the most honor and the least anger.

To write your own family constitution, start by determining which main principles you want to guide your family. In other words, what should be the foundation upon which your family is built? Ask each other the following questions:

- What key principles do we believe are important for our family?

- What standards of conduct do we want to model for other families?

- Which values and convictions need to be a part of our family?

- Which biblical principles should we stress within our family?

- Are there any unhealthy doctrines that we want to keep from infiltrating our family?

- What should our "mission statement" be as a family?[1]

- What are the most important principles that we want to pass on to the next generation as part of their family heritage?

These questions can help your family develop a constitution that will guide you toward emotional and spiritual health and happiness. We encourage you, before proceeding further, to take some time and ask your family these questions.

The following is our final family constitution. We probably had 50 "constitutional convention meetings" over the years as we constantly tried to find what worked best for our family. This striving for clarity communicated to the kids that we were serious about their worth and loved them enough to keep working at it.

THE SMALLEY FAMILY CONSTITUTION

We, the Smalley family, hereby declare on this day and do solemnly swear to abide by the following articles as we each commit ourselves together to honor and love one another through the good and difficult times as best we can.

1. We promise to encourage one another to understand that *God honors and loves us* so much that He has promised to meet all our personal and individual needs much better than anyone or anything else could ever do. We will each strive to rest in this belief so as not to become anxious about anything. We are each looking forward to being so *full* of His Spirit that whatever each of us gains during our lifetime will be viewed as only *overflow* to His complete fulfillment. We also recognize that God will transform within us all our individual *trials*, making us more loving and more like Him in all His character, thus allowing us to remain at peace through all our unique circumstances.

2. We each purpose to *highly honor God and His creation* above ourselves and remain grateful to Him for all that He is and does for us.

3. We agree to *honor our father and mother* through obedience. This means that when they ask us to do something, we will not complain, nag, or argue. However, we will be allowed to ask questions as long as we do so in honor. We agree that Mom and Dad are the final authority and have the right to ask us to do something that is not up for debate.

4. We also promise to *treat one another with honor.* This means that each person has unique needs and interests that must be valued. In addition, we agree that using proper manners is another way to honor each other.

5. We agree to *honor our home* through cleanliness and the completion of household chores.

6. We will strive each day to choose *forgiveness* for any offenses received from any source. It is our solemn promise to resolve any level of anger between ourselves and anyone or anything before the sun sets each day, thus allowing our hearts to remain open to both God and people.[2]

7. We resolve to discover the special needs each member of our family has with regard to *physical care.* We will strive to meet one another's need for touch in loving and meaningful ways.

8. We understand the value of *spending meaningful time together* as a family. Therefore, we agree to schedule regular times of fun and mutually enjoyable activities as our individual schedules will allow. We also agree to avoid arguments during our fun times and schedule them for a later time.

9. We agree that all good things come from above, including the financial resources available to us. We will strive to remain *responsible stewards* of any and all of our individual and family resources.

10. We recognize that each family member is a unique person with differing personalities, interests, and dreams. We purpose to not only understand one another's uniqueness, but also to *accept, honor, and praise* each one's individuation.

11. We recognize the importance of *understanding and valuing*

one another's unique thoughts, feelings, and needs. We purpose to lovingly and meaningfully communicate with one another as needed by listening and repeating what the other person is saying until mutual understanding is achieved.

12. We resolve to care for one another in an *affectionate and tender* manner.

13. We agree to believe the best about one another and to trust the words and actions of one another as honest. If this trust is broken in any way, we resolve to *restore the trust* by confessing the untruth, seeking forgiveness, and making any necessary restitution.

Once you have a family constitution in place, you create a document to deal with the day-to-day functioning of the family. We call this second document a "family contract." The difference between a family constitution and a family contract is that the contract flows out of the principles in the constitution. The constitution acts as an umbrella covering everything the family does or believes about life together. That's why it's crucial that you develop a constitution first.

What Is a Family Contract?

We define a family contract according to psychologists Spiegler and Guevremont: "A contract is a written agreement between one person and one or more other people that specifies the relationship between a target behavior and its consequences."[3] In other words, it specifies who is to do what, for whom, and under what circumstances.

A family contract is a great way to help children of all ages learn limits, take responsibility for their actions, and "own" their place in the family. It's important to teach children that the world has controls and limitations. Just as the seatbelt law restricts our freedom, it also ensures our safety and increases our chances of surviving an accident. It's there for our welfare. Likewise, a family contract protects a child.

Most teenagers roll their eyes or stomp their feet at the mere mention of the word *contract*. Since they're attempting to become autonomous from the family anyway, rules or contracts seem to restrict their freedom, and tension or conflict can result. (Autonomy is simply another name for independence or not being controlled by others.)

You may be thinking, *Great, you guys are suggesting that I do something that's going to* increase *conflict with my teenager!* That's not the case, though. In fact, your teenager ought to get excited about a family contract, because rather than limiting her freedom, it actually *produces* freedom! How? Having clearly defined rules and limits allows your teen to make informed decisions about how to behave within those boundaries. This freedom can only happen when your teen is clearly aware of the responsibilities expected of her and the consequences that will follow her behavior. Real freedom is having the inner power to do what she knows is best for all concerned. Immaturity is lacking the power to do what she knows is right and not being able to delay gratification. As adolescent expert Dr. John Santrock, author of *Adolescence,* notes:

> Psychologically healthy families adjust to adolescents' push for independence by treating the adolescents in more adult ways and including them more in family decision making. Psychologically unhealthy families often remain locked into power-oriented parent control, and parents move even more heavily toward an authoritarian posture in their relationship with their adolescents.[4]

Let us illustrate what we mean by *freedom.* When I (Greg) was 14 years old, I needed less parental control and more autonomy than I had enjoyed when younger. One night, however, Dad did something that made me think he didn't care about my feelings or understand my need for freedom.

At the time, my favorite TV program was *M.A.S.H.,* the show about the silly antics of Army medics during the Korean War. It was the last season that *M.A.S.H.* was going to be on TV, and I had been anticipating the final episode for months. Several minutes before the show was to start, I made some popcorn and sat down in my favorite chair. Everything was perfect except for one thing—Dad!

> ### *A family contract is a great way to help children of all ages learn limits, take responsibility for their actions, and "own" their place in the family.*

He was in a foul mood when he approached me about my homework. "Is your homework finished?" he said in a rough voice.

"Shhh!" I blasted back at his interruption. "Can't you see I'm watching *M.A.S.H.?* It's the last episode. I'll do my homework later."

That kind of sarcastic and controlling response had never worked on him before, so I don't know why I thought it would work this time. But I wish I hadn't picked that night to experiment with a new negotiation technique. It didn't go over well at all.

Click! was the next sound I heard as the TV was turned off. "No!" he stated firmly. "You'll finish your homework now!"

"But . . . But . . ." I tried to explain. "No way! . . . Last one. . . . Not fair. . . . Mom!"

My pleas were useless. Mom couldn't save me this time. Dad forced me to leave my precious show several minutes before it even started. I was so upset that I ran to my room in tears. My freedom had been taken away, and I wasn't too happy about it.

Several days later, we were able to resolve our conflict. I explained to Dad that I had been hurt not so much because I didn't get to watch *M.A.S.H.,* but because I hadn't understood that I would lose my TV privilege if my homework wasn't finished. I hadn't had the freedom to choose whether to lose TV because I hadn't known the possible consequences of my actions.

As that story illustrates, one of the most common reasons teenagers argue with their parents is a lack of clearly defined rules. But by using a family contract, you can almost completely eliminate that ambiguity and confusion. As this happens, freedom is born. And when teens know their limits, they can accomplish what's expected of them in ways we parents never dreamed possible.

How Teenagers Feel about Rules and Limits

Do teenagers really want to be held accountable and disciplined? You may be skeptical. But a woman at one of our seminars captured the truth in her touching story:

As a teenager, I was angry and rebellious. My curfew was finally pushed to 2:00 A.M. Yet I continually violated it, so my parents moved it again, this time to 3:00 A.M. However, there is nothing positive about a 16-year-old girl being out until the early morning. As a result, I got involved in immoral activities. I didn't feel good about myself. Looking back, I now see that I wanted limits. I desired for my mom to say, "I don't like what I see happening. I don't want you to be out that late—hanging around with people you shouldn't be with." I desperately wanted her to give me rules that would demonstrate her love and concern about me and the person I was becoming.

No matter what you see on TV or in the movies; regardless of what some popular books or magazines insist—don't be fooled. Teenagers really do want limits. A report entitled "Voices from the Classroom" noted that of the 1,365 high-school students surveyed at North Kansas City High School in Kansas City, Missouri, many suggested that their parents aren't involved enough in school. As one teenager said, "I just have so many friends who wish their parents would say no—no to talking too late on the phone at night, no to going out when they should be doing their homework."[5] Likewise, the 5,000 adults in our own survey reported that when they were teenagers, their parents didn't set or enforce family rules either.

What's the solution? We believe it's to find a simple method that provides both freedom for teens and the necessary amount of control for parents: a family contract. It can do several key things for your family.

Why Develop Family Contracts?

Why do we so strongly advocate a contract between parents and teens?

- It decreases problems at home.[6]

- It brings family unity.

- It creates consistency in behavior for both parents and teens by reducing the temptation to establish "double standards."

- It gives teens ownership of any rule or limitation the family establishes.[7]

- It reduces prolonged or angry arguments by forcing meaningful and honorable communication.

- It requires negotiation and cooperation, which can provide structure for and improve troublesome relationships between teenagers and parents.[8]

- It provides greater security and stability for each family member.

- It allows a family to prioritize its most-important values. And then it serves as a continual reminder of those values and rules.

- It can become the "policing force" at home. The parents are then free to focus on relational issues.

- Signing one tends to make the family members more committed to fulfilling their roles.[9]

- It can reduce stress and bring peace.

A written and signed document has tremendous power to keep people in harmony with agreed-upon, loving rules.

Developing Your Own Family Contract

How, specifically, does a family contract work? The essence is that parents and teenagers work out some form of agreement on acceptable behavior at home and in one another's lives—and on the consequences of violating the agreement. Contracts can cover such practical matters as schoolwork, housecleaning, and driving the family car.

For example, at one point when the Smalley kids were teenagers, our family contract said they had to maintain at least a C average in school. Anything below a C and they would forfeit their TV privilege for an entire semester. I (Greg) actually came up with that harsh punishment for low grades. Unfortunately, I would soon regret it.

"I got a D!" I screamed in disbelief that fateful day. "That's impossible! Give me that report card!" And with that, I grabbed the card from my mother to inspect it myself. There it was, bigger than life—a D. Math had never been my strongest subject, but a D?

"Give me a break!" I said, now fuming. "There must be some mistake. Don't you worry, Mom, I'll take care of it."

She gave me "the look." You know the one—the look most mothers are born with, the one that says, "Do I look like the dumbest person on the face of the planet?" In other words, she wasn't going to let me "take care of it."

Sadly enough, after my math teacher, Mr. Stark, confirmed that the D was no typo, I lost my TV privilege for an entire semester. "For the whole semester, Mom?" I pleaded. "But . . . but . . . that's like six months! I've got to be able to watch *M.A.S.H.!* That's not fair! Dad!" (What was I thinking? Like Mr. "You can't watch the last episode" was going to be any help!)

Sure enough, night after night, week after week, I sat at the kitchen table and stared at my family watching TV. I continued this pitiful behavior until my mother could no longer take it. She called an emergency family meeting to discuss my predicament. "This is more of a punishment on me than it is for Greg," she explained to the family. "When the rule was made, I don't think any of us thought we'd ever really have to use this extreme punishment."

"That's right," I agreed joyously. "So what should we do about this unfortunate situation?"

After about an hour, we all concluded that I had been punished enough. I had to complete a math summer-school course to make up the

D, but at least I got my TV back. Wouldn't you know it, though—by the time I was allowed to watch TV again, the season was over and only reruns were showing. The good news is that I never got another D on a report card.

Keep in mind that the contract will need to be changed from time to time to fit the changing needs of your children.

All the ideas that we felt were important for the daily operation of our family were written into our unique contract. We found that it worked well for us in all aspects of family discipline.

The Smalley kids were first exposed to a family contract when they were around three to six years of age. Naturally, that contract was simple. They were taught to obey God and their parents, and to be kind to people and things. As their physical, emotional, and mental abilities grew, so did the contract. In its heyday, our family contract covered these six areas:

- Honoring God, others, and His creation

- Obedience

- Cleanliness

- Chores

- Manners

- Inner character qualities (e.g., honesty, integrity, and humility)

We've reproduced the final version of our family contract in the last few pages of this chapter.

By the way, Mom and Dad are governed by the contract as well as the kids. For example, if I (Gary) left my things scattered around the house, I would lose the morning newspaper privilege for 24 hours. Having *each* person held responsible for his or her behavior enabled us to function as a team, supporting one another.

What ingredients are essential to an effective family contract? Just as preparing your favorite meal requires the correct ingredients, so also creating a family contract requires several elements. The five most important are discussed below.

1. Precise wording

A good contract begins by clearly defining the exact behaviors the child is expected to do or refrain from doing. Limit the use of vague words that are open to different interpretations. Instead of saying that the child needs to obey, carefully define the exact behaviors and meaning of *obey*. You might write, "Once Mom or Dad gives a direction, you are to immediately do it without complaining, arguing, or nagging." Remember that a child is better able to conform to his parent's wishes when he understands the exact expectations. A written contract reduces the possibility of misunderstanding and provides an objective reference when disagreements about contract terms arise.

2. Clear rewards and consequences

A helpful contract will specify the rewards that can be gained and privileges that may lost as a result of the child's behavior. For example, if a teen is required to take the trash out after dinner, she needs to know that *not* doing this will result in no TV for 24 hours (or whatever consequence your family chooses). Likewise, it's important for the teen to understand that positive behavior leads to rewards like allowance, special dessert, or extra use of the family car.

3. Bonus clause

According to the research of psychologist R. B. Stuart and colleagues, an effective family contract contains a "bonus clause" that rewards contract compliance.[10] For example, adherence for five out of the seven days in a week might yield a bonus in the form of a special activity or a "dividend" added to the teen's usual allowance.

4. Teenager and parent as co-creators of the contract

The key in setting limits is to work *with* the teenager. Together, establish the important rules, consequences, and rewards. When teens are involved in creating the rules, they consider them *their* limits rather than standards being imposing on them. They also take more ownership of the contract because the rules seem fair.

Keep in mind, too, that the contract will need to be changed from time to time to fit the changing needs of your children. In the Smalley household, we held meetings like the one described earlier when someone thought a rule should be modified. We added and subtracted clauses in our contract. The best part was when one of the kids came up with the particular contract idea, because he or she would then own the responsibility to obey the rule.

Part of the reason the contract has to be open to renegotiation is the ongoing need of teenagers to separate and individuate, as well as to form their own identity. When parents place severe restrictions on their teens, it can literally disrupt their development.[11] So teens need opportunities to earn rewards that allow greater independence and individuation. A teenager's need for separation from the family, however, sometimes makes her a reluctant contributor to the negotiation process. In that case, let her know that while she can choose not to participate, she will still be bound by the family contract.

Let us illustrate how our family contract (*not* the basic, core principles of our family constitution) changed to meet the needs of our adolescent children in five different areas.

ASKING QUESTIONS

When the kids hit the teenage years, we had a family meeting and decided that it was still important to obey Mom and Dad without complaining, arguing, or nagging. But it was also important for our young teens to be able to ask questions and understand why we were asking them to do or not do something. Adolescent expert John Santrock makes an important point about this:

> In terms of cognitive changes, the adolescent can now reason in more logical ways with parents than in childhood. During childhood, parents may be able to get by with saying, "O.K. That is it. We do it my way or else," and the child conforms. But with increased cognitive skills, adolescents no longer are likely to accept such a statement as a reason for conforming to parental dictates. Adolescents want to know, often in fine detail, why they are being disciplined. Even when parents give what seem to be logical reasons for discipline, adolescents' cognitive sophistication may call attention to deficiencies in the reasoning.[12]

We all agreed that Mom and Dad still had the final authority and the right to ask the kids to do something occasionally that was not up for discussion. But for the most part, they were allowed to ask questions in order to understand the reasons behind an instruction.

CLEANLINESS

When the Smalley kids were younger, our family had a rule in the contract that their rooms needed to be cleaned before leaving for school.

If not, they lost their TV privilege for 24 hours. Yet when the two oldest, Kari and Greg, were in high school, they became so active in after-school activities like sports and clubs that keeping their rooms in "tip top shape" was difficult. Norma was the most frustrated by this. So we had family meeting number 1002.

"What should we do about this?" I (Gary) asked. "Our contract clearly states that rooms must be clean before school, yet the kids are so busy now. How can we solve this?"

Sensing a possible opportunity, the kids chimed in immediately, "We agree with Dad. We just can't keep up with everything!" Their craftiness might have worked had it not been for their "high fives" and a chorus of "Dad, Dad, he's our man. If he can't do it, no one can!"

Norma, being accustomed to my erratic ways, countered with, "We can't live in a pigpen."

"I agree with Mom," I stated intelligently. "She can't handle a big mess." As I defended my wife, I reminded the kids that Mom was a very important person within our walls and that we needed to come up with a win-win solution. (Now you can see why my family refers to me as "Mr. Switzerland.")

Eventually, we all agreed to amend the phrase "clean room before school" in our contract. We decided our rooms didn't have to be perfect. In addition, Mom reduced her expectations and chose to place a higher value on the kids and their activities than on a totally clean house. That was a freeing decision for the family. But the main point is that *we were united and solved the problem as a team*. We kept the principle of cleanliness but amended the daily functioning of our family contract.

SPANKING

When the Smalley kids were younger, our contract called for Mom and Dad to spank them when they were openly rebellious or boldly dishonoring. We didn't have to spank often because we had started using the contract when they were young. Nonetheless, the time came when spanking needed to be removed from the contract altogether.

One day when Greg was about 14 years old, the two of us were working in the yard. We had been there most of the morning and had reached a point where we were both tired and grouchy. "I'm done doing yard work," Greg suddenly informed me (Gary), "so I'm going inside to watch TV."

"Oh, you are!" I responded. "How about we finish the work and *then* you can go inside."

Greg came back at me with some very disrespectful language and then headed for the house. I stood there for a few seconds, stunned at what he had said. Before he reached the front door, however, I had caught up to him and grabbed him, and we headed to the backyard.

After I gave him a few swats, we looked at each other. Then Greg started to laugh. It wasn't a funny laugh; it was more like an uncomfortable giggle. Suddenly I realized he was too old for that kind of discipline.

Following that experience, we met as a family and agreed on other ways to discipline the older kids when they dishonored or disobeyed Norma or myself. We used grounding, natural consequences, and removing privileges—methods more appropriate and effective for adolescents.

DATING

Many parents of teenagers cringe at the word *dating*. After all, it's one of the most common areas of conflict between parents and their adolescents. "Is he mature enough to date?" "How old should she be before we let her date?" "Is he strong enough to resist peer pressure?" Such questions haunt parents. Yet Norma and I (Gary) knew that teenage dating is an important part of growing up. The benefits, according to many studies, include:

- Plays a vital role in the development of identity and intimacy.

- Shapes the course of adult romantic relationships and marriages.

- Can be a source of fun and recreation.

- Teaches manners, sociable behaviors, and how to get along with others.[13]

Therefore, as our children approached the age when they were likely to start wanting to date, we added a dating clause to our family contract. It took the pressure off trying to determine when each child was ready, since each child is different and matures at his or her own rate. We structured the first part of our dating clause around character traits and signs of maturity. When a particular teen was able to meet the contract criteria, he or she was ready to date.

The second part of the dating clause dealt with actual dating practices. For example, we all agreed that during the first few years of dating, each dating situation would be evaluated on its own merits, but we especially favored well-organized, school-sponsored activities that were adequately chaperoned. Next, every member of the family had to approve of the potential dating partner. This was an effective safeguard designed to protect against a potentially harmful relationship. It also reflected that we were a close-knit family, with each member concerned about the well-being of the others.

Further, we discussed and set a curfew for dates. The greater a teen's trustworthiness, self-control, and purity of heart, the greater freedom in dating privileges. Likewise, if any of the character qualities were tarnished or violated, the dating privilege was lost for an agreed-upon period of time. For example, if one of the children lied about some activity, even if it had little to do with dating, he lost the privilege of dating for a week or two, depending on the severity of the offense.

We all agreed to this addition to our contract, and as the children got older, we continually reevaluated it and revised it as needed.

In my (Greg's) clinical practice, I've also found another good way to resolve conflicts over dating. I get both the parents and their teenager to sign an agreement stating that the teen will date only if he or she is in an accountability group of some kind. The group can consist of a leader who shares the parents' values and a few peers, or it can be just the teen and a responsible adult (e.g., a youth pastor, mentor, teacher, coach, or family friend). If the teen chooses not to be in such a group, he or she is also choosing not to date—it's the teen's decision. But if the teenager agrees to join a group, the parents can relax in the knowledge that someone is asking their child the tough questions of accountability. And the teen gains a measure of independence from Mom and Dad.

DRIVING

Driving a car is another privilege that comes with age and character development. Even before the Smalley kids were old enough to drive, we agreed as a family on the following clause in our family contract:

1. Upon receiving my driver's permit, I will be allowed to drive on local errands when accompanied by either parent. I will assist in driving for extended periods of time on long family vacations under all types of driving conditions.

2. Before using the car, I will ask either Mom or Dad if I can use it and explain the purpose.

3. If I want to go somewhere for fun, both my homework and other chores must be completed first.

4. During the first month after receiving my driver's license, the radio will not be used while driving.

5. During the school year, I will be allowed to drive to activities at night but cannot take anyone home without permission.

6. I will not allow anyone else to use the car under any circumstances without permission from my parents.

7. I will not carry more than five passengers at a time.

8. I will not give rides to hitchhikers under any circumstances, and I will use extreme caution in accepting assistance if I should have difficulty with the car.

9. I will pay half of the increase in insurance costs whenever my grades fall below a C average. In case of an accident, I will assume half of the deductible costs.

10. If I receive any moving violations, I will lose my license for up to one month. On the second violation, I will lose it for up to three months.

It took us several weeks to negotiate these changes to our contract, and the Smalley teenagers signed it only after a number of revisions. We were certainly open to future changes, but again, they would have to be understood and agreed upon by each of us.

5. Everyone signs the contract

After the family contract has been created, it's important to make a place for everyone to sign and date the document. This shows that everyone agrees with the direction the family is going. And as psychologists Ollendick and Cerny note, "Written contracts are preferred since they reduce the possibility of misunderstanding and provide an objective reference when disagreement about contract terms arises. Having teenagers sign the written contracts may also increase their commitment to the contract."[14]

Enforcing the Family Contract: Family Meetings

Dr. James Dobson says this about parenting teenagers: "It is not wise for parents to be too demanding and authoritative with an older teenager; they may force him to defy their authority just to prove his independence and adulthood." Going along with that, the 5,000 adults we surveyed provided these as the third- and fourth-most-common answers to the question "As a teenager, what did you least appreciate from your parents":

- Demanding or overprotective

- Too strict or too lenient

Likewise in the Smalley home, we realized that the two most dishonoring patterns any family can fall into are *demanding too much control* or the opposite, *remaining too aloof and uninvolved with the family.* These two extremes can usher in a lot of anger for kids. To combat them while at the same time enforcing the family contract, we relied on family meetings. We found that they're a great way to inspect and evaluate each teen's behavior regularly.

Instead of having to continually correct a teen's behavior throughout the day, the family meeting provides a specific time for it.

Up until the kids' high-school years, we met for 5 to 10 minutes after dinner every day to review how everyone was doing in each area. Once they entered high school, we limited our family meetings to several times per week or on an as-needed basis. We usually kept a small chart on the refrigerator so we could mark it with a grease pencil and erase it the next evening.

Instead of having to continually correct a teen's behavior throughout the day, the family meeting provides a specific time for it (unless, of course, the child commits a serious offense that has to be dealt with immediately). This avoids both overcontrol and noninvolvement.

One of our most amusing family meetings took place on Catalina Island off the coast of Southern California. We had just arrived for a week's vacation after a one-hour boat excursion over rough seas. When we had unpacked at the hotel, we sat down to decide what we would do for fun during our stay. The discussion soon turned into mass chaos, as we found we had several very different definitions of the ideal Catalina vacation.

"We want to go scuba diving!" demanded the boys.

"Mom and I want to lay out on the beach," Kari countered.

"That's a stupid idea," yelled Greg, giving Michael a high five.

"Now, boys," Norma said, entering the pandemonium.

Just as she was about to rebuke Greg, he added, "The only reason Kari wants to lay on the beach is because if she lays in the water, she might get harpooned!" The boys broke into laughter at Greg's dishonoring comment.

I (Gary) figured I'd better try to calm everyone down, but then Kari jumped up and tried to kick Greg in the shin. However, as she swung her leg, Greg moved, and her foot smashed into a metal bar hidden under the bed. *Bong!* It sounded like some disgusting noise from *The Gong Show.* Kari immediately began hopping on one foot and screaming, "I broke my toe!"

As fast as I could, I suspended our "family meeting," and we rushed Kari to the emergency clinic.

It turned out that Kari actually had broken her little toe. Unfortunately, all the doctor could do was tape it. So, $200 later, we continued our argument as we walked down the street.

"Thanks a lot, geek!" Kari hissed at Greg as she hopped along.

"You're welcome, pogo stick!" Greg snapped back.

I was just about to strangle them both when a voice broke through the banter. "Stop!" Norma shouted. "It just occurred to me what's happening here. We all took Dramamine before we left the mainland, right? It's the medicine that's making all of us grouchy."

We glanced at each other and collectively said, "Ohhhh!" After realizing what was happening to us physiologically, we became more relaxed. We continued our meeting in a restaurant and finally agreed on what we'd do during our vacation. Needless to say, Kari was somewhat limited in her activities.

Over the years, we've had hundreds of such family meetings, and they proved effective in resolving disagreements. Because of that, I (Greg) believe that I can enter a negotiation with anyone today and feel comfortable and confident. Here are some of the other lifelong benefits we all got from our family meetings:

- A safe place to resolve conflicts, because emotions were allowed to cool off
- The opportunity, as teens, to practice making decisions both routine and significant
- A sense of shared responsibility
- The involvement of every family member
- Better cooperation between family members
- A pattern and a place for organizing the family
- Greater family unity
- Improved communication skills (using drive-thru talking)

As we look back on those years of family meetings, we still chuckle at the freedom we all had in expressing our ideas and concerns. Everyone's feelings and needs were listened to with respect. We sometimes had to keep the boys in line (see below), but for the most part, everyone left those meetings feeling honored.

How to Organize and Run Family Meetings

To organize our family meetings, we simply scheduled them for a time when everyone could attend. We would announce the subject we wanted to discuss and ask each person to think about what he or she would like to contribute. When the meeting started, I (Gary) usually asked the family members to state their thoughts and opinions one at a time, because everyone has the right to speak without being interrupted. I would emphasize that each opinion was valid and there was to be no dishonoring one another through sarcasm.

That was a necessary caution, because it wasn't uncommon for Greg or Michael to respond to one of the other kids with something like, "Only a moron would want to do that." When they did, we'd stop the meeting and discuss why we couldn't say that, and then we'd continue. If apologies were needed, the kids were most often willing to cooperate. Honor was such a part of everything we did that it just seemed natural to correct any dishonoring comments or actions.

We also tried to make our meetings short and light, have a sense of humor, avoid using them as a dumping ground for massive complaining, and keep the focus on solutions rather than on blaming.

In summary, one of the best ways to deal with discipline issues during the adolescent years is develop both a family constitution and a family contract. The constitution lists the guiding principles that make up the family's foundation. The contract flows from the constitution and manages the daily functioning of the family. Together, they provide the necessary rules and accountability all children need, especially teenagers—as well as their parents.

Further, family meetings are one of the best ways to enforce the family contract. They provide parents with a good balance between being too demanding or too uninvolved with teenaged kids.

We encourage you not to become discouraged if your first attempt to write a constitution and a contract with your own family doesn't go well. Many teens will fight over the use of a contract. Keep working at it for several weeks or even months before you assess its value.

Finally, we would like to end this chapter with the example of what the Smalley family contract looked like when the children were adolescents.

The Smalley Family Contract (Kids' Part)

RESPONSIBILITIES

1. **CONFORMING**: Honoring God, parents, and others in authority. This means obeying the Scriptures and the laws of our country, state, and city. Obeying Mom and Dad means not complaining, arguing, or nagging. We may ask questions for clarity, but Mom and Dad have the final authority.

2. **CLEANING:** Clean up after using something. Clean room once per week or before company comes over.

3. **CHORES:** Each person is responsible for completing his or her chore by the agreed-upon time. Mom or Dad will make up a new chore list every month and post it on the refrigerator.

4. **CARING:** Honoring others, self, and things. (Others) This means resolving conflicts honorably. Being kind and sensitive to each other. Asking questions—not arguing; playing gently—not roughhousing; praying for our "enemies"—not hitting. (Self) Maintaining one's own health by eating right and exercising. (Things) Protecting house and furniture.

5. **GRADES:** Each child must maintain at least a C average in each course.

LOST PRIVILEGES

Social activities with friends for the weekend

Television for 24 hours

One of the following: Television or phone privilege for 24 hours

One of the following: Phone privilege, TV, or social activities for 24 hours or weekend

Loss of TV privilege for an agreed-upon time and repeating the course

RESPONSIBILITIES

6. **DATING:** During the first few years of dating, each dating situation will be evaluated on its own merits, but we especially favor well-organized, school-sponsored activities that are adequately chaperoned. Every member of the family must approve of the potential dating partner. Each person must agree to a curfew for dates.

7. **DRIVING:** Before using the car, we will ask either Mom or Dad if we can use it and explain the purpose. If we want to go somewhere for ourselves, both our homework and other chores must be completed first. During the school year, we will be allowed to drive to activities at night but cannot take anyone home without permission. We will not allow anyone else to use the car under any circumstances without permission from Mom or Dad. We will not carry more than five passengers at a time. We will not give rides to hitchhikers under any circumstances, and we will use extreme caution in accepting assistance if we should have difficulty with the car. We will pay half of the increase in insurance costs whenever our grades fall below a C average. In case of an accident, we will assume half of the deductible costs. If we receive any moving violations, we will lose our license for up to one month. On the second violation, we will lose it for up to three months.

　　　Signed:
　　　Gary Smalley
　　　Norma Smalley
　　　Kari Smalley
　　　Greg Smalley
　　　Michael Smalley

LOST PRIVILEGES

If the curfew or any of the character qualities are tarnished or violated, the dating privilege will be lost for an agreed-upon period of time.

Depending on the offense, driving privilege will be lost for an agreed-upon period of time.

7

STRENGTHENING YOUR RELATIONSHIP WITH YOUR TEENAGER

Fifty years from now it will not matter what kind of car you drove, what kind of house you lived in, how much you had in your bank account, or what your clothes looked like. But the world may be a little better because you were important in the life of a child.
Anonymous

Because teenagers are going through the process of individuation and sometimes seem more interested in their peers than in their families, parents tend to wonder just how close a relationship it's possible to have with them. The answer is that it's not only possible to have a great relationship with our teens, but it's also important that we work at it intentionally and regularly. In this chapter, we're going to show how it can be done.

Norma and I (Gary) were close to all our kids when they were teenagers, and we're still close now that they're older and have their own children. The following story illustrates one way in which we developed that friendship—by taking advantage of our mutual love of the outdoors.

When Greg was about 13 years old, he and I heard about this unbelievable fishing river called Lee's Ferry in northern Arizona. The fishing was so good that people were catching 12- to 13-pound trout. The mere thought of catching such a fish caused our mouths to salivate. As it turned out, however, the fishing was not the best part of the trip we soon made together to Lee's Ferry.

The drive took six hours, so we arrived late that evening. Because our hotel was about 40 miles from the nearest town and we were surrounded by the Grand Canyon, the sky was lit up with stars that looked like millions of tiny diamonds. The scene was breathtaking and far more interesting than the thought of sleep. So, wanting the perfect place to watch the show, we decided to take our pillows and perch on top of a big stone wall behind the hotel. We just lay there, talking and watching the shooting stars. Our comments of "Hey, did you see that one!" and "Look over there!" were the only sounds. Minutes went by when we didn't say a word. We just kept staring up at the beautiful night sky.

At one point in our reverie, without any warning, a stray cat leaped up and landed right on Greg's chest. In sudden terror, with a high-pitched scream, Greg flung the cat at my unsuspecting head. We both tried to dodge the flying cat claws, but we lost our balance and fell off the wall.

Needless to say, we never saw that cat again. And after regaining our composure, we couldn't stop laughing as we watched the stars well into the next morning.

Unfortunately, many teens don't get to build such memories with their parents. In our survey of more than 5,000 adults, we asked them, "What did you least appreciate from your parents as a teenager?" The number-one response was that "They were not involved in my life." By the same token, those who apparently had a closer relationship with their parents reported that love, affection, and encouragement were the things they most appreciated receiving from them. Both of these survey results indicate the same thing: *Teens want their parents' friendship.*

We need to clarify what kind of friendship we're talking about, though. We're not saying parents should become "buddies" or "pals" with their teens, like another set of peers. In the family team, the parents aren't teammates with their children—they're the coaches. We can have close relationships with our "players," but there still must be a distinct boundary between who is a player and who's a coach.

We need, in short, to maintain a healthy balance between authority and camaraderie. If we become buddies, we tend to lose our authority. Therefore, when we advocate building a friendship with our teens, we're referring to strengthening our relationships with them as their "coaches," not to becoming chummy like fellow players.

Perhaps you want to deepen your relationship with your teenager. Or maybe you feel your friendship isn't what it used to be. Regardless of the situation, you're wise to want to do something about it. Let's examine just what benefits can come from developing a closer friendship with a teenage son or daughter.

Why Developing Friendships with Our
Teenagers Is So Important

As the two of us experienced on our fishing trip, spending time together as parents and teens not only creates precious memories, but it also causes us to *become bonded.* And when things go wrong during such times, ironically, the bonding can be even greater than it might be otherwise.

Have you ever noticed how quickly things can go awry when you're together as a family? Whether it's being startled while star gazing, the car breaking down, or someone falling out of the bleachers, those crisis experiences, and the memory of them, can unify a family. So, contrary to popular "wisdom," difficult times don't have to pull a family apart. Instead, they can be the very glue that bonds the family into tight friendships.

Of course, such bonding doesn't take place immediately. When our family was in the middle of a crisis, you didn't find us saying, "Isn't this great? We all feel so close right now!" No way! In most cases, it takes about three weeks for a shared crisis or experience to set and permanent bonding to take place. Once set, though, it's usually so tight that virtually nothing can tear apart the memory.

When difficult times happen in the family,
having a long and positive history between the
different members gives everyone hope that
things will work out.

This bonding is vital when the relationship between teens and parents begins to strain, as so often happens. Many times, Norma and I (Gary) faced difficult trials with our teenagers. Looking back, we're convinced that a major reason we were able to deal constructively with those crises was that we were so close with our kids. The bonding experiences caused "history" to form between us. *When difficult times happen in the family, having a long and positive history between the different members gives everyone hope that things will work out.* History derived from shared crises says that "Although things seem bad now, we've made it before."

Another important reason for spending time with our teenagers is to foster a "secure attachment." Developmental experts like psychiatrist John Bowlby and psychologist Mary Ainsworth suggest that such an attachment is central to a teenager's development of social competence, higher self-worth, and well-being.[1] Attachment to parents during adolescence may also provide the secure base from which teens can explore and master new environments, widening their social world in a psychologically healthy manner.[2]

What we're talking about is a progression that looks like this:

Time —> Bonding —> History —> Security —> Better Well-Being

As we spend time together, we become bonded. This creates family history, which helps our teenagers to feel secure. And that increases their well-being. If we use the suggestions that follow—10 things that worked well for the Smalley family—then over time, the quality of friendships we desire can blossom.

10 Ways to Build Closer Friendships with Teenagers

1. Make a lifetime commitment.

Developing closer friendships with teens begins with making an unconditional commitment for life. Such a commitment says, "No matter what happens, I will never stop loving or supporting you."

As I (Greg) was growing up, we Smalley kids got a daily reminder of Dad's love and commitment. At the entryway of our home hung a wall plaque that read: "To Norma, Kari, Gregory, and Michael, in assurance of my lifetime commitment to you." This plaque gave me (and the rest of our family) a feeling that it was safe to be close to him, because I knew that no matter what I did—good or bad—he was committed to me for life.

Are love and commitment really that important to teenagers? After all, they're in the midst of separating emotionally from the family. Yet the 5,000 adults we surveyed said that the five things they most appreciated from their parents when they were teenagers were:

1. love and affection

2. encouragement

3. independence

4. trust

5. security

One of the best ways to communicate unconditional commitment is to regularly use words of affection—expressions such as "I love you" and "You're the greatest son I could ever ask for." If teenagers don't hear such words from Mom and Dad, they make up their own minds about how their parents feel about them.

I (Greg) remember an incredibly valuable thing my father said to me when I was about 13. We were driving in the car one day when I caught him smiling at me. When I asked what was so funny, he replied, "Nothing. I just enjoy being with you." Then he said something I'll never forget: "Greg, having children is like creating your own best friend."

I don't think he knew how much I appreciated those words as a teen. And now that I have children, I really understand what he meant.

When teens know that we're committed to them for life, it allows them to become close to us—like best friends.

Remember, however, that teens may not respond outwardly to words or expressions of commitment. They may say, "Dad, you're embarrassing me" or "Stop with the mushy stuff." Don't be discouraged. Whether they admit it or not, they will remember those words of endearment for the rest of their lives. So Mom and Dad, ignore their moaning and let them hear how committed you are to them. Just don't embarrass them in front of their friends!

2. Become a student of teens by discovering their built-in "parenting manual."

As we carefully listen to and observe our teenagers, we'll see that they each have a built-in "parenting manual." In other words, they usually know what it takes for them to feel loved and, therefore, how we can improve our relationships with them. They also know whether it feels as if we have a friendship with them.

It seems too simple, but I (Gary) often asked my teens what it would take for me to be a best friend with them. If their anger level was low toward me at the time, I was always amazed at how much information they provided about how I could improve our relationship.

Here are some of the questions I used over the years to open the pages of their built-in "parenting manuals":

- What would it take to improve our relationship?

- What's one thing that brings you the most happiness when Mom and I do it for you or with you? How could we do it better?

- If you could wave a wand over our heads, what would you change or improve about us?

- What do you think makes for a great family relationship?

Sometimes a straightforward question like one of these is the best approach. Once the question is asked, the parent needs to listen carefully and respectfully.

In addition to the general questions above, we recommend three specific questions that, if answered honestly, can dramatically improve the parent-teen relationship. We've used these questions for years with our family, in counseling, and at seminars, and they do a great job of drawing out valuable parts of a teen's built-in manual. Let's look at how they helped settle a dispute between a teenager named Chris and his parents.

Chris was strong willed. One day his mom got extremely frustrated when she discovered he hadn't taken out the trash as he was supposed to do. "How many times do I have to ask until you take the trash out?" she questioned angrily.

"I heard you the first time," Chris shot back. "I'm watching TV right now [probably *M.A.S.H.*]! I'll do it when the show is over."

"You always say that, Chris!" his mother replied. "Forget it! I'll just take it out myself."

Rolling his eyes at his mother's "melodramatic" response, Chris answered back, "Fine! Whatever! You do what you want, but I'm finishing my show!"

Just as Chris was finishing his words, his father walked by. "How dare you talk to your mother that way!" Dad yelled. "If you don't take that trash out right now, you're grounded from now until the end of the world or when I say different—whichever comes first!"

Suddenly convinced to take care of the trash, Chris got up and carried it outside without bothering to put on shoes. When he returned, his dad was still upset about what Chris had said. The dad glared at Chris as he walked by, and then he noticed that Chris didn't have any shoes on. "That does it!" he said. "I can't . . . What were . . ." but he couldn't find the right words to yell at his son. Finally he blurted out, "Why don't you have more respect for your socks?"

As soon as the words left his mouth, Chris's dad paused and then started laughing at the humor in his statement. Ten seconds later, everyone was laughing and the tense situation had ended.

After everyone's emotions had settled, Chris and his parents sat down to discuss the conflict. And the way they settled it was by asking the three questions we referred to earlier. Here they are:

1. On a scale from 1 to 10, with 10 being the best, what kind of relationship do we both want?

Maybe the teen or parent would be satisfied with being at a seven or eight most of the time. It's important for both the parent and the teen to respond to this first question; it sharpens the print in the manual. Furthermore, when a teen hears that we desire to have a 10 relationship, it strengthens the sense of commitment. When Chris's parents asked him this question, since they all had a fairly solid relationship, it was easy for him to answer, "9.2." (We always have to be prepared for humor when dealing with teenagers.) Chris's parents agreed that they also desired a 10 relationship.

2. *Considering all things, on the same scale, where are we today in our relationship?*

Every teen we've ever talked to has had an accurate answer to this question. That's because it reflects how teens feel at the moment, and it indicates whether their deepest needs are being met. Norma and I (Gary) would listen carefully to our teens' responses, and if they said all was not well, we tried not to react with something like, "I can't believe you brought that up!" or "I thought we were over that." We need to let our teens express their feelings in an atmosphere of safety and love.

When Chris's father asked him this question, he responded, "I think we're at about a 5.1." That made it obvious that the conflict was real but not severe. And his numerical response provided a better picture of the state of the relationship than a vague verbal answer like "all right" would have, since that could have meant something totally different to parent and teen.

3. *As you consider our relationship, what are some specific things we can do over the next week that would move it from where it is now closer to where we want it to be?*

This last question is the most powerful, because this is where the pages of a teen's parenting manual jump open. Almost always, the answer will involve the kinds of things we're looking at in this book—more security, affection, better communication, less anger, and so on. But the statement we most often hear from teens after being asked this question is, "If you could better understand me, or if you could just admit it when we both know you're wrong about something between us."

Chris and his family all agreed instantly that they needed a better, less-stressful method of reminding him to take out the garbage. What they came up with was a sign hanging on his bedroom wall that he couldn't miss.

This question is so helpful because it changes the focus of the relationship—away from the difficulties and onto solutions. Being caught up in a parent-adolescent conflict can feel like being stuck in quicksand. The more we dwell on the problem and who's to blame, the faster and deeper we sink. But solutions are like a rope tied to a tree. They provide the means to change, the way out of the quicksand.

Over and over, we've seen these three questions allow parents and teens to shorten the time it takes to improve their relationship. But we need to remember that teens may be reluctant to answer at first. They may fear that our feelings will be hurt if they're honest—or even worse, that we'll hurt their feelings with a defensive response. So it's crucial to provide reassurance that the relationship is secure no matter what is said. When both parents and teens feel safe in their love, answers can be given that will strengthen the family.

3. Notice what's happening to teens when they hit puberty.

To keep valuing our teenagers and continue building the friendship when they hit puberty, we need to understand the changes taking place inside them. So let's consider what occurs during this turbulent time.

We've heard puberty described as an out-of-body experience, one in which the child is stuck between looking like an adult and acting like a child. I (Greg) learned the truth of this in an embarrassing incident. The summer after my freshman year in college, I worked as a counselor at a camp for kids ages 7 to 13. During the first week at camp, the guys went to a party over on the girls' side. This was a big deal, because we got to interact with the girls only rarely. Everyone was excited, but especially us counselors. This was our chance to mingle with each other and possibly get a date for our night off.

At the party, I spotted a beautiful young woman I wanted to meet. After several minutes of working up the nerve to speak with her, I finally approached her, and to my delight she was very friendly. *This is great,* I thought. *She seems really interested.*

For the next few minutes, we had a wonderful conversation. I poured on all the charm I could muster in hopes of getting a date with her. Finally, sensing the right moment, I took a deep breath and said, "Would you like to go out with me sometime?"

"I'd love to," she said with enthusiasm.

Not only was her answer a yes, but it was an enthusiastic *yes.* I was feeling pretty good . . . until her next statement.

"When camp ends," she said, "it will be so much fun to go out with you."

"When camp ends!" I responded. "Why do we have to wait that long? When is your first night off?"

"Campers don't get nights off, silly," she said innocently.

My mind tried to compute what I had just heard. *Camper!* I thought. *Did she say camper?* Suddenly I realized I had just asked a 13-year-old out on a date. I couldn't believe it. She looked like a college student! I quickly glanced around the room to make sure no one was watching, because I knew that if any of the other male counselors had witnessed my mistake, I would never live it down. Fortunately, no one had heard me. I quickly explained to the girl that we'd better wait about *six years* before dating.

Puberty can sneak up on parents and shock them the same way Greg was shocked. One day you have this young son or daughter, and the next day a young man or woman stands before you. Puberty is a rapid switch to physical maturation involving hormonal and bodily changes that occur primarily during early adolescence.[3] Since the early 1990s, the average age of menarche (first menstruation for a female) has been declining an average of about four months per decade.[4] If this pace continues, by the twenty-third century we might start to see toddlers with breasts or six o'clock shadows! (It won't really go that far.)

What are some of the other physical facts of puberty?

- For girls, the onset of puberty occurs at approximately 11 years of age.[5]

- Adolescent boys typically reach puberty at around age 13.[6]

- The growth spurt for girls occurs at approximately 10.5 years of age and lasts for about two years.[7]

- The growth spurt for boys begins at approximately 12.5 years of age and also lasts for about two years.[8]

- During early adolescence, girls tend to outweigh boys. But, just as with height, boys begin to surpass girls by about age 14.[9]

- The male genitalia may take from two to five years to reach adult size.[10]

- For adolescent girls, the time from the appearance of breast buds to full maturity may range from one to six years.[11]

Often unprepared, teenagers may face difficult issues with the onset of these sexual characteristics. Therefore, it's essential that we discuss with our sons and daughters what is taking place—for instance, what to expect during her first menstrual period, and why he might experience a spontaneous ejaculation ("wet dream"). One way we can honor our teens is to help them to understand these changes and to feel comfortable talking about them with us or some other qualified adult.

Another way to be a friend to teens during puberty is to be sensitive to how quickly they're developing. Slower-developing boys may have emotional problems and may be more argumentative than the norm. Faster-developing girls may experiece problems as well.[12] We need to look realistically at how our teens are developing physically in comparison to other adolescents. Many of the problems we face with our teens (e.g., emotional distance, depression, shyness, isolation, rebellion, or anger) can be connected to their physical development.

They may be embarrassed if we confront them with this new understanding. But we can be more empathetic as conflict appears around the house. This doesn't mean we ignore the conflict or fail to hold them accountable for their behavior. Instead, our friendships deepen as we understand their predicament and empathize with their pain.

4. Listen in an understanding way.

One of the most common complaints from adolescents is that even though they want to communicate with their parents, they become frustrated when Mom and Dad don't listen attentively. But the converse is that listening in an understanding way is another great means of developing a friendship with your teenager.

We encourage you to become an active listener, using eye contact and stopping other activities—putting down the newspaper or turning off the television—to give your teen your undivided attention.

Good listeners never assume they know what others are saying. Instead, they ask questions to clarify what someone has said. They repeat, using different words, what they think the other person meant, as in drive-thru talking. If we want to be good listeners, we might ask, for example, "Is this what you're trying to tell me?"

If our teen says, "Well, Dad, that's close, but that's not quite it," we could then say, "Well, we have plenty of time. What do you mean by that?"

As this back-and-forth process continues, we will be communicating that our teenager's words and feelings are extremely important.

5. Understand a teenager's need for peer friendships ... but be available.

Teenagers have a great need to feel connected to a peer group in order to realize who they are as individuals, which means they usually start to spend more time away from home. We encourage you not to take this need for friends as a personal attack on you or your family. It's an appropriate developmental need that teenagers must satisfy.

A peer group as defined by adolescent expert Dr. Eastwood Atwater is "people who regard one another as equals because of their age, grade, or particular status."[13] Dr. Atwater also notes that peer groups play four primary roles in a teenager's life. These include:

1. Helping a teen transition to adulthood by providing social support during a critical developmental period.

2. Serving as a reference point, providing alternative standards that the teen can use to judge his or her own behaviors and experiences.

3. Providing opportunities to develop interpersonal relationships that resemble future adult relationships.

4. Becoming the main context in which a teenager redefines his or her sense of self and identity.[14]

Hanging out, going to the mall, having sleepovers, and talking with friends on the phone are activities that seem to increase automatically when children become teenagers. Adolescents' newfound peer groups help to satisfy their need for companionship and fun, along with emotional support, understanding, and intimacy. They still need these things from their families and other adults as well, but it's vital in their development to receive these things from friends.

Good listeners never assume they know what others are saying. Instead, they ask questions to clarify what someone has said.

Parents are usually unwelcome intruders when peer groups associate. I (Gary) remember a time when I picked up the phone and found my daughter, Kari, on the line with her friend. Just as I began to say "Pardon me," Kari shouted at me, "Dad, do you mind! I'm on the phone!"

I was shocked that she reacted that way. I felt like saying, "Yeah, well I pay the phone bill, so you get off!" I'm thankful that I didn't, however.

A study by Hans Sebald showed what types of issues teenagers seek advice from their peers about and which from their parents. It gives us hope that our teenagers don't stop seeking our advice on important matters. Sebald found that teens are likely to seek their friends' advice on personal, day-to-day matters such as which social events to attend, whom to date, and which groups to join. In contrast, they're more likely to seek their parents' advice about basic life decisions and matters that concern their futures, such as personal problems, career plans, education, and finances.[15]

Another benefit of peer-group involvement is that adolescents can develop the social skill of learning to look beyond initial friendship offers and assess the group of which the potential friend is already a part. They learn to ask, Do I want to affiliate with that group of people? This skill will continue to help them throughout life. We can encourage our teens to develop this perspective as they start to make friends outside the family.

At the same time, teens need to learn balance in where they spend their free time. They shouldn't spend *all* of it with friends. This is where a family contract can be useful.

A good way to complement our teens' need for peer relationships while continuing to develop our own friendship with them is to simply *be available*. They might go days without seeking our help. But as Dr. Ross Campbell explained in his book *How to Really Love Your Teenager*, teens have something like a "gas tank" built into them, and every once in a while they run out of "emotional gas." That's when they need to be close to us for a few minutes—when they need touching, listening, understanding, and our time.

When they come to us, if we say, "Not now, I'm busy," they'll observe what we're doing and conclude they're not as important to us as that activity. This doesn't mean we always have to drop what we're doing; most teens don't expect that. Be we do always need to be available to listen carefully, give a hug, and fill that emotional gas tank—to show that they are more valuable than our activities.

Then they're usually off to be with their friends again. Maybe we haven't explained everything we wanted to say, but they're filled up. And that's okay.

6. Schedule fun times together.

The stress in our family lives from school, work, household tasks, and the demands of society can feel overwhelming at times. We need to find ways of coping with it. One of the best is family play.

In her excellent book *Traits of a Healthy Family,* Dolores Curran made this observation about healthy families: "The primary hallmark of a [strong] family seems to be its absence of guilt at times of play. Individuals and the family collectively give themselves permission to sit back, relax, dream, and enjoy. Further, they schedule play times onto the calendar; they don't wait for free time."[16]

Making that time to play with our teens can be difficult because we all have more to do than can be done in one day. But we need to develop the ability to separate ourselves from work and other responsibilities in order to have fun.

What things does your family enjoy doing together? Walks or hikes? Board games? Backyard barbecues? Swimming? Going to the movies? Window shopping? Camping? Miniature golf? Bicycling? Going out to eat? Football? Helping out together at your church or favorite charity? Whatever things you and your teens enjoy doing side by side, schedule more of those activities—as many as you can. Remember that friendships don't develop by chance or accident but as a result of spending time together regularly.

7. Become involved in a teenager's activities.

As we've seen, teenagers, unlike young children, don't necessarily want special times with their parents every day. But our teens do need for us to become involved in their activities—to attend their games, band or choir performances, and school plays. A deeper friendship can develop as a result, because a valuable message is conveyed: *Your interests are important to me!*

8. Discover each person's most meaningful activity.

Once we understand that it's still important to spend time together as a family, we should ask each member to list the activities he or she would enjoy most. We might use the 1 to 10 scale to rate how much we'd like to do each activity, with 10 being the most fun and fulfilling. After learning everyone's wishes for family activities and experiences, we can design a trip, vacation, special outing, or family night that meets as many of those as possible. For example, the Smalley family spent a number of family nights at the mall, because the women loved to shop and the men enjoyed browsing through bookstores.

If it's impossible to go to one place that satisfies everyone, split the night between places, or pick one person to choose the activity that night and someone else to choose the next week. Or use the fishbowl method. Simply write everyone's favorite activities on small pieces of paper, fold, and place them into a small bowl. Each week, someone draws one from the bowl, and that's what the family does.

9. Protect family fun times from conflict.

As we've said, having fun with teens is crucial in developing friendships with them. But the relationship can be damaged if we mix arguments with the fun times. If conflicts do arise during family activities, agree to deal with them later—after the fun has ended. That will greatly increase the chances of everyone remaining friends.

Our family found a good way to handle an argument during an extended vacation in Canada when I (Greg) was a teenager. Early in our time there, it rained for 12 days in a row. Plans got canceled, and tempers grew short. A huge argument broke out between us one day about where we should go next. No two of us agreed. Finally, when our conversation grew loud, I interrupted and said, "We're all at each other's throats, so why don't we just go out to the camper and shoot each other?"

As the laughter died down, we all agreed to calmly write on a slip of paper where we wanted to travel next, put our choices in a bowl, and pick one out randomly. That solved the conflict. But more importantly, we agreed to postpone any other major arguments that arose until we got home. That protected our fun, and it also kept our anger levels low and helped us to bond. Remember, prolonged anger melts the bond between parents and teens.

If conflicts arise too often in our recreational times, it becomes difficult to relax and enjoy each other, and our teens may lose the desire to try fun things. When tempers got out of control in Canada, we needed to call a time-out. As happened there, humor can provide such a break.

We need to be prepared, then, to interrupt arguments or sensitive discussions by agreeing to talk about them later, when we can provide the attention they deserve. By not allowing conflict to harm our recreation, we communicate that protecting the relationship is more important than impulsively arguing about a problem.

10. Start a collection of memorable places.

One last idea for building better relationships with our teens is to get in the habit of collecting things while doing fun activities together. As a family, the Smalleys collected something from every experience. Whenever we went on a family vacation, for example, each person gathered pictures, souvenirs, or dinner mats. A few weeks after returning home, we would each describe something we remembered from the trip during dinner. Norma and I (Gary) also reinforced lessons we'd learned or things we should have done differently.

To summarize the main points in this chapter, we encourage parents (or anyone influencing teenagers) to strengthen their relationships with their teens, not by surrendering their authority and becoming "buddies" but by becoming better true friends. According to the *American Heritage Dictionary*, a friend is a person whom one knows, likes, and trusts. Also, a friend is one who supports or sympathizes with another. This is the kind of friendship we're talking about. And we can develop that kind of relationship by doing the 10 things discussed above.

8

HELPING TEENS MAKE LEMONADE OUT OF LIFE'S "LEMONS"

*It is difficult to make people miserable when they
feel worthy of themselves.*
Abraham Lincoln

"No! I am not leaving this town! My friends are here!" I (Gary) shouted at my parents that day when I was 15. "I'm not going to move to California! *This* is my home. I won't go!"

"You'll go if we tell you to go!" my dad shouted.

But my mom, sensing that my spirit was closing, knew a different approach was needed. "They have beaches and fun parks, Hollywood, and blonde-haired girls," she cleverly informed me.

"Gary, you know how you love blondes," Dad said, finally catching on to Mom's logic. "Can't you see how much fun it will be? Your brother Frank is down there; he wants to be with you. He's never had the opportunity to hang out with you." My mom and I both turned toward my dad at the same time and rolled our eyes. He was starting to sound pathetic. "What?" he exclaimed.

"Okay," I finally agreed, "I'll go for a vacation. But I'm not moving!"

I had this conversation with my parents many years ago. It was one of the first major trials I faced. Looking back, I can see why God wanted me to leave the state of Washington. But at 15, leaving my friends and my home was very painful. I was convinced my parents hated me. It seemed strange that they wanted me to leave paradise, where we had streams with salmon to catch and mountains with wildlife to hunt.

Our small town, Benjen, was great except for one problem—I'd gotten caught up in the wrong crowd there. My parents wanted to move me because they had heard about something that could have had a tremendously negative impact on my life.

My friends and I, as high-school freshmen, didn't have goals like those of most other kids who dreamt of straight A's and sports achievements. Instead, our goal was to get sexually involved with as many girls as we could. (In terms of teenage boys, not much has changed in 40 years!)

My sister overheard me explain the goal to a school friend and immediately told our parents. As they discussed it, my life was destined for change. They decided we needed to relocate in Southern California. For some odd reason, they thought Hollywood would be better for my moral development. Talk about being as naive as the Beverly Hillbillies!

Several days later, my sister and I left for California on a Greyhound bus. I didn't know it at the time, but I would never return to my parents' home. For my benefit, they made the extreme sacrifice. They were hoping my older brother could get me involved in a church and praying that his church friends would have a positive influence on me.

My first year in the small town of Artesia was difficult. For example, I still remember my sister putting tiny Bible verses around my cigarette packs. "Pollyanna!" I'd scream, and then I'd throw the slips of paper away on my way to school. Walking home, I'd usually find the verses on the ground and read them.

Looking back, I realize that had it not been for my family's influence, I probably would have given in to sexual temptation. A number of my Benjen buddies got their girlfriends pregnant. But I wasn't able to see this reality back then. When I first left Washington, I was devastated and angry at my parents. Only through treasure hunting the event years later did I discover the rewards of leaving home.

Treasure Hunting

What do we mean by *treasure hunting?* We mean learning to take any negative experience and actively reverse the damage by turning it into something from which we benefit. It's like, as the cliché says, making freshly squeezed, refreshing lemonade out of life's lemons. The principle comes straight out of the world's greatest book of wisdom: "And not only this, but we also exult in our tribulations, knowing that tribulation brings about perseverance; and perseverance, proven character; and proven character, hope; and hope does not disappoint."[1]

It will help our teens so much if we teach them to say, "I don't like this pain. I wish it weren't here. But since it *is* here and it's beyond my control, I want to express appreciation to God. I'm grateful that He'll bring good from this hardship." Being able to thank God in the midst of a trial is a sign of maturity and gratefulness, because we realize our pain is producing great things.

Teenagers, like the rest of us, can easily become bitter and resentful in the face of life's difficulties, but treasure hunting has the power to transform *bitter* into *better*. When we're bitter, we're angry and feel low self-worth. When we're better, we feel grateful and enjoy an elevated sense of value. So treasure hunting is a great way to help our teens increase their sense of self-worth and decrease their anger.

When Hurt Comes Wrapped as Opportunity

The Scriptures, as well as history and personal experience, assure us that trials and difficult times are unavoidable. We may work overtime to protect our teenagers from pain, but we'll never be able to isolate them totally from being hurt by their own or others' actions. They may experience moments or even days of doubt, discouragement, loneliness, disappointment, or depression. They may be betrayed by a friend, fail to get into the college or the profession of their choice, be dumped later in life by a spouse, or perhaps experience the disabling results of experimenting with drugs or alcohol. And with each painful experience a teenager suffers, Mom and Dad feel the aftershocks in their hearts.

If teens don't know how to deal with trials in a positive way—if they're mired in fear or saddled with deepening bitterness and resentment—they stand an increased chance of being emotionally and spiritually handicapped, and their relationships later in life can suffer. Nor can they deny problems, ignore them, or try to explain them away. One of the all-time significant truths is that life is difficult and often unfair.

The healthy perspective, the one we as parents need to live by and pass on to our teens, is that the better we are at seeing the good that trials can produce in our lives, the more calm, secure, and genuinely loving we'll be. The very things we fear can make us stronger people, depending on how we respond to our difficulties. What are some of the benefits we can gain from life's trials? Here are a few:

• Strength

• Courage

- Genuine love

- Righteousness

- Perseverance

- Sensitivity

- Wisdom

- Endurance

- Humility

- Maturity

- Greater family closeness

- Increased awareness of others' needs and pain

Before we proceed any further, please understand that we're *not* saying parents should stand by and let their teenagers suffer if it's in their power to help them, nor that parents should create or actively seek out difficulties for their teens to experience. The apostle Paul was asked whether we should create evil that "grace may increase."[2] Put another way, should we cause troubled times for our teenagers so that God can build good things into their lives? In Greek, his answer was *Me genota*. That was the strongest way possible in his language to say, "Absolutely not! No way! Don't even think about it!" Teens who are mistreated may one day gain positive things from their trials, but that's because of God's grace, not their parents' sin.

Our emphasis in this chapter is on how we can teach teenagers to uncover the benefits in their trials, but many parents who read this may need the same kind of help. With God's grace, anyone can take control over the past, relinquishing things they may not have been able to shake loose of before. The secret is discovering how to find the treasure buried in every trial.

When Should We Start Treasure Hunting with Our Teenagers?

When is the best time to start talking about the value that can be found in troubled times? Several days, weeks, or even years may go by before a person is ready to hear the message that God can bring good out of hardship. We must allow enough time to grieve painful and discomforting experiences; it's the first step toward healing.

When a person doesn't grieve, it's as if he's looking for buried treasure without a map. He can't go out in the front yard and dig hole after hole without some idea of where to start. Grieving provides the time needed to prepare for finding the treasure—to learn which tools to use, the correct way to dig without injury, and the exact location to start.

The better we are at seeing the good that trials can produce in our lives, the more calm, secure, and genuinely loving we'll be.

After someone has experienced a trial, therefore, we need to let him set the pace. Only when the person is ready do we try to help him discover the wonderful treasures that await.[3]

When my (Gary's) kids seemed ready, one way I brought up the subject was to say, "Are you satisfied with what you're experiencing out of the trial you've been through?"

If they hadn't talked about the trial yet, they'd almost always say, "No, I'm not. I'm miserable and unhappy."

At that point I asked, "Would you like to spend some time this week 'unwrapping' the treasure you've received?" I'd usually give them a hug and a reassuring smile.

If the answer was yes (and 9 times out of 10 it was), that's when I would start to help them find the good in their troubled times. If the answer was no, I didn't panic. I just came back another day and softly but persistently presented another opportunity.

How to Treasure Hunt Life's Trials

Treasure hunting life's trials involves four steps. To do it, we suggest that a teen (or anyone else) take a clean sheet of paper and divide it into four vertical columns. Each step will have its own column. Use as many sheets of paper as necessary—the more the better. Here are the four steps:

1. Write down several things you like about yourself.

2. Write down the most painful trials you've been through.

3. List the people you can turn to for help as you treasure hunt.

4. List all the benefits you can think of from each trial.

As we explore this process, you'll see how all four of these steps are extremely positive. Let's look more closely at each one.

1. Write down several things you like about yourself.

For some of us, it's easy to write down things we like about ourselves, but for others it's quite a challenge. Young Amanda found the assignment terrifying.

Amanda had been brought in for counseling because she was experiencing nightmares. For several months, she had been having disturbing dreams about killing her father and stepmother.

During the second session, Amanda asked if she could talk to me (Greg) alone. Once her mother was out of the room, the frightened girl explained a terrible secret. She said that when she visited her father, his wife was cruel to her. Her stepmother would push and scream at her and call her names. Once, she even killed a dog in front of her. After each visit, the stepmother would tease Amanda by threatening to keep her, saying she would never see her mother again! Amanda tried to tell her father, but he didn't believe her. Amanda kept this secret from her mother because the visitations were court-ordered and she didn't want to worry her.

After we discussed the situation a little more, we let her mother know what was happening. Then, to deal with the nightmares, I told Amanda that we could find hidden treasure even in this difficult experience. Although she didn't believe me at first, she reluctantly joined me in the process of treasure hunting.

First, I asked Amanda to write down all the things she liked about herself. This was hard for her; she could only do it with help from her mother and I. But after we had brainstormed her good qualities, we had a full-page list. Amanda beamed with pride as she read off her positive traits. (Later, we'll see more of how treasure hunting helped her.)

As we work with our teenagers, we can likewise assist them in writing down their positive qualities in the first column of their sheet of paper. They need to understand that self-appreciation is not an unhealthy, narcissistic indulgence but a healthy exercise in personal value. This is not the time for them to be overly humble. We're looking for an accurate view of their good traits and what they truly appreciate about who they are.

Good questions with which to prompt them include the following: What are your strengths? What types of activities are you good at? What do other people seem to like about you? In what hobbies have you developed skills? What do you most enjoy doing in your free time? What do you bring to relationships? (Loyalty? Creativity? A sense of humor?) If they still

can't think of several strengths, we can suggest one or two to get them
started, and we can encourage them to ask a coach, youth pastor, or
friend as well.

2. Write down the most painful trials you've been through.

In step two, using the next column on their piece of paper, we ask our
teens to list the most-difficult trials they've gone through—especially the
ones that have lowered their self-esteem or created guilt or shame. It may
be too painful to list them all, but they should do just that if they're able.
If it becomes unbearable, they can focus on two or three now and deal
with the others another time.

Sometimes, reliving hurtful times can uncover major pain. That's
precisely what happened to an older teenager named Jill.

I (Greg) had been counseling with Jill for several months when she
decided to treasure hunt a recent humiliating experience. In preparation,
I had her list several other trials she had been through so we could see the
treasures she had already received. As Jill reviewed her life, she was forced
to deal with an extremely painful experience.

Shortly after her parents divorced, Jill's mother started dating Ken. In
the beginning, Ken seemed like the ideal boyfriend. He was kind and
loving toward the mother and showed great interest in developing a relationship with Jill. Soon, however, the fantasy turned tragic.

One night shortly after Ken moved into the house, he snuck into Jill's
room and sexually molested her. Even worse, that attack was only the first
of many. Jill was devastated. She knew how happy her mother was, and
she feared that her mother wouldn't believe her if she reported what he
had done. After all, Ken was a nice man. As a result, Jill blamed herself and
vowed never to tell her mother.

The nightmare continued throughout Jill's high-school years. Consequently, the once fun-loving and outgoing adolescent slowly became shy
and refused to trust any boy. And still her mother remained unaware of
the abuse.

When Jill graduated from high school, she jumped at the opportunity
to attend an out-of-state college. Although she was now free of Ken's
nightly visits, his past behavior continued to torment her.

Several months later, the news that Ken and her mother were going to
marry made Jill sick to her stomach. What if they had more children? Would
he do to them what he had done to her? These thoughts terrified her.

As the wedding approached, Jill wanted desperately to tell her mother
what Ken had done to her. But she was afraid her mother would marry

him in spite of her revelation, and that prospect was more terrifying than keeping quiet.

Finally, after Jill received counseling, she decided she needed to tell her mother after all. Jill called her mom and asked if they could meet. To Jill's surprise, her mother said that she, too, had something she needed to say. Jill's heart skipped a beat. *Has she known all along?* Jill wondered.

Sitting at the restaurant, after a moment of silence, Jill's mother started to talk. "There's something I must tell you," she said. "I know this will be painful, and I don't know any other way than to just come right out and say it. Jill, I have cancer. I'm dying!"

Her mother's words caught Jill completely off guard. And she couldn't help thinking, *How can I tell her now that Ken sexually abused me?* Shortly thereafter, her mother went to her grave, never knowing the truth.

Several days following her mother's death, Jill experienced severe guilt. She felt ashamed for not telling her mother about Ken. And she blamed herself for letting him off the hook.

Now, as Jill relived these events, the pain she still harbored was evident. How could anyone find good in such horrible experiences? Yet she did, as we'll see when we look at step four.

Because it can be so difficult to revisit hurtful past events, we may need to prompt our teens patiently and compassionately. But the effort will be well worthwhile when they get to step four and see that good really can be found in those experiences.

3. List the people you can turn to for help as you treasure hunt.

In the third column, our teens write down the names of those people who can help them heal the wounds of their more serious trials. These are the kind of people King Solomon had in mind when he wrote, "A friend loves at all times, and a brother is born for adversity."[4]

Their lists will probably include the names of people like parents and other family members, close friends, relatives, youth pastors, co-workers (if they have jobs), or counselors. But we can also remind them that the best support is found by turning to a loving God. Even when we feel as if no one else loves us, God does. This is a powerful realization for someone going through hard times. He loves us so much that He gave His only Son to die on the cross for our sins.[5] And He extends this invitation to us: "Cast all your anxiety on Him because He cares for you."[6]

4. List all the benefits you can think of from each trial.

Finally, here in step four, we get to the heart of finding treasures in life's trials. When our teens realize the wealth they have because of what they've gone through, they'll wish they had learned to do this long ago.

At this point, in the last column on their paper, they start listing the positive effects of each painful event they listed in step two. For example, crisis situations tend to make us more loving and compassionate. Other common benefits are thoughtfulness, gentleness, carefulness, kindness, patience, and greater self-control. In addition, when we go through a trial, we almost always become more sensitive to the pain of others in similar circumstances. (The people our teens listed in step three can often add helpful insights here as well.)

In the case of young Amanda, mentioned earlier, she and her mother and I (Greg) discussed how her painful experience at the hands of her stepmother helped to develop those positive qualities we had listed in step one. For instance, one of Amanda's favorite qualities was her sensitivity toward kids who were teased at school. We talked about how this may well have grown as a result of being teased by her stepmother. Once she understood what she'd gained, it was amazing to watch how the painful experience was transformed in her eyes into a priceless treasure.

If you have an insensitive teenager, wait until he goes through a few trials. He may then become more grateful, loving, empathetic, and sensitive to others in pain.

Another common benefit is that difficult experiences cause us to slow down. We can then realize that people are more important than anything else, and we're able to enjoy deeper emotional intimacy because we know better the feelings and needs of others.

Jill, the young woman who suffered sexual abuse, illustrates this concept well. When she looked for the treasures in her trials, she realized she had gained such benefits as increased sensitivity toward others in pain, a closer relationship to Jesus, a heightened ability to identify other girls who were being abused, greater compassion, a desire to work with younger girls who'd been abused, and a conviction about not keeping family secrets. That was a lot of good to come out of a terrible ordeal!

Several years ago, my (Greg's) wife, Erin, learned to do her own treasure hunting as she faced one of the most painful experiences of her life.

Erin is adopted. At the age of 22, after years of dreaming about finding her birth mother, she decided to start the search. Many times she had wondered about this person, *Is she pretty? Does she live very far away? Did she have any more children? Why did she give me up?* After much thought and prayer, she realized she needed these questions answered. Most importantly, though, she knew that her heart's desire was to simply say, "Thank you for giving me life."

Erin wrote to the agency that had handled her adoption and requested the necessary forms and information. After filling out numerous documents, the search began. Finally, after two long weeks, she received a phone call. They had found her mother.

Erin's heart beat faster with each passing moment. She listened as the agency representative explained the procedure, and finally she heard, "Your birth mother cannot make contact with you at this time . . . *but she thinks of you all the time.*"

"That's it?" Erin demanded. "She thinks of me all the time but can't make contact?"

Erin was devastated. *She doesn't want to meet me!* she thought. *How could she? I'm her daughter. Doesn't she want to know how I've turned out? How could she reject me a second time?* Tears streamed down her face. With one short phone call, her dream had been shattered.

Erin wept for the remainder of the day and finally fell asleep out of exhaustion. The next day, she awoke realizing something important. She'd never understood before how much finding her birth mother meant to her. Ever since her adopted parents had told her the news, she had denied this reality. Out of a need for survival, she'd buried the feelings deep in her heart. Now she realized the tremendous desire she had to know her heritage.

To Erin, her life felt like a 20,000-piece puzzle. Over the years, she had worked faithfully, trying to connect the pieces. Finally, she had reached the last one. It was the most important piece—the one that would make sense of the mysterious picture. When she received that phone call, however, it was like discovering that the last piece was missing. The disappointment was severe as she realized the picture might never be complete. Somewhere lay the final piece. And it could not make contact with her at this time.

After suffering through the pain and disappointment, Erin began to realize something special. As she gave the entire puzzle over to God, she saw her adoptive parents in a new light. They had truly and wonderfully blessed her. They were her parents, the ones who chose her, who raised her and molded her into the woman she is today. They had given her the greatest love of all.

The experience turned into a priceless treasure as Erin discovered that she wasn't looking for her birth mother's love or acceptance. She simply wanted to know her history and to say thanks. Instead of feeling anger and hatred toward her birth mother, she now felt compassion. She started to imagine what her birth mother must have gone through in order to give her away.

Four years later, Erin's understanding crystallized when she gave birth to our daughter Taylor and realized the severe emotional pain her mother must have felt as she handed Erin over to the nurse. The instant, incredible bond Erin felt with Taylor, her birth mother enjoyed for only a brief moment. What fear she must have felt, hoping that Erin's new parents would love her! Yet unselfishly, she let Erin go, praying her daughter would have a better life than she could provide.

Erin is now so thankful for her birth mother's sacrifice. Without that painful decision, Erin most likely never would have met her parents or her husband or given birth to our two wonderful girls.

She did not arrive at these feelings instantly. The pain of being rejected bore a deep and painful hole into her heart. But when she finally saw the treasures, she gained a new perspective on the experience. Here are some of the things God developed in Erin as a result of her suffering:

1. A deeper love, respect, and appreciation for her adoptive parents.

2. Increased awareness of and sensitivity to others who have been adopted.

3. The discovery of very real longings for her birth mother. No more would these need to be buried.

4. A new love and thankfulness for her birth mother for giving her up.

5. The awareness of the pain her birth mother must have undergone in giving her up.

6. A peace that God is in control and is working in the life of her birth mother.

As parents, we can encourage our teenagers to take their time listing the benefits from their trials. There are always a number of them, but our kids may not see them all at once. The experience can be like discovering a trainload of gold, one car at a time.

We could go on and on with stories from our lives and from many others who have found great treasures in their trials. And all these experiences make us confident that your teenagers can also benefit greatly from this process.

Continue to Treasure Hunt as Long as Needed

As we've said, treasure hunting trials is not something we do quickly. We can continue the process until we're confident we've identified all the riches to be found. Also, with such serious trials as unwanted pregnancy, major accidents, grave illness, death of a parent, and other traumatic events, we can't expect teenagers to see the benefits immediately. In some cases, it may take a year or longer. But once they start to treasure hunt, and learn to keep at it with the help of our loving persistence, they will soon begin to recognize the remarkable growth that has taken place in their character.

Writing out the four steps in the process we've described can also be done like keeping a journal. Over the weeks, months, or even years—whenever we uncover a treasure that's the result of a trial—we write it on the paper. This helps us to continue seeing benefits long after the trial is over. And it provides written proof that treasures flow from difficult times.

What About Anger?

We realize that some people can go through difficulties and become anything but more loving as a result. Anger is a natural stage for someone experiencing a trial to go through, but choosing to *remain* angry can desensitize a person to spiritual truth. It can also lead to bitterness and resentment, hardening the heart and weakening one's relationship with God and others. This is why it's important, both during and after our teens' trials, to listen and watch for their reactions to make sure the after-shocks of emotion won't chip away at their self-worth. Are they disappointed? Are they staying angry? Do they get discouraged or depressed easily?

If you find that your teenager remains angry after a trial, especially at you, review the four steps to opening a closed spirit in chapter 3. If the anger is causing your teen to "walk away" from God, read chapter 12. The entire chapter is devoted to describing what to do if a teen is angry and remains in spiritual darkness.

If a teen still continues to struggle with anger, perhaps a mentor, youth pastor, coach, teacher, or counselor could provide extra help. On the other hand, if the child is handling the problem well, we can be just as quick to encourage and praise him or her.

The number of tears we cry does not determine how much we grow through trials. Rather, it's the degree to which we're willing to take God at His Word. If we listen to the wisdom of the world, trials will almost always lower our sense of self-worth. But if we listen to God's unchanging Word, even when we hear it only as a still, small voice in a troubled time, our spirits will mature and grow.

The Rest of the Story ...

At the beginning of this chapter, I (Gary) described my first major trial—when my parents moved me to Southern California. Although it was painful at the time, I can now see God's priceless gift in it as well. Here's the essence of what I received through it:

First, my parents demonstrated that God is valuable and that a life centered on Him is extremely important. The word *worship* in essence means falling before the Lord on our knees because He is extraordinarily valuable. And to this day, the single most important thing in my life is my relationship with Him through His Son, Jesus Christ. He's everything to me. If I have a need, either He meets it or He leads me to the place where I'll have it met. He gives me wisdom, guidance, strength, and grace. My appreciation for Him grew out of the seeds my mom and dad planted by their concern for me.

Several years ago, during a casual conversation with my sister about that move, I got chills as I realized how God had intervened in my life. He led me to Southern California, where my older brother got me involved in his church, as my parents had hoped and prayed. But it was a rocky road. Shortly after we moved to California, my father died and I got into a fist fight with the church's youth director. (That's not exactly the best way to bond with a person.) But then God brought a caring man named Rod Taves to become the youth pastor. He also became my "dad" and mentor. He took me on trips, counseled me, and even gave me my first job. Eventually, Rod Taves got me into the ministry. I never would have met Rod if my mom and dad hadn't insisted that I move to California.

The number of tears we cry does not determine how much we grow through trials.

That conversation with my sister also brought other things to mind—small things, really—that my mom did to help shape the man I am today. For example, she took me to different churches when I was little. And though she never said much about God and was, in fact, often discouraged about life, she did always say, "God is good, and God will take care of us." We said a prayer at dinner each night that was strictly memorized words for me. But the fact that we said it every day made a lasting impression. Furthermore, I recalled coming home from a date one time and listening to my mother praying on her knees for her children. She never lectured me, she didn't know much about Bible teaching, and we never had any formal devotional times as a family. But I watched her, and I never knew until later what great lessons I was learning.

Through treasure hunting, I now can cling to the priceless riches my parents gave me. For example, my dad was an angry person, yet because of his hostility toward me, I became extremely sensitive to anger toward my own kids. I also have tremendous empathy when a child or adult is in my office crying because of the influence of "Dad" in his or her life. And when I see others hurting, I can now guide them to greater worship with the Lord through my past sorrow.

I get the best of both worlds, actually: I benefit from all the good things my parents did for me, plus I get the treasures resulting from all the bad things they did. I choose, as a responsible individual, not to let anything they did influence me in negative ways, but instead to turn those things into positives. And in the same manner, whenever anything negative happens to me now, I immediately start looking at how God can use it to benefit me and develop my love for others.

In summary, one of the greatest gifts we can give our teenagers is to help them see the positive things they gain in troubled times. If we don't give them that—if they don't learn how to deal with trials in a positive way—they stand a strong chance of being emotionally and spiritually handicapped.

The essence of treasure hunting is captured in one of our favorite poems, which provides a good ending for this chapter:

My life is but a weaving, between my God and me,
I do not choose the colors, He worketh steadily.
Oftimes He weaveth sorrow, and I in foolish pride,
Forget He sees the upper, and I the underside.
Not till the loom is silent, and shuttles cease to fly,
Will God unroll the canvas and explain the reason why.
The dark threads are as needful in the skillful Weaver's hand,
As the threads of gold and silver in the pattern He has planned.
                                                                    Anonymous

9

HELPING TEENAGERS MAINTAIN OR REGAIN THEIR VIRGINITY

Puberty: The time of life when the two sexes begin to first become acquainted.
Samuel Johnson

As we all know, adolescence marks the time when boys and girls get seriously interested in one another. And it has never been easier for teens to make bad choices in this vital area of sexual relationships. As parents, we want them to resist all the temptations they'll face and remain morally pure, saving sex for marriage. We're like the father who told his wife, "I think I'll go downstairs and say good night to Sally's boyfriend. He's been here long enough."

"Now, Sam," his wife said, "don't forget how we were when we were young."

"That does it!" Sam shouted. "Out he goes!"

Yet, as the title of this chapter suggests, even those who have committed sexual sin can *regain* their virginity. "How is that possible?" you might ask. "And what does it mean exactly?" Let us begin to explain by telling you the story of Sandy.

Sandy approached me (Gary) at one of our seminars. She was glowing and full of enthusiasm. The tale of her youth, however, was anything but pleasant. "All I remember about my family was one fight after the other," she said. "Dad was physically abusive. I hated him for what he did. On the nights he got drunk, we'd all shiver in fear, hoping he'd pass out before he could terrorize us. I'd go to bed most nights wishing that he would die and be gone forever."

It was difficult for her to tell the story, but she continued, "As a result of my home life, I welcomed every opportunity to get out of the house. I could hardly wait to meet 'Mr. Wonderful' and be whisked away on a white horse to our faraway castle. As you can imagine, I did everything possible to find him. I dated extensively. But this way of thinking led to multiple sexual experiences. Sadly, I can't even remember them all. It seems like all those guys wanted anyway was my body—they didn't seem interested in loving me. Many nights, I cried myself to sleep. My whole life was a mess. My home was the pits, my social life reeked, and Mr. Wonderful was nowhere to be found. I finally concluded that I was created to fail. I not only felt guilty about my behavior, but I felt worthless and dirty. It was like leprosy covered my entire body."

But then Sandy started to smile again as she said, "During my junior year of high school, I attended a special teen appreciation night at a nearby church. I went with a few of my friends, thinking we could flirt with the boys. But what happened that night, I never could have dreamed possible. For the first time in my life, I heard that someone loved me unconditionally. And it wasn't just anyone—it was the God of our universe! At first I thought, *He loves everyone? Right! God couldn't love me. I'm unlovable. God surely knows what I've been doing. He must know about my parents, too—He wouldn't love them.* I continued trying to rationalize what I heard, thinking, *I've gone too far. I'm too dirty.*"

Sandy continued explaining that special night. "I can't tell you why," she said, wiping away a tear, "but after hearing the pastor's invitation, I got up and walked down the aisle. I knelt before a small wooden cross and listened as he explained how God loved me. I had finally found someone."

Tears were now streaming down both our faces. Without pause, she whispered, "That man—I don't even remember his name—shared the most wonderful story of how Jesus gave His life for me. And he explained that if I invited God into my heart, He would make me new again. Imagine that—a new person! Free from all the filth and pain. But I began to doubt this was true, so I asked him to explain it again. Then I asked, 'Are you saying that no matter who I am, no matter what I've done, He will accept me? Forgive me? Wash away my sins forever? Make me new again?' He assured me it was true. So that night I accepted Jesus into my heart. I had finally found Mr. Wonderful.

"Not long after, I met Mrs. Winters at that little church. She became like a second mom to me. It was great to finally have someone I could talk with about my deep secrets. We read the Bible together, and she taught me how to let God be my passion instead of boys. They had left me with emptiness, but God filled my life. I truly started becoming a new person."

Then Sandy went on to explain that several years later, God also fulfilled her dream of finding a human Mr. Wonderful in the person of Chip, a young man who was able to forgive and see beyond her past to the new, pure woman she was in Jesus. On their wedding night, knowing that his bride often still felt ashamed about the immorality of her adolescence, Chip did something that finally convinced her, once and for all time, of his love and devotion. "Sitting on the bed," Sandy explained, "he carefully grasped my feet. He then pulled out a beautiful silver washbasin from under the bed. My anxiety level shot through the roof. But something about his eyes enabled me to trust him.

Is it really possible to regain one's virginity after having premarital sex? We say a resounding yes!

"With tender movements, Chip slowly dipped a monogrammed wash-cloth into the warm water and began stroking my feet. As he washed, he prayed words that instantly healed my heart and set me completely free from my past. 'Lord, as I wash my bride's feet,' he softly spoke, 'let her experience Your forgiveness. Show her how You bury our sins in the depths of the ocean—never to be remembered again. Please, Lord, let Sandy hear that I've forgiven her. As she sits before me, she is a virgin. Lord, I love her with all my heart. Allow her to feel that purity. Thank You, Lord, that I have the high privilege of being with such a beautiful virgin. Amen.'

"Since that day," Sandy concluded, "I've felt like a totally new person— the kind of wife Chip deserves. God has truly blessed my life. First and forever, He became my Mr. Wonderful. And then He gave me a second Mr. Wonderful."

Sandy was made pure—a new virgin—by God's love and forgiveness. Her understanding husband affirmed that fact in his wedding-night prayer. And we'll see even more of what it means to regain one's virginity as we continue through this chapter.

A Morally Confused World

For today's teenagers, few issues are more critical than sex. Unfortunately, in modern Western culture, it's an extremely confusing issue.

Many teens have heard that premarital sex is in contradiction to God's Word. But they must wonder, *If it's so wrong, why is sex—and encouragement to think about it and* do *it—everywhere I look?* It's present at the mall, in the movies, on TV, on billboards, and in popular magazines and books, not to mention the Internet.

Sex is one of the strongest drives your son will ever face, and it can be your daughter's security in a relationship. It's one of life's biggest pleasures, yet it's also one of the biggest killers of our time. Teens can't seem to live with it or without it. So unless we raise our children on desert islands, we need to be aware that teenagers will have to deal with sexual temptation many times in their young lives—perhaps even many times a day.

Our point is not to attack the media or anyone else. But we have to face the reality that our teenagers—even Christian teens—are falling sexually by the millions. Consider the following statistics:

- A study of college students' sexual practices and attitudes from 1900 to 1980 reveals two important trends: First, the number of young adults reporting to have had intercourse has dramatically increased. Second, the number of females reporting sexual intercourse has increased more rapidly than the number of males, although the initial base for males was greater.[1]

- In a recent national study, 54 percent of teenagers in grades 9 through 12 said they had had sexual intercourse. Also in this study, 54 percent of teens reported having had sexual intercourse with two or more partners. Nineteen percent reported having had four or more partners.[2]

- Teens typically engage in their first sexual intercourse around 16 or 17, though the age varies widely depending on sexual maturation, gender, ethnicity or race, and socioeconomic status.[3] As teens get older, the percentage of those who have had sex increases. According to some studies, at age 15, fewer than one-third of teenagers had begun sexual intercourse. By age 17, more than half of the males and fewer than half of the females had become sexually active. But by age 19, almost 9 out of 10 males and 8 out of 10 females had engaged in sexual intercourse.[4]

- Every day in the United States, 4,219 teenagers contract a sexually transmitted disease. The World Health Organization estimates that by the year 2000, more than 20 million men and women will be infected with the deadly AIDS virus.[5]

- More than 1 million teenage girls become pregnant each year in the United States—one of the highest rates in the world.[6]

These studies and others like them portray a sad reality: *Large numbers of American teenagers are sexually active.* Since our teens are having sex or are at least being severely tempted, what can we do as parents or other adults working with teens to help them maintain their virginity or recover from the consequences of sexual activity?

In this chapter, we'll focus a lot on helping teens who have already experienced sex. But regardless of whether a teen has had sex or is still a virgin, the nine steps in this chapter can be used to establish the personal boundaries necessary for abstaining from premarital sex in the future.

Is Regaining Virginity Really Possible?

The idea of someone "regaining" lost virginity may seem ludicrous to some. After all, one's physical experience of sex can't be undone. The consequences that go with violating God's principles—some of them life-long—can't be dismissed either. But there's much more to a person than just the physical part. When we advocate regaining one's virginity, we're talking about the *emotional, mental,* and *spiritual* aspects as well. All four of these are part of anything we do.

To say that losing one's virginity is only a physical act is to ignore these three other distinct and important aspects of a person. In this chapter, we'll explain how to deal with each of these four areas in regard to sexual purity. Specifically, here's what we want to accomplish:

- *Spiritual.* We want to help teenagers commit to following God's will and realize that He is the ultimate answer in maintaining and regaining virginity.

- *Physical.* Although teens can't undo what has happened physically, they can develop a plan for avoiding any further sexual activity until marriage. We will offer several methods any teen can use to stay pure.

- *Emotional.* Our desire is to help teens who have fallen sexually to deal with the guilt and shame. It's easy for them to be locked into feeling like failures. But, like Sandy, they can turn those emotions around and begin to feel like virgins once again. For those teens who are still virgins, we'll explore some emotional issues that could lead to stronger temptations.

- *Mental.* To behave like virgins, teens need to deal with the way they think about themselves. If they think they're worthless and dirty for having premarital sex, they'll probably act in a manner consistent with that self-image. Once they believe they can remain pure or regain purity, however, they can act like virgins. So our desire is to give them the mental strength to guard against premarital sex.

Is it really possible to regain one's virginity after having premarital sex? We say a resounding *yes!* To suggest anything else would be to accuse God's Word of fraud. God said, "All things become new to those who are in Jesus." New means new—not secondhand or used, but brand-new. We know the answer is yes because we've met Sandy and others like her. They're living proof that the God of the universe can completely restore our soul.

How, specifically, can teens maintain their sexual purity or regain it after it has been lost? For the rest of this chapter, we'll look at nine steps that will enable them to do just that.

Nine Steps to Maintaining or Regaining One's Virginity

1. Turn to *Jesus.*

Not surprisingly, several researchers have found that teens who value religion and frequently attend religious services have more restrictive attitudes concerning premarital sex and less sexual experience.[7] That supports our conviction that the first step in keeping or regaining their virginity is for teens to turn to Jesus.

What usually happens when they have premarital sex is that they place their own desires above the Lord's wishes. Whether they never had a relationship with Jesus or have turned away, we need to help them understand that God desires to have a new relationship with them. As a matter of fact, before they can have any truly successful dating relationship, they need to experience His love. He wants to be their *first love.* Only when we have discovered how to find satisfaction in Him—to have Him "fill our lives," as Sandy put it—are we capable of truly healthy human relationships.

Making God our first love begins with confession and repentance. The word *confession* simply means to admit it when we know we're doing something that grieves God. In other words, it's agreeing with God that our behavior is not His best for us. When Sandy, in our opening story, became a Christian, she admitted that her immoral lifestyle was not pleasing to God. She also asked Him to forgive her for sinning.

Repentance means to turn around and go in the opposite direction. We stop our sinful behavior and make a 180-degree turn. The Bible says to run from anything that takes us away from God's best.[8]

When we turn back toward God, He promises that all things become new. As Sandy experienced, the almighty God can restore anyone who has fallen—no matter how far. This is a major theme throughout the Bible.

Before becoming a Christian, for instance, the apostle Paul killed many of Jesus' early followers. He did all he could to destroy Christianity. God not only restored Paul, but He also made him a key leader in the church. Paul would later say, "You were once immoral and doing all sorts of despicable things before God and the Lord has forgiven and restored you. You no longer do those same things."[9]

Another important part of turning back to God is developing a strong, working faith in Him. Our teenagers who want a second virginity must have a faith that believes what God says and trusts Him until the renewal actually happens—no matter how long it takes. If God promises to restore our lives, it's just a matter of time before it occurs. So a working faith is one that allows us to wait for God to renew us—to make us pure again.

Here's a brief list of Scripture verses that assure us of God's faithfulness to restore us after we sin in any area:

- The Lord is my shepherd. He restores my soul (see Psalm 23:1-3).

- Inwardly, we are being renewed day by day (2 Corinthians 4:16, NIV).

- If anyone is in Christ, he is a new creature; the old things passed away; behold, new things have come (2 Corinthians 5:17).

- He will renew your life and sustain you (Ruth 4:15, NIV).

- Yet those who wait for the Lord will gain new strength (Isaiah 40:31).

- Rest in His promises; He will be faithful (see Hebrews 10:23).

2. Understand the *consequences* of premarital sex.

The more we know about something, the easier it is to make an informed decision. This is as true regarding teens and their sexual involvement as it is of anything and anyone else. So they need to know the terrible potential consequences of sex before marriage.

Such knowledge can be a powerful motivator because we all do almost everything in life for one of two main reasons: (1) desire for gain or (2) fear of loss. The fear of loss is usually the stronger motivation. If teens can fully understand what they may lose as a result of sexual involvement, they stand a better chance of keeping their commitment to purity.

As a family, we came up with close to 30 reasons to leave sex alone before the wedding ceremony. (It was so convincing that the information helped me [Gary] resist any extramarital sexual temptations as well.) Here are some of those reasons:

- It dulls our soul toward God and His ways.

- It lowers our self-worth by making us feel guilty or shameful.

- It reinforces our self-centeredness, strengthens our sensual focus, and pulls us away from our loving focus on God and others.

- It makes us more susceptible to sexually transmitted diseases.

- It increases our need for greater stimulation in sexual contact, which then increases the potential for conflict in marriage.

- It can reduce our satisfaction in the marital sexual relationship because the marital relationship can't compete with the "backseat of a car."

- It increases one's chances of developing a sexual addiction.

- It reinforces the wrong notion that sex is an act instead of emphasizing the true meaning of sex, which is that it's a reflection of a loving, committed relationship.

- It can cause either the man or the woman to feel like an object instead of a valuable person in God's sight.

- It creates the possibility of pregnancy outside of marriage.

- It also creates the possibility of being tempted to have an abortion.

- When a relationship becomes sexual, it no longer grows but instead becomes a need or a dependency.

- When we have premarital sex, we lose control of our lives and become controlled by another person.

If we don't clearly understand what we're getting into, we will rely on impulse or the "heat of the moment" in making our decisions. But by explaining to our teens the potential consequences of premarital sex, we can counteract the impulsive nature of adolescence. We encourage you to investigate the facts for yourself and create your own list of consequences, and then discuss them with your teen.

3. Learn the *facts* about sex.

If you asked teenagers where they learned about sex, sadly, many of them would not list their parents as a main source of information. In a large study, researchers asked 1,152 Midwestern high-school students that very question. The sources were as follows:

Friends or peers	37.1%
Literature	21.9%
Mother	17.4%
Schools	15.2%
Experience	5.4%
Father	2.2%
Minister	0.5%
Physician	0.3%[10]

The sad reality of this study is that teens are getting most of their information about sex from the least-reliable source, their friends. The good news is that those same teens said that when they're able to have open and straightforward discussions with their parents, they're less likely to be sexually active.[11] As parents, then, we need to reverse the above trend—especially the fathers' lack of involvement—and become a more helpful source of sex education to our teenagers.

Why is it hard for parents to discuss sex with their children? Some of the more common reasons include embarrassment and not knowing how to present good information. Teens often feel it's difficult because the parent may respond negatively. For example, the parent may disapprove, tease, deny reality, or avoid the situation entirely. The key is for parents to be clear on their own standards and then agree about what they're going to teach their kids.

After that, parents need to *listen*. We can't overemphasize the value of listening to teenagers. We don't have to know all the answers to be good sex educators. We *do* need to clearly model our own standards regarding sex, have some good information, and then listen to our teens without teasing or getting defensive or angry.

4. Discover *why* a teen might have sex or have had sex.

Trying to change a behavior without first understanding why it occurred is difficult. It would be like telling a chef who made a terrible dinner to simply stop cooking so badly. Did he use the wrong ingredients? Were his measurements off? Did he use spoiled food? Whatever the reason, it's necessary to find it out so it can be corrected.

Why might teens engage in premarital sex? Too much peer pressure? Fear of losing a boyfriend or girlfriend? These reasons and many more are important to understand in order to help teens maintain or reclaim purity. The following common reasons provide specific "talking points" we can use with our kids.

Weak relationship with Jesus. Immoral behavior can be the result of a poor relationship with Jesus. It might be that our teens have never made a commitment to follow Him. Or they may have fallen into sin and moved away from God's will.

Family influence. Younger adolescents (11-13 years old) are usually more emotionally connected to their parents than older teens, so their sexual behavior is more influenced by such factors as the absence of a parent or weak parental values. One study found that teens from single-parent families and unhappy intact families begin dating at an earlier age than those from happy, intact families.[12] When teens start to date too young, sexual temptation increases. Research shows that 91 percent of the girls who begin dating around 12 years of age will have sex before graduating from high school.[13] Other family members can also be a factor in teens having sex. For example, sisters of teenagers who had babies had more-permissive sexual attitudes and were more likely to have already had sex than the younger sisters of nonchildbearing teens.[14]

Anger or closed spirit. Teenagers with unresolved anger or closed spirits become more vulnerable to sexual temptations. According to the Scriptures, anger clouds our judgment, keeps us from achieving the righteousness of God, and produces self-abuse, sin, and strife. Moreover, it stirs up dissension, makes us jealous, withholds compassion, is cruel and foolish, makes us act impulsively, and moves us far away from God. All these things can lead a teen toward immorality.[15]

Society. As mentioned earlier, sex is everywhere. We receive countless messages promoting it each day. Some experts on adolescent sexuality believe we're moving toward a societal norm that says sexual intercourse between any two willing people is acceptable as long as it's within the boundary of a loving and affectionate relationship.[16]

Friends. Around the age of 14, teens begin to examine, evaluate, and possibly adopt values different from those of their families. Friends become a large factor in whether a teen gets involved in sexual behavior.[17] For example, studies show that teens usually begin dating when their friends do, regardless of their age or maturity level.[18] Further, teens who depend heavily on their friends and are less involved with family are more likely to be sexually involved.[19] Many teens also believe that experiencing sex will increase their popularity or will impress their friends.[20] Finally, male teenagers report considerable pressure from their peers to be sexually active and have intercourse.[21]

Dating at a young age. As we saw briefly above, early dating tends to lead to increased sexual temptation. Most adolescents have their first date sometime between the ages of 12 and 16, with the average being age 14 for girls and 14.5 for boys.[22] The problem with dating too early is that young teens often aren't ready to handle the intense nature of an intimate relationship. They're often focused on themselves. They also tend to have an immediate-gratification orientation toward dating.[23] The combination can lead young teens right into sexual behavior.

Manipulation. Some teens get manipulated into having sex through a faulty belief that it's the only way to get or keep a boyfriend or girlfriend. A major report indicated that many teens feel this pressure to begin having sex.[24]

When teens have no goals or plans for the future, they're at greater risk for engaging in premarital sex.

Vulnerability. Teens who feel inadequate or depressed, who don't have adequate opportunities for education and work, or who feel the need to prove something to themselves through having sex are particularly vulnerable to sexual temptation.[25]

Curiosity. One study reported that 75 percent of teenagers say curiosity was a major factor in their premarital sexual behavior.[26]

Lacking goals for the future. When teens have no goals or plans for the future, they're at greater risk for engaging in premarital sex. For example, research found that teenagers who don't plan to go to college are less likely to postpone having sex than those who do.[27]

Rebellion. The more teens become involved in rebellious kinds of activities, such as drinking, drug abuse, and truancy, the more likely they are to engage in sexual activity as well.[28]

Communication problems. Teenage girls who are sexually active report less-frequent and less-supportive communication with parents than do those who are not sexually active.[29] And one adolescent expert suggested that the more openly parents communicate their sex-related values and beliefs, the less their teens display either negative sexual attitudes or promiscuous sexual behavior.[30]

Low self-worth. When teens have a negative self-image and feel they're not worth much, they're more likely to be involved in sexual activity.[31]

Confused about the meaning of love. Teenage girls, more than boys, report being in love as the main reason for being sexually active.[32] They tend to rationalize their sexual behavior by believing they were "swept away by love."

Puberty hits too young. Another reason teens become sexually active is they experience adult levels of sexual development. In one study, early-maturing boys and girls reported more sexual activity than did late bloomers.[33] The bodies of early-maturing girls are more likely to elicit responses from males that lead to earlier dating and sexual experiences.[34]

Mental factors. Adolescence is marked by idealism and the ability to think in more abstract and hypothetical ways. So young teens can get caught up in a mental world far removed from reality, one that may involve a belief that bad things can't or won't happen to them and they are omnipotent and indestructible.[35] This way of thinking can lead to an increase in sexual activity.

As Sandy began to understand why she had been promiscuous, she came to realize that several factors were involved. For example, she realized she had been confused about love. She had thought that having sex with boys would finally make her feel loved. Unfortunately, it had the opposite effect. So to remain pure in the future, Sandy had to change her ideas about love. Once she did, she no longer had a desire for premarital sex.

In addition, we parents need to be aware of how our example affects our teenagers. I (Gary) remember trying to convince Ann, the mother of a sexually active teen, that her daughter had developed the same pattern she had received from her parents. Ann had conceived her daughter before she married the father, but she had never realized that her child was now imitating her. This mother had transferred her resentment of her husband to her daughter in many subtle ways. The lack of transparency and covering of guilt had alienated her daughter, and the daughter had her own learned resentment. This kind of resentment grows out of family patterns of unforgiven dishonor and can be passed down from as many as four previous generations. We believe it's the biggest factor in steering a child toward sexual involvement before marriage.

Our teenage boys also need to be aware of something significant that can take place when they're "making out." They may think the activity is harmless and have every intention of staying virgins, yet they can lose control without even realizing what's happening. One psychological study found that some males who are getting "worked up" during passionate times can actually blank out due to a shift in the nervous system.[36] What happens in lay language is that they can become "heated up" to a certain point and then lose their awareness of events. Once they reach that level, the drive for sex becomes so strong that a different nervous system is activated, and it can inhibit their plan to go only so far sexually.

That's scary, isn't it? But teens need to realize how their bodies work so they can remain in control—not allowing themselves to reach such sensual and dangerous states.

Some good friends of the Smalleys who have a beautiful teenage daughter have laughingly talked about inventing a device that would fit on the wrist of any young, testosterone-loaded male who wanted to date their girl. If his sexual excitement reached a certain level, an alarm would sound both on his arm and at our friends' house. The device would also contain a homing beacon so they could immediately locate the kids. The boy could take the device off his arm only with a special key—and of course that would be held by our friends!

5. *Treasure hunt* the pain of the sexual experience.

As we saw in the last chapter, one of the best ways to increase teenagers' self-honor is to teach them to find value in a difficult experience. A trial such as losing one's virginity might produce things like increased sensitivity, empathy, humility, and a renewed desire for a relationship with God. Whatever gifts are buried under the pain or hurt, we can help our teenagers to find them.

6. Develop strong *values* and *convictions*.

"Stand for something or you'll fall for anything." That truism capsulizes the sixth step in maintaining or regaining virginity. Having strong values and convictions is vital in staying pure.

Imagine that maintaining one's virginity is like walking across a gymnastics balance beam. The smaller the beam, the easier it is to fall off. Think of how simple it would be if the beam were six feet wide instead of a mere four inches. We could all probably score a perfect "10" if that were the case.

We want teenagers to have the greatest possibility of success as they try to maneuver across the balance beam of virginity. The best way to help them do that is to help them establish clear values and convictions that, in effect, make that beam six feet wide.

As we will discuss more fully in chapter 10, convictions enable us to know where to draw the line morally. They help us to know when to say no and when to proceed. The kinds of temptations teenagers confront today are intense, and facing them with unclear convictions is like tumbling on a one-inch-wide balance beam over the Grand Canyon.

Where do we need to teach our children to go to develop clear moral convictions? The Bible. Its principles provide our moral foundation. The more teenagers read it, the wiser they will become in making decisions that affect their purity. Here are a few of the Bible's many verses that deal with the conduct of our lives, sexual and otherwise:

1. 1 Corinthians 6:9-20
2. 1 Corinthians 7:1-2,7-9
3. 1 Corinthians 10:6-8,14
4. 2 Corinthians 12:21
5. Ephesians 5:3-6
6. Ephesians 2:3
7. Ephesians 4:19,29
8. 1 Thessalonians 4:3-8
9. 1 Thessalonians 2:3
10. 1 Thessalonians 1:9
11. Galatians 5:16-19,24
12. Romans 8:3-8,13-14
13. Romans 1:24-25,28
14. Colossians 3:5-6,8
15. Hebrews 13:4
16. Mark 7:21
17. 1 Peter 1:15
18. 1 Peter 3:16
19. 2 Peter 2:2,7-9,18-19
20. 1 Timothy 1:5,18-19
21. 2 Timothy 2:20-23
22. 1 John 1:5-10
23. 1 John 3:4
24. 1 John 5:17,21
25. Matthew 12:33-34

26. Colossians 1:13-14,21-22
27. Romans 6:6
28. Galatians 2:20

For further help in answering our teens' questions about values and convictions, we need to teach them to turn to a parent or a youth minister, coach, teacher, mentor, or counselor who shares the same commitment to the Bible.

7. Become *aware* of the impact of *choices,* and draw a line to provide a *margin of safety* from sexual temptation.

As Edwin Hubbel Chapin said, "Every action of our lives touches on some chord that will vibrate in eternity." Our teens need to realize that their every decision leaves a lasting impact on them and others. Even the smallest action can have a major effect. My (Greg's) younger brother, Michael, and I once got a simple yet memorable demonstration of this fact in the mountains of Colorado.

I was living in Denver at the time, and Michael, then an older teenager, came to visit me during the winter. Since he was into photography that week, we decided to take pictures of a frozen waterfall. We found the perfect spot about an hour west of Denver. We parked my truck on the side of the road and hiked down to the icy river. The gorgeous waterfall now stood about 20 yards away. Michael carefully walked a few feet onto the frozen river and concluded that it would support our weight. He planned to walk briskly out to the falls, snap a few pictures, and then return to the bank. The plan sounded insane, but Michael talked me into it. "Trust me!" he said.

I followed Michael toward the falls like a sheep being led to slaughter. Suddenly we heard loud cracking sounds, and Michael fell through the ice. *Mom is going to kill me for letting this happen!* I thought, panicked. But then I noticed that the river was only about four feet deep where he fell in, so the water was only up to his waist. "Get me out!" Michael begged as the shock of the cold water hit him.

"But I thought you said 'Trust me,'" I blurted out while trying not to fall over from laughing so hard.

In hindsight, I shouldn't have laughed at Michael. The moment I reached for him, *I* fell through the ice. Now we were both stuck in the freezing water. After a few minutes, we finally managed to pull each other to shore. But the real challenge still remained.

It was getting late, and we hadn't dressed to go swimming in freezing water. The trail back to the road was about a quarter mile from where we had fallen in. As Michael surveyed the situation, he noticed a small opening in the trees on the surrounding cliff. It looked as if we could hike straight up to the truck. "Trust me," he said again, "the shortest distance between two points is a straight line." I'm not sure who was more of a nitwit, Michael for concocting this plan or me for trusting him again.

As we started scaling the cliff, I realized Michael's math teacher must not have explained that the straight-line principle doesn't work in every situation. It took us about an hour to ascend the snow-covered cliff without gloves. When we finally reached the truck, our hands were numb. We couldn't get the key into the door. I pictured tomorrow's newspaper headlines: "Two Boys Freeze to Death with Truck Key in Hand." I could have killed Michael myself at that moment.

Finally, after rubbing and blowing on my hands, I was able to get the door open. Of course, I then had to repeat the process to get the engine started.

What Michael and I learned that day is the same thing teens trying to stay pure must understand: *Every choice we make has consequences for ourselves and others.* When we stepped out onto that frozen river, we suffered the consequences of our poor choice: We almost froze to death.

One of the things that can lead to a poor choice is rationalizing. We rationalize when we use statements like: "It's no big deal"; "It's all right—everyone's doing it"; "I'm not really hurting anyone"; "It's only wrong if you get caught"; or "Trust me!" Such statements can start a tragic pattern. Each time a moral line is crossed (no matter how small the step), we risk stepping out-of-bounds.

> ### *In addition to helping our teens set safe boundaries, we need to teach them to stop asking what's* wrong *with certain choices and instead ask what's* right *with them.*

To avoid crossing those boundaries, teenagers committed to purity must learn to draw personal lines in such areas as these: how far to go physically on a date; what type of clothes to wear; how much time to spend alone with a date; whether to watch R-rated movies on a date; and how much kissing to do. Every teen is different in where the lines need to be drawn, but many lines need to be drawn or the results can be tragic.

Let us explain this concept of drawing a line another way. During a football game, have you ever noticed which part of the field is most worn? It's the middle. That's because the closer the players get to the sideline, the more likely they are to run out-of-bounds. So most of the time, the action takes place in the center of the field.

Morally, we're much better off if we stay in the center of God's will as revealed in the Bible. But we're constantly tempted to step out-of-bounds. "But each one is tempted when he is carried away and enticed by his own lust. Then when lust has conceived, it gives birth to sin; and when sin is accomplished, it brings forth death."[37] The closer we get to the sideline, the closer we are to a potentially tragic decision to cross over a moral line.

Teenagers need to learn how to keep from stepping out-of-bounds. As Dr. Gary Oliver noted in the book *Seven Promises of a Promise Keeper,* the key is teaching teens to create a new sideline—10 yards back from the original line. In other words, they need the protection of a margin for error. For example, teens who have had sex need to develop a new purity line. If their previous mistake started with passionate kissing, they might decide that until marriage, no matter how much they care for the person they're dating, they will not kiss while lying down or engage in any open-mouthed kissing.

Wherever a particular teen needs to draw the line, the principle is this: Since everyone makes mistakes, having room before you step out-of-bounds can make the difference between losing a few yards and losing the "game" of virginity.

In addition to helping our teens set safe boundaries, we need to teach them to stop asking what's *wrong* with certain choices and instead ask what's *right* with them. For example, a great question to ask is, "How will this decision lead to the enrichment of myself and others?" If we can help teenagers to consider whether their actions are moving them closer to or further away from purity, a major battle has been won.

A short poem I (Greg) came across helps me to remember the impact of my own choices, and I often share it with teenagers:

The choices we make every day,
Dictate the life we lead.
To thine own self be true!

For me, "to thine own self be true" simply means understanding what God wants for my life and being true to His wishes. I start each day by thinking about the decisions I'll make and how they might affect my life. If we desire purity, we must carefully watch our choices.

8. Seek out *accountability.*

One of the most important ways to help teens maintain or regain their virginity is to get them to be accountable to someone. This person could be a family member, friend, coach, or youth pastor. Or it could be a group of people who have made a similar commitment to purity. Whoever provides the accountability, we have found that it greatly strengthens a teen's ability to say no to sex before marriage. One of the most powerful stories we've heard in this regard came from a close family friend named Jane.

When Jane was in the seventh grade, her brothers, Jason and Travis, gave her a special ring called a purity ring. She was to wear it on her left hand to show she was reserved for her future husband. Her older brothers had both graduated from high school, and they knew how challenging it is to keep one's virginity intact through adolescence. By giving Jane this ring, Jason and Travis were holding their sister accountable.

As Jane told us this story, she said with a gleam in her eye, "It's one of the most honoring things anyone has ever done for me. Each morning when I place the ring on my left finger, it symbolizes how much my brothers love me. But most importantly, the ring reminds me to save myself for my mate." When Jane goes out on dates, sometimes the boy asks why she wears a ring on her left hand. He wonders if she's engaged. With pride Jane kindly explains, "I'm not engaged—I'm just reserved." Hearing that explanation no doubt makes her date think twice about his agenda.

Jane's purity ring powerfully illustrates the benefit of having accountability, which is simply being responsible to another person or persons for goals and commitments we've made. Jane is gladly accountable to her older brothers.

When our sons and daughters become accountable to someone, they must choose a person who will ask the difficult questions. For example, "Did you compromise your standards on your date last night?" or "Have you been tempted sexually this week?" Ideally, these questions force us to carefully and prayerfully consider our choices because we know someone will be checking up on us.

Accountability is so important that not having it can weaken or even block the commitment to purity. Sometimes, virginity may be lost unless someone else keeps a watchful eye. The moment teens "cross the line," they need to have someone willing to help them find the way back. What a great source of strength when a teen faces difficult times!

If your teenager desires to be pure, encourage her to ask an older friend, youth minister, teacher, or like-minded coach for accountability. And then begin praying that the right person or people will come around. As this accountability begins to work in your teenager's life, she will understand why Ecclesiastes 4:9-12 says, "Two are better than one, because they have a good return for their work: If one falls down, his friend can help him up. But pity the man who falls and has no one to help him up! Also, if two lie down together, they will keep warm. But how can one keep warm alone? Though one may be overpowered, two can defend themselves. A cord of three strands is not quickly broken" (NIV).

9. Be *persistent!*

One time in a college history class, I (Greg) heard something incredible about George Washington. Apparently President Washington had described one of his lifelong desires this way: "I hope I shall possess firmness and virtue enough to maintain what I consider the most enviable of all titles, the character of an honest man."

It takes the character of an honest person to maintain virginity. When we strive to have integrity and purity, we develop an honest character. But as our first president recognized, this is a lifelong process. It can't be developed overnight. Instead, it's something that we make the daily decision to possess. In other words, we need to be *persistent.*

In Luke 18, we find a story that illustrates beautifully the power of persistence. A wicked judge was assigned to a small city in Israel. He was dressed in judicial robes and had two large Roman guards on each side of his bench. The look on his face revealed that he was angry. And with each passing day, his anger and frustration grew stronger. He had no respect for God or man. Sometimes those in line to have their cases tried could hear him brooding about how he would rather be in Rome, the capital of the empire. Instead he was stuck with a bunch of farmers, shepherds, and religious fanatics. Every day, people lined up to present their grievances to him, and he passed judgments according to his mood.

In this same town lived a poor woman whose husband had died. She had no one to look out for her best interests or protect her. Her situation appeared hopeless. Appearances can be deceiving, though. Many looked at her as helpless, but she knew the secret of success.

An adversary had unjustly risen up against her, so the widow decided to seek legal protection. Every day, she took her place in the judge's line. The first time she presented her petition to him, he abruptly dismissed her. The look of disgust on his face would make many people stay far away in the future. But the widow was determined. She needed the legal protection. Day after day, week after week, she stood in line. Finally, just to get her to stop bothering him, the judge granted her request. "Otherwise by continually coming she will wear me out," the judge said.

That parable pictures an important truth teenagers need to understand. *The judge* didn't make the widow's desire a reality—*her persistence* did. Jesus went on to say, "Will not God bring about justice for His elect who cry to Him day and night, and will He delay long over them?"[38] If teenagers want to maintain or restore their virginity, then, they need to:

1. Make their requests known to God.[39]

2. Come before God every day as the widow did with the judge— "praying without ceasing."[40]

3. Act like virgins, because God will maintain or restore them if they're persistent. "And all things you ask in prayer, believing, you shall receive."[41]

Remember, however, that God does things in His timing, not ours. Although He promises to grant any request consistent with His will,[42] that doesn't mean we should expect immediate gratification. We may get our answer the next day, week, month, or year. But the bottom line is that if we desire to maintain our purity, God will be faithful if we remain persistent.

Through Jesus, our teens *can* remain sexually pure, and anyone who has experienced premarital sex *can* become a virgin once again.

10

TURNING BELIEFS INTO PERSONAL CONVICTIONS

Strong beliefs win strong men, and then make them stronger.
Walter Bagehot

One of the most difficult issues parents or anyone who works with teenagers face is how to help them develop their own beliefs and convictions. If they do *not* take personal ownership—if they only parrot what has been force-fed to them—their values may well crumble under pressure. Greg faced this dilemma as an adolescent. But then he went through an experience that helped him begin the process of making his faith his own. What happened to him illustrates what all teens need to turn their beliefs into personal convictions.

When Greg was 15, I (Gary) took him with me on a speaking trip to Romania, which at the time was still a communist nation. When we arrived at our guide's home, we were told that the Romanian government hated any religious teachers coming into their country, so we were advised to be extremely cautious.

The first day, our "paranoid" guide, John, spent hours rehearsing with us the story we were to give the authorities when questioned. However, at the first border crossing, John left some spiritual tracts in his camera case, and we were detained for three hours.

A few days later, we were to meet a pastor for a confidential meeting. Once again, John went overboard practicing the secret password. He even wore a trench coat and hat, thus earning our nickname: *John Bond Jr.*

As we were walking toward the rendezvous point, we passed a prison. It was an incredible sight, so I slowed down to take a photo. I had to be quick because John had warned us against taking pictures. But Greg, mischievously curious about how John would react, told him what I was doing. John immediately scolded me for my "adolescent" behavior and confiscated my camera. Shocked, I glared at Greg for getting me "busted" and warned him with a smile, "I'll get even!"

When we finally reached the meeting place, John sat Greg and I down and instructed us on the finer points of espionage. "Don't say anything," he barked. "Let me do all the talking. Don't make any sudden movements or noises of any kind!"

Greg, our family comedian, raised his hand and said, "John, is it too late to ask a question?"

John rolled his eyes and sternly said, "What is it?"

I could tell Greg was setting poor John up for something. I squeezed Greg's hand to get his attention, but it was too late. "John," he inquired, feigning innocence, "I know we're not supposed to move or make noise, but is *breathing* permitted or should we hold our breath?"

I had to bite my lip to keep from laughing. I thought, *At least I won't be the only one in trouble.*

Wrong! Instead of lecturing Greg, John glared at me and whispered, "You'd better get control of your kid! He could get us into trouble!"

If anyone is going to get us in trouble, I thought, *it's certainly not going to be Greg.* John was taking this "spy" stuff a little too seriously.

The tension mounted as we waited for the guy with the "code word." Suddenly, from the crowded sidewalk someone shouted, "Gary Smalley! It's great to finally meet you. Follow me and I'll take you to where you'll be staying."

John jumped out of his seat as if someone had just shot a gun. He "shushed" the man and whispered, "What's the code?"

The man stared at John as if he were insane. Greg and I smiled and thought, *Buddy, you have no idea!* (In John's defense, however, Romania was a dangerous country at the time. Later, we heard horror stories of what could have happened to us.)

Entering the man's house, Greg saw how little the family had. He soon felt ashamed as he realized he was so materially blessed, yet he lacked this family's passion for the Lord. As the trip progressed, Greg started longing for what they had.

The most meaningful experience of the trip, however, came on the last day. During my final speaking session, Greg and I met Joseph. His love and excitement for Jesus were obvious. And Joseph told Greg something that Greg will never forget. "In order to hear your father's seminar," Joseph said, "my family will lose a week's salary." Joseph's boss hated Christians, so Joseph would be punished for missing work. "But that doesn't matter," Joseph explained. "My family and I feel nothing is more important than hearing about God."

As Joseph walked away, I watched Greg's eyes. Earlier, I had seen that his first thought had been, *Why would anyone give up a week's pay to hear my dad?* But now I could see that Joseph's words had made a tremendous impact on Greg's young life. Later that night, I asked him what he had been thinking about.

"Dad," Greg said softly, "Joseph made me realize that I have no clue about real Christianity. To me, being a Christian is having fun traditions and hearing interesting stories. It's going to church on Sunday and then forgetting about God on Monday. My Christian faith isn't something that I would give up money or my life for—not like Joseph would."

Through the eyes of Joseph, Greg had seen an image of God that he had never thought about. Joseph's love for Jesus was passionate, a love that surely had come to him through pain and suffering. Greg had been truly touched.

He continued, "As we left, I secretly gave Joseph the money I'd been saving for souvenirs. Somehow, buying gifts didn't seem very important anymore. Was that a dumb thing to do?"

I assured him it wasn't. And, seeing the excitement in his eyes, I suggested that we also give Joseph everything we had already bought. Greg was thrilled. The thought of his "stuff" buying food for Joseph's family gave him a new sense of pride.

When we arrived home, our family met us at the airport. After we exchanged greetings, Michael asked if Greg had brought him a present. With great joy, Greg winked at me and said, "Yes, but I don't have it with me. God has already used it."

That experience began a process in which Greg started to turn his values and beliefs into real convictions. The journey doesn't have to begin so dramatically, but it does need to happen. So the essence of this chapter is: *How can we help our teenagers develop their own beliefs and convictions?* But first, what can happen to a teenager who does *not* develop a personal set of beliefs and values?

What If Beliefs Are Not Turned into Personal Convictions?

As a youth director in my twenties, I (Gary) came to recognize an interesting phenomenon. I saw many parents who were "Rockys"—world-champion Christians—but whose teenagers struggled to step into the boxing ring of commitment. In other words, the kids who grew up in Christian homes did not seem to possess the same religious commitment as did kids who were raised by unbelievers and became Christians after the age of 12. Many of these teens from devout homes continually made compromises that resulted in a hollow faith. Even worse, when those adolescents grew up, they tried to pass down a compromised faith to their own children.

The Scriptures powerfully illustrate this reality in the experience of King David and his family. We've all heard the stories about the great spiritual commitment of David. Sadly, however, his son Solomon made various compromises and never had the same kind of passion for the Lord: "And his heart was not wholly devoted to the Lord his God, as the heart of David his father had been."[1] So King Solomon was unable to pass down a strong belief and commitment to his son Rehoboam: "Rehoboam the son of Solomon reigned in Judah. . . . [And] Judah did evil in the sight of the Lord, and they provoked Him to jealousy more than all that their fathers had done, with the sins which they committed."[2]

If you feel frustrated trying to get your teenager turned on to the Lord, take comfort in knowing that no one is perfect. Even King David—who had tremendous spiritual passion—could not pass down strong convictions to his son and grandson.

The three generations of King David confirm that God has no grandchildren; He only has children. It's impossible to inherit a personal relationship with Jesus from our parents. Norma and I (Gary) learned this firsthand with Greg. Through the years, we tried to live out Psalm 78:4: "We will not conceal them from their children, but tell to the generation to come the praises of the Lord, and His strength and His wondrous works that He has done." By passing down strong values and beliefs, we gave Greg something upon which to build his own faith. But Greg had a difficult time translating what he was taught into a personal relationship with God. As we said earlier, the real growth in his spiritual life began with his encounter with Joseph in Romania.

Ironically, Greg seemed to grasp his need to develop his own convictions even before I did. A few years later, as he was pursuing his doctorate in psychology, I was eager for him to finish so we could work together full-time. Talk about a father and son's dream come true! As a result, I was putting pressure on him to finish quickly. One time in particular I said, "You don't really need a doctorate. Will you hurry up and finish already!" Although I was joking, he became very frustrated. Greg then provided a word picture to explain his feelings, one that really opened my eyes.

If you feel frustrated trying to get your teenager turned on to the Lord, take comfort in knowing that no one is perfect.

Here's what he said: In the movie *Rocky V,* Rocky Balboa trains a young fighter who ends up turning on Rocky. In one scene, Rocky's wife tries to explain what went wrong. "Rocky," she says, "you can teach this kid to look like you, move like you, and punch like you. But you can never give him your heart."

Rocky's mistake with his protégé was the same mistake I had made with my son. Greg could write, speak, and counsel like me, but if he didn't have the right heart, all our dreams would be in vain. Greg explained to me that he needed to get his own training, develop his own heart for God and ministry, and earn the right to work with me.

In the same way, all teenagers need to develop their own convictions. As parents, we can teach our teens to look, act, and sound like Christians, but we can never give them the heart of a Christian. We must not try to hand them a prepackaged faith. Teens need to struggle with their beliefs before they can take ownership.

Greg's word picture helped me realize that in our attempt to pass on our values, Norma and I had made being a Christian too easy for Greg. And what tends to follow then is a weak faith. Only when a child works for something does it becomes dear to him. The beginning stage of working for our faith is to question it, and Greg was still in the process of questioning his values.

In his excellent book *The Dangers of Growing Up in a Christian Home,* Dr. Donald Sloat explained:

> Because each generation is different, we have to take what we have learned from our parents and the church, examine it, struggle with it, understand ourselves, and modify or build what we have learned into our own lives. No matter how good and meaningful our parents' spiritual experiences are, the fact remains that they

are our parents' experiences and we cannot simply transfer their values into our lives without adapting them to suit our personalities and experiences.[3]

So how do we do enough and yet not too much in our effort to instill beliefs and values in our teens? How do we avoid passing on a weak faith and instead help them struggle their way through to solid personal convictions? We have found seven steps that parents or other adults working with teenagers can take to facilitate the process.

Seven Ways to Help Teens Turn Their Beliefs into Convictions

A young teenager was arguing with his father about going to church. "It's good for you to go," the dad explained. "Church helps you to develop good morals and values. You need those." The father then had what he thought was a clever idea. He pulled out an old painting of a pilgrim family on its way to church. "See," cried the father, "the pilgrim children liked going to church with their parents, and we know how strong their morals were!"

"Oh, yeah?" the son replied. "Look carefully at that picture, Dad. Do you see what the father is holding? I'd follow you to church, too, if you were carrying a gun!"

As that father knew, trying to motivate teens to develop their own convictions can be frustrating. But instead of feeling we have to carry a rifle, we can do seven parent-tested things that will give our teens the right foundation for developing strong beliefs.

1. Remember that the *relationship* always comes first.

Let's never forget that the two biggest factors in building loving relationships with our children are to honor them regularly and help them keep their anger levels low. The more honor and the less anger they feel, the greater the probability that they will want to make our values and faith their own. Of course, the more these two principles are violated, the greater the chance that they will reject our ways.

At times we'll get frustrated watching our teens question their faith. Yet they still need to feel—above all else—that we love them and highly value them. In our survey of 5,000 former teenagers, they reported that the things they most appreciated from their parents in terms of their spiritual development were *listening, supporting,* and *encouraging*—in other words, having a strong relationship.

To keep the bond strong, we need to find different ways to express our love. For example, we might decide as a family that it's important to be patient, trusting, and never failing in our mutual support. So we list these things in our family constitution and review them from time to time by asking our teens, on a scale from 1 to 10, how they feel we're doing at keeping the relationship as a top priority. If they respond with a low number, we ask for specific ways that we can improve.

Their answers need to be put in observable terms. For instance, instead of saying something vague like "You could listen more," they should say, "I feel like a top priority when you listen to me while I talk about my school day." The first statement was open to individual interpretation, but the second is behaviorally specific. Parents and teens will both know if it's being done. In chapter 7, we called this questioning "discovering your teenager's built-in parenting manual," and we offered several questions that can dramatically improve the relationship and maintain it as the top priority it ought to be.

With the relationship in good shape, we next need to sharpen our own convictions.

2. Sharpen our *own convictions* so we can be *effective models.*

Sharpening our own convictions is necessary because we are the foundation of our teenagers' beliefs. They adopt our values first and then begin questioning them when they reach the adolescent years.

Because they build their convictions on the foundation we provide, it's vital that we carefully evaluate what we're passing down—which we do largely through our example. In our survey of 5,000 former teenagers, they said that the second-most-important thing their parents did for their spiritual development was to *provide a good example.*

If we want our teaching to be effective, we must show our teens consistency between our words and our actions. If we don't, they'll usually imitate our actions rather than obey our words. If we tell "little white" lies, for example, we can expect our teens to be liars as well.

Norma and I (Gary) have been brought up short by our inconsistencies countless times. For instance, we've always been good at playing practical jokes on people. Our kids have said that it's fun watching us and our friends "getting" each other. Wanting to be just as funny, one time Greg decided to play a joke on his high-school English teacher.

Greg's friend had brought a "whoopee cushion" to school. Throughout the day, the two boys reveled in their ability to "get" people. Finally, they got up the nerve to go for the ultimate challenge—a teacher. Their well-mannered English teacher, Mr. White, seemed perfect for such a prank. Since it was winter, Greg hid the cushion under Mr. White's coat, which was draped over his chair. When the class began, Mr. White lectured for a short time and then gave the class some desk work. As he situated his chair to sit down, Greg could hardly wait. His heart raced in anticipation of completing the perfect joke. It was going to be awesome!

As Greg expected, Mr. White sat down hard, and the loudest noise blew out from under his seat. The entire class erupted in laughter.

Mr. White was not amused. "Who did this?" he shouted as he looked around the room.

Instantly, Greg's classmates pointed at the two guilty parties. As loyal as teenagers are, when faced with detention, they can be quick to betray their comrades.

Mr. White sent the boys straight to the principal's office. When Norma arrived, she felt humiliated. *How could my own flesh and blood have committed such a devilish prank?* she thought. *Where did Greg learn this behavior?* "His father!" she whispered to herself. But that was a problem she'd have to deal with another time.

Sitting in the principal's office, Norma was not a happy camper. "What were you thinking?" she finally asked Greg. "Why?"

"Because you guys do it!"

Greg's response took her by surprise. When I heard what he had said, I had to admit his point was not without merit. Nonetheless, later that night we explained the difference between playing a joke on someone and humiliating him. We reaffirmed how we need to honor people in everything we do. "Embarrassing a teacher was not very honoring," we explained. Greg understood and apologized to Mr. White the next day in class, but Norma and I were also reminded that we had to take care not to dishonor our friends when joking with them.

This story illustrates what Jesus said: "How can you say to your brother, 'Let me take the speck out of your eye,' when all the time there is a plank in your own eye?"[4] As parents, we need to make sure we don't have a "plank" in our eye before we try to remove "dust" from our teenager's eye. Our everyday words and actions must match what we claim to believe.

We must also be clear about our convictions. Otherwise, our teens can turn away from our values simply because they don't understand them. One way to make sure we're presenting them clearly and living them out is to ask our mate or a close friend if they see anything that needs to be changed. What we must *not* be are parents whose words and actions promote two different sets of values.

At this point, we encourage you to write down your key beliefs and values. Clarifying your convictions in the following areas will help you determine if you're passing down the right message. What are your convictions with regard to . . .

> Jesus/spirituality
> church
> school/education
> integrity
> honor
> family
> work
> sex
> character traits
> serving
> friends/social activities
> money
> health

Are there any other critical areas that need to be addressed in your life? If so, write those down as well.

In addition to making the relationship a top priority and being aware of our informal actions (modeling) as parents, a third way to assist in value ownership is by providing formal teaching.

3. Once we're aware of what we're modeling, we can provide *formal instruction* to our teens.

Moses certainly recognized the importance of providing formal instruction to our children. He said, "You shall teach [God's standards] diligently to your sons and shall talk of them when you sit in your house and when you walk by the way and when you lie down and when you rise up."[5] In other words, we're to spend time with our teenagers, consistently teaching them the Word of God. It should be a normal, natural part of our conversation as we use life's "teachable moments" to pass along the lessons and truths we've learned.

The importance of this biblical command was underscored by the 5,000 adults we surveyed. *Teaching beliefs* and *teaching morals/values* were among the things they most appreciated from their parents in terms of their spiritual development. Conversely, the things they least appreciated were their *father's lack of spiritual involvement* and that their parents *didn't talk about their own relationship with God, did not attend church,* and *did not have a personal spirituality.* When we asked how parents can

motivate their teens to develop their own spiritual beliefs and convictions, the top two responses were *lead by example* and *talk to them.*
Teenagers are crying out for us to teach them with our words and our
example.

To help teenagers develop a conviction in a particular area, they must
first develop a belief. This is the primary focus of our formal instruction
as parents. *A belief is an acceptance of the truth without a real, personal
conviction.* In other words, there's no ownership of the idea yet.

At the belief stage, their acceptance of the truth is also more dependent
on their parents. They haven't yet examined and "proved" the idea for
themselves, so to a certain extent they're taking it on faith. During adolescence, of course, teens often aren't as accepting as when they were
younger. Instead, they question their parents' beliefs. Although it may not
feel like a good thing, it is. Like babies learning to walk, questioning is
how teens learn to take their first steps of conviction. (We'll say more
about the questioning process in the remaining sections of this chapter.)

It's encouraging to note that one study found that teenagers are more
interested in religion and spiritual beliefs than younger children are.
Teens' maturing thought processes and search for their own identity
seem to draw them toward such matters.[6] According to another study,
more than 90 percent of teenagers say they believe in God and prayer.[7]
Teens *do* want to develop strong spiritual convictions.

All the beliefs and values we pass on, of course, should be consistent
with the teachings of the Bible. Otherwise, there can be severe consequences: "But whoever causes one of these little ones who believe in Me
to stumble, it would be better for him to have a heavy millstone hung
around his neck, and to be drowned in the depth of the sea."[8]

How can we know, in those areas of life where we can't find a verse that
speaks directly to the matter, that the values we're teaching are consistent
with Scripture? To answer that, the Smalley family has long relied on what
we call the "1 Timothy 6:3-4 test." Those verses read, "If anyone advocates
a different doctrine and does not agree with sound words, those of our
Lord Jesus Christ, and with the doctrine conforming to godliness, he is
conceited and understands nothing." So we ask, Do our words or actions
in this case lead to godliness? If the answer is yes, the values we're teaching are probably compatible with the Bible.

Once we've instilled beliefs through formal instruction, the fourth step
in helping teens develop personal convictions is to allow them to find
their own answers to the questions they've raised.

4. After providing instruction, allow teenagers to *find their own answers.*

One of our favorite sayings is "Give a man a fish and he'll eat for a day; teach a man to fish and he'll eat for a lifetime." When helping our teenagers develop their own convictions, this should be our battle cry. If we want them to remain spiritually dependent on us, we'll give them the answers to their questions. But if we want spiritually independent sons and daughters, we'll teach them how to find their own answers.

As we already stated, when we give teenagers too many answers to their questions, we can keep them from developing their own strong convictions. The following story illustrates this truth. It took place during America's Depression era. As a young, married math student was finishing his college education, he realized that the job market for someone with a math degree was extremely limited. The only job he could find was at a soup kitchen. He became discouraged thinking he would not be able to support his family.

A few days before his final exam, however, he heard some encouraging news. A teaching position had opened up in his school's math department, and the job would go to whoever got the highest score on the final test.

The young man studied diligently because he *had* to get that job. He again reviewed his notes and textbooks the entire night before the test. When his wife came down to start breakfast the next morning, she found him fast asleep at the kitchen table. "Honey, wake up!" she shouted. "Aren't you supposed to be in class?" He had overslept! He looked at his watch and realized his classmates had already been taking the test for nearly an hour.

When he dashed into the classroom, he looked around for his professor, but the man was nowhere to be found. Instead, a teaching assistant handed him eight questions on a piece of paper and added that there were two more questions on the blackboard. The young man worked relentlessly for the next few hours. When the assistant called for the tests, the young man felt discouraged because he hadn't gotten to the two problems on the board. He knew that someone else would probably solve them.

Still determined to get the job, however, he went looking for his professor. When he finally found the man, to his surprise, he was given permission to work on the two problems over the weekend.

When Monday arrived, the young man handed in the problems. But he still felt discouraged because he had only solved one of them.

Later that day, the dejected young man heard a knock on his door. He was shocked to discover his math professor on the front porch.

"You've made history!" the professor shouted in greeting. "You solved one of the extra-credit problems!"

Confused, the young man lowered his head and said, "I'm sorry I couldn't complete both problems."

"No, no, young man!" cried the professor. "You came late to class and missed my announcement about these two problems. They were put on the board only for your amusement. Until now, these problems had no solutions. People have spent their entire lives thinking about them. *Einstein* died without ever solving them. But you did it! The job is yours!"

And that young math student went on to become one of the most influential mathematicians of his time.

Imagine, however, if he had thought before he started that the problems couldn't be solved. Would he have even tried? Or what if his wife or parents or math instructor had known what he was doing? They might have told him it was impossible. Worse, they might have unintentionally sent him in the wrong direction.

In short, there's great value in allowing our teens to struggle while finding their own answers. The process of turning beliefs into convictions is like solving a math problem. If we allow our teens to look for their own answers, they may do things and develop convictions we never dreamed possible.

We define a conviction as *an ownership in a belief that becomes part of the foundation from which the person thinks and behaves.* If teens are denied this opportunity to form their own values, they tend to stay dependent on their parents' beliefs. And then false convictions may develop.

A false conviction is *a deceptive, incorrect, faithless, or counterfeit belief in something that becomes part of an unstable foundation from which the teen thinks and behaves.* False convictions seem like true convictions for a time, but they're unstable—like sand. Teens can't build their lives on them. What's erected on false convictions will need to be reconstructed again and again until the foundation is solidified. Teens need to build the type of foundation described by Jesus: "The rain came down, the streams rose, and the winds blew and beat against that house; yet it did not fall, because it had its foundation on the rock."[9] Those are the convictions that will stand against the storms of life.

We can rejoice, then, when our teens begin to question their faith. In

Romania, as Greg spoke to Joseph and struggled to understand his own faith in light of the experience of Christians there, I (Gary) was thrilled. My son was beginning to take ownership of his beliefs and think for himself. Up to that point, he had maintained his spiritual life and other values through Norma and me.

I could have interfered in this process by providing easy answers to his questions. Unfortunately, I had done that many times in the past. For example, Greg had asked one day why the Bible didn't mention anything about "petting" with girls. "The Bible talks about not having intercourse," he said. "What about all the other stuff?" What a great conviction-building question! But instead of encouraging to him look up several scriptures on his own or read a Josh McDowell book, I explained what I thought was the correct answer. And because Greg didn't have to wrestle with the issue, he developed a passive stance toward petting and experienced difficulties with it when he got into college.

We're not saying, of course, that Greg's struggle with sexual temptation was all because I gave him an easy answer to his question years before. He was still responsible for his own choices. But we do encourage parents to refrain from trying to give their teens all the answers. If I had allowed Greg to wrestle with the sex issue, I would have given him a better chance to think it through and develop his own, more meaningful standards.

Other types of conviction-building questions that teens ask and we need to let them explore may include:

- Should I go to college? Is school really that important?

- What should I do if my friends are negatively influencing me?

- How should I handle social activities like parties where drinking is involved?

- What's my position on attending R-rated movies or listening to hard-rock music?

- Am I lacking any valuable character traits?

- How much time should I spend with my family and siblings?

- How much money should I put into savings?

- How far should I go on a date? What are my convictions about premarital sex?

- Do I really need to go to church?

- What should my eating and exercise habits be?

- How many extracurricular activities should I get involved in?

Understand, we're not suggesting that teens should be given total free-dom to make decisions in these areas. Just how much autonomy they should have depends on the levels of maturity and responsibility they've demonstrated. But let's remember that our goal is to teach our teens to fish and not simply give them fish to eat. So we moms and dads need to talk and determine how we can best allow our teens to question their beliefs and build their own convictions. With some issues, we may need to set boundaries so they won't get injured (physically as well as emotion-ally). But what those issues are depends on each family and each teenager.

We know that having our children question our beliefs can be frustrat-ing. At times they may belittle, accuse, abandon, or interrogate our long-standing values. But the process marks the beginning of the development of their own convictions. The next step, then, is learning how to encour-age our teens during this confusing belief-questioning time.

5. Provide *encouragement* during times of *belief questioning*.

When teenagers question their beliefs and values, they usually go in one of three directions:

1. They walk completely away from the faith.

2. They remain dependent on their parents' beliefs.

3. They develop independent beliefs based on all or parts of their parents' values.

If we become angry and defensive during this period, we may suffocate our teens' ability to question their faith. We must decide whether we're going to aid or hinder them in developing their own convictions. To help them grow, we need to encourage them during this process.

For example, when they do something that looks like honest wrestling with issues surrounding convictions, we can tell them how proud we are that they're thinking and struggling with these matters. We can empathize with their confusion and frustration as they try to solidify their own values. Instead of being defensive or providing too many answers, we can be silent and listen to their pain.

We can also ask our teens if they feel we've been good encouragers.

Although this takes courage, it can provide a gold mine of information. We can say something like, "From 1 to 10, with 10 being awesome, how do I rank as a source of encouragement to you?" If they answer "Definitely a 2!" we know we need to do a better job. We can then ask, "What can I do this week to move that 2 closer to a 10?" Their answers will give us specific handles on how to improve in this vital area.

You may be thinking, *Encouraging teenagers to question their faith sounds reasonable, but how much freedom should we grant them?* It's true that too much freedom can be harmful, so we'll address that question in the next step.

6. *Monitor* teenagers during the belief-questioning process.

We previously stated the principle "Inspect what you expect." My (Gary's) wife, Norma, has used this phrase countless times because she knows that if we want something to happen, we can't leave it to chance. "Positive results," she says, "happen because you inspect them." She regularly surveys every part of her life, and she especially looked at how her children were doing when they were still living at home.

As we give our teenagers the freedom to question their values and beliefs, we still need to maintain some rules and limits in a healthful balance. Let us illustrate how this works.

One day while sitting by the side of a swimming pool, we watched as a father tried to get his young son to jump off the diving board into his arms. The father kept saying, "Don't worry, son, I'll be right here to catch you. You can do it. Don't be afraid."

But the boy *was* afraid, and he resisted for a few minutes. Finally, just when he had gathered his courage and was about to jump, his mother called to her husband. He turned to answer her, and as he did the boy closed his eyes, squeezed shut his nose, and leaped off the board. The father wasn't ready. The boy stretched toward the water and did a perfect belly flop. *Smack!* The sound echoed over the pool. People everywhere turned to see what had caused the awful noise. A second later came the boy's scream when he finally surfaced.

"Are you okay?" begged his father, taking him in his arms. "I wasn't ready. Why did you jump?" But the father's concern didn't matter now. Nothing he could say would make a difference to the young boy. He had jumped, and no one had caught him.

That scene illustrates teenagers as they begin to question their beliefs. They need the freedom to "jump off the board of life," but they also need someone to catch them. Family rules and limits are like the father in the pool. If they're not in place, it's like the dad turning away—they may jump and end up doing a belly flop. Sadly, many of the belly flops teens experience have consequences that go way beyond a red stomach. On the other hand, when we maintain good rules and limits, we provide an enormous amount of trust and security. Further, having rules will not leave to chance the development of their convictions.

> *As we give our teenagers the freedom to question their values and beliefs, we still need to maintain some rules and limits in a healthful balance.*

One way to establish this balance is to add an article to the family constitution that could read, "We agree to give each teenager the opportunity to develop his or her own beliefs and convictions. We will allow the questioning of our family values. However, if we feel that harm will result from the questioning process, we will intervene and provide a boundary."

We urge you to become a student of your children, checking on them regularly during this growth process. And remember that it takes time and will not be done overnight.

7. Remember that conviction building is a *process* and not a quick fix.

Building meaningful convictions is a lifelong process. At times, however, the road can be filled with potholes. It may get narrow and seem impossible to maneuver. Our teens may experience rock slides and bad drivers who run them off the road. They may even choose the wrong fork and go completely away from Jesus' path. As these things happen, we need to remember that God has forever to mold their character. Detours are not the end of the journey; they're painful realities of life. The *beauty* of detours is that they're the very things that can produce a strong faith. The apostle Peter recognized this truth in the Scriptures:

> In this you greatly rejoice, even though now for a little while, if necessary, you have been distressed by various trials, so that the proof of your faith, being more precious than gold which is perishable, even though tested by fire, may be found to result in praise and glory and honor at the revelation of Jesus Christ.[10]

Negative experiences, or trials, provoke the questioning of one's beliefs, and that leads to conviction. But the process can be painful. As parents, we can take refuge in God's promise that when our teens' convictions have been "refined," they will be "more precious than gold." It's still not easy watching our sons and daughters go through tough experiences. But knowing what can come out of them, through treasure hunting and the questioning process, certainly helps.

My (Greg's) life provides a good example of how this process is not a quick fix. I first began to really question my beliefs during our time with Joseph in Romania. But it's not as if the next day I had strong, new personal beliefs or a complete list of my own convictions. Instead, it took me years of searching and making mistakes to reach the place I'm at now.

We don't have to travel across the ocean to find great opportunities for our teens to grow, either. They have plenty of chances all around them. Let's look for those opportunities and pray every day that our teens will begin to question their beliefs and values.

One way to jump-start the process is to ask our teens to write out the major values, beliefs, and convictions they presently hold in the following areas:

school
parents
friends
vocation
character
social activities
family/siblings
money
dating
spiritual life
health
sports/extracurricular activities

Then we can challenge them to consider over the coming months, prayerfully and biblically, just what they think their values, beliefs, and convictions *should* be for the rest of their lives, and *why*. Of course, we also need to pray diligently for them as they go through this essential questioning process.

We now want to turn our attention to one of the most important ways Norma and I (Gary) helped our teenagers to *maintain* their convictions. What we discovered was that having different people mentor our teens provided a special kind of accountability. We believe good mentors can be an incredible asset in your teen's life as well.

HOW A MENTOR CAN HELP TEENS MAINTAIN THEIR CONVICTIONS

If a child is to keep alive his inborn sense of wonder, he needs the companionship of at least one adult who can share it, rediscovering with him the joy, excitement and mystery of the world we live in.
Rachel Carson

Once our teenagers start questioning their beliefs and values, which we looked at in the last chapter, one of the best things we can do for them is to help them find a mentor—someone outside the family to provide another role model and a "safe" place to discuss and sort through important issues.

A special mentor to Greg during his teen years was a man named Terry Brown. Terry has worked with me (Gary) for more than 15 years. Although I never formally asked him to mentor Greg, a relationship blossomed between the two. Throughout Greg's high-school years, they met regularly. During those times, Terry reinforced the beliefs and convictions that Norma and I taught. It was great! Because Terry was younger and athletic, Greg felt he could relate better with him and so was much more open to hearing some things from him. Norma and I could have suggested the same things, but Greg probably would have resisted us because of his need to separate and individuate.

I didn't realize the extent of Terry's influence, however, until after a big game in Greg's high-school football career. I was heartbroken about not being able to attend because I had to be away on business. So I asked Terry to take pictures and a video that I could watch when I returned.

Late in the fourth quarter, the game was tied 17-17. Greg's team was on the opponents' 10-yard line. As Greg stood in the huddle, his heart began to race, because the coach had sent in a pass play that would give him a chance to score the winning touchdown.

Greg could barely keep his hands from shaking. As he looked around, he noticed Terry standing with a camera near the end zone. "21 . . . 44 . . . 8," barked the quarterback, "Hut! Hut!" The ball was snapped and the crowd fell silent. A few seconds later, Greg made an incredible diving catch near the back of the end zone. "Touchdown!" Greg heard. But it wasn't from the referee. Terry was standing near Greg, pointing and screaming. Finally, the referee raised his arms in agreement. Greg had won the game! Terry and Greg embraced until they were both mauled by his teammates.

When I returned home the next day, everyone described the big game in great detail. Greg talked about how close he'd come to stepping out-of-bounds. Terry explained how he had wanted to take pictures of the winning catch but was afraid the flash would have blinded Greg. Everyone was so excited that my stomach grew sick because I'd missed the game. But I did have the next best thing, a video of the entire contest. Greg and I sat and relived every moment.

Later that night, as the family continued laughing and discussing the big game, I again asked Greg to describe his catch. "Terry said it was the best catch he's ever seen," Greg stated with pride. "And Dad, he knows a lot about football!"

Experiences like that are what bonded Terry and Greg for life. From Greg's comment, it was obvious that Terry meant a great deal to him. And Norma and I really appreciated the way Terry gave our son another example to follow. Terry was able to affect Greg's life in many positive ways. For instance, he was able to teach scriptural principles much more easily because Greg was open to listening to him. Those lessons made more of an impact on Greg than a lifetime of sermons.

Mentors can be a powerful force as teens develop convictions, because "outside instruction" can make a special impression on their lives.

What exactly is a mentor? In the excellent book *Seven Promises of a Promise Keeper*, Dr. Howard Hendricks wrote that it's someone committed to "developing a person to his maximum potential for Jesus Christ."[1] The Bible gives a clear mandate for mentoring in these words: "The things which you have heard from me in the presence of many witnesses, entrust these to faithful men who will be able to teach others also."[2]

Mentors can be a powerful force as teens develop convictions, because "outside instruction" can make a special impression on their lives. We're not suggesting that a parent's words no longer have an impact, but teens do seem more motivated to listen to those outside the family.

For example, Norma and I (Gary) told our children at least six million times as they were growing up that we should resolve family arguments before going to bed. We also modeled that practice when the opportunity presented itself. Just when I started thinking I had done a good job in this area, in strutted Greg from youth group one day. "Guess what I learned today?" Greg said as if he had discovered some fantastic new insight. "Pastor Huey said that we should never let the sun go down on our anger. We should really try to do that the next time we get into a fight!"

My jaw hit the ground. I started gasping for air as if Greg had just set off a smoke bomb. "You're joking, aren't you?" I uttered in disbelief. "Haven't you been listening for . . . oh . . . *your entire life?* We've said the same thing over 400 million times!"

As Greg walked out of the room, he shot me that look teenagers develop when they turn 13—you know, the one that means, "Dad, get a clue!"

Exposing Teenagers to Other People

When we expose our teenagers to a mentor who invests in their lives, a special process is launched that, ideally, will never end. But it can be intimidating to envision a son or daughter getting involved with a mentor. We may feel that we've failed, thinking, *If I need someone else to help raise my child, it must mean I didn't do my job right.* In fact, however, a mentor is the perfect person to enter our teens' lives and help them build their own values and convictions on the foundation we've laid.

We might also fear that our kids will expose our weaknesses to their mentor. That may well happen as our teens discuss frustrations they're having at home. But the benefits of involving a mentor will far outweigh the negatives.

Consider, for example, that getting our teens involved with a mentor can help to satisfy three important needs. According to Dr. Bruce Narramore and Dr. Vern Lewis, in order to become healthy, well-adjusted adults, all adolescents must:

1. Develop their own distinct identity and a sense of their uniqueness and individuality.

2. Progressively separate themselves from their childhood dependency on their parents.

3. Develop meaningful relationships with peers and others outside the family.[3]

A good mentor helps in all three of these areas.

A mentor can also compensate in part for the fact that teens often tire of attending church as a way of growing spiritually. Many teens say that organized religion has little meaning for them and that the church's doctrines are outdated. Only 25 percent of teens say they have a high degree of confidence in organized religion.[4] Although it's still important for teens to find churches where they can feel connected, a mentor—like Terry Brown in Greg's life—can have a tremendously positive spiritual impact.

Exposing Teenagers to Experiences Outside the Home

In addition to getting other people involved with our teenagers, another form of mentoring is exposing them to "outside experiences." In our survey of 5,000 adults, for instance, the former teens reported that encouraging their attendance at church and youth events was a key way their parents helped them develop their own spiritual beliefs and convictions.

I (Greg) once got a good (but embarrassing) chance to grow through an experience that was literally outside our home. Dad and I had traveled to the mountains of northern Arizona to fish on a secluded river. As we hiked to our spot, we noticed signs prohibiting fishing with worms. I wasn't happy about that, because worms were the perfect bait for this river. "That's not fair!" I shouted as we split up to go after "the big ones."

The more I thought about it, the more upset I got. *Why can't I use live bait?* I wondered. *They have no right to limit my opportunity to catch fish. I paid for a fishing license—I should be able to fish however I want.* So I put a worm on my hook and started fishing.

Everything was going great until—out of nowhere—a game warden appeared about 20 yards downstream. He startled me. I figured he'd bust me if he caught me fishing with illegal bait, so I immediately cut my line. The only problem was that since I was upstream, my bait floated right to him! He plucked it out of the water and walked toward me.

When he asked if it was my line, I wanted to lie. I was seriously tempted. But I didn't. Something about being there in such a beautiful part of God's creation made it seem wrong. I felt proud of myself for telling the truth. And I realized later that this had been a defining moment for me in terms of my own commitment to honesty.

The "fish policeman" didn't find it in his heart to forgive me, however. There in the middle of nowhere, I got a ticket for using illegal bait. And to top it all off, I wasn't allowed to fish for the rest of the day.

That's just one example of how exposing our teenagers to outside experiences can give them opportunities to take ownership of their important beliefs. Other types of activities they could be involved in include:

- summer camps

- missions trips

- after-school activities like choir, clubs, cheerleading, sports, etc.

- youth group

- Boy Scouts or Girl Scouts

- boys' and girls' clubs, YMCA, YWCA

- city parks and recreation department programs

- Big Brothers and Big Sisters

- any kind of volunteer services

If our teens aren't already engaged in these kinds of things, we can brainstorm the possibilities with them, especially activities they could do with their friends. Whatever they might want to try, they only need to commit to trying it for six weeks or so (rather than a longer time frame, which might seem overwhelming).

Any situation can be used to teach or strengthen a value or belief. The key is recognizing the opportunity. But sometimes, after teenagers return from their experience, it's better to wait a week or two before asking what they might have learned. They may need time to let their emotions settle and deal with any negative feelings they could have experienced. At a later date, we can reinforce the value of the experience. Sometimes there won't be any major lesson that was learned, and that's okay. God can still work through those outside experiences to teach our teens about His will.

Now let's turn our attention to the specific ways we can get a mentor involved in the lives of our teenagers.

Getting a Mentor Involved

We hope by now that you realize the incredible positive power of a mentor. If you want the same thing that Greg received from our friend Terry Brown for your teen, we invite you to read on about how you can help bring home that person God wants to be ministering to your child.

1. Begin asking *God* to bring someone into the teenager's life.

Before we begin looking for a mentor, the first step is to turn the process over to God. He knows exactly what our teenagers need. We can pray that He will start preparing both them and their future mentors, and that He will give wisdom and patience to everyone involved. We can also pray that He will deal with any fears we might have about involving another person in our teens' lives. If we are faithful in prayer, God will be faithful to us. The Bible promises, "Therefore I tell you, whatever you ask for in prayer, believe that you have received it, and it will be yours."[5]

A single mother in Denver, Colorado, began praying for someone who could mentor her angry teen. This boy, Kevin, had been in and out of trouble. The mother feared she was losing her son. But her prayers would soon be answered.

I (Greg) was working as a social worker in Denver at the time. My job was to counsel young teenagers who had recently been released from a psychiatric hospital. Kevin was one of those to whom I was "randomly" assigned. As I spent time getting to know him, I learned that his dream was to go fishing, so we made plans to spend an afternoon at a nearby lake.

The day we were to go fishing, Kevin, like a typical adolescent, started dating a girl. He begged me to take Becky with us. When we got to the lake, we found a concrete drainage unit that was about 10 yards from the shore. We all pulled up our pant legs and waded out to it. After I helped the kids with their fishing poles, I was ready to cast my own bait into the water.

We were standing together near the edge of the concrete slab, with me positioned between the two "lovebirds." As I prepared to cast, I turned to make sure the worm was still on my hook. That's when Kevin leaned in to kiss Becky. So when I twirled back around, I smashed into Kevin, sending young Romeo flying into the lake.

"Help me!" Kevin screamed. "I'm drowning!"

Becky and I doubled over with laughter as Kevin splashed around in the water. "Kevin," I yelled, "just stand up!" He hadn't realized the pond was only about five feet deep.

As Kevin regained his footing, he shrieked, "I want to go home!"

During the ride back, Kevin refused to speak. He sat with arms folded and glared at me. Later, when we were alone, I began to get irritated because Kevin was so angry at me. I tried to explain that people make mistakes and sometimes accidentally hurt others.

"Shut up!" Kevin screamed. "I'm not upset just because you knocked me into the water. I'm angry because you laughed at me. You embarrassed me in front of Becky. You're supposed to be helping me, not hurting me!"

"Kevin," I said softly, "I had no idea I hurt your feelings, and I'm sorry for being so blind. This may not be the best time, but could you forgive me?"

Kevin was shocked that an adult was apologizing to him. As his anger melted in response, he was able to forgive me.

Over the months that I mentored Kevin, I watched this angry teen soften. He returned to school and ended up graduating. By God's grace, I had been the answer to his mother's prayers. She and Kevin had so many problems that her words could no longer penetrate his heart. But I—who had no negative history with him—was able to reach him.

2. *Model* the importance of learning from another person.

Many times our teenagers' actions will amaze us. Sometimes we'll be astonished by their mistakes, like the time Greg put the whoopee cushion under his English teacher's chair. But there will also be times when our children surprise us with their brilliance. If we watch closely enough, we will discover that sometimes they can be our greatest teachers. When this happens, we can point it out and let them know we're not above being taught by them, saying things like "I didn't know that," "That's amazing," "You're brilliant," or "I'll give that a try." As they see us willing to learn from them, they can, in turn, be more open to learning from others. Again, by doing these things we will be sending a subtle yet powerful message: *Being taught by others is important.*

3. Understand which *character qualities* are important for a mentor to possess.

When we're searching for someone to invest in the lives of our sons and daughters, it's important to think through what character traits we want the mentor to have. For example, do we want someone who is sensitive, confrontational, well versed in the Bible, intelligent, humorous, full of integrity, perfectionistic, or worldly wise? When I (Gary) looked for mentors to build into the lives of my teenagers, one of the most important qualities I looked for was the ability to seek forgiveness when wrong. I knew that even mentors aren't perfect, so I wanted someone who'd try to make things right. I personally valued this quality as well. I tried to model it with my kids, and I got plenty of practice!

In their book *As Iron Sharpens Iron,* Howard and William Hendricks provided 10 marks of a mentor for which every parent should look. We include it because, just as we suddenly start to see everywhere the type of car we've just bought, so this list can help us see in a new way people who might make great mentors for our teens. The ideal mentor, then, is a person who . . .

1. Seems to have what our teens need.

2. Cultivates relationships.

3. Is willing to take a chance on them.

4. Is respected by other Christians.

5. Has a network of resources.

6. Is consulted by others.

7. Both talks and listens.

8. Is consistent in his or her lifestyle.

9. Is able to diagnose our teens' needs.

10. Is concerned with their interests.[6]

We encourage parents to sit down with their teenagers, as we did in the Smalley family, and make a list of the qualities they consider important in a mentor. One word of caution, however: We shouldn't limit ourselves to a list like the one above. We've provided it only as a guideline. And we must remember to bathe the selection process in prayer.

4. Become aware of the *places where mentors can be located.*

Several years ago, something mysterious happened in Canada that illustrates an important point when looking for a mentor. The rabbit population diminished drastically. Intrigued, scientists searched for an explanation. They thought it must be an illness, but they couldn't identify any. A few years later, scientists again noticed something unexplainable: The rabbit population had increased. Adding to their perplexity, shortly thereafter it decreased once more. Still, scientists discovered no explanation for these variations in the rabbit population.

At approximately the same time, population fluctuations in foxes were noticed as well. As with the rabbits, scientists looked for illnesses that might be responsible, but none were discovered.

Reports about the cycles in the rabbit and fox populations were read by another scientist who finally put together the pieces of the puzzle. He noticed that as the number of foxes grew, the number of rabbits diminished, and that when the number of rabbits grew, the number of foxes diminished. He figured that as the rabbit population multiplied, they provided an ample food source for the foxes, which resulted in larger numbers of foxes. When the increased number of foxes ate the rabbits, the food supply diminished, which eventually resulted in the foxes dying off. When the fox population declined, the rabbit population increased, creating a new food supply for the foxes. The cycle was self-perpetuating.[7]

Let's not limit God with our thinking. A mentor can be found in practically any place.

The point of this story, when it comes to looking for a mentor, is that if our focus is too narrow, we might miss someone special. Trying to find a mentor can become overwhelming. We may develop prejudices or limitations concerning who our teens' mentors should be. I (Gary) hardly thought someone from Communist Romania would have such a powerful influence on Greg's spiritual development, so I almost discouraged Greg from speaking with Joseph. If we limit our vision to certain people and places, we might miss someone who could change our teenagers' lives forever.

Several parents at an inner-city high school never thought someone from a completely different background could influence their teenagers, yet I (Greg) was able to do just that. During my doctoral work in psychology, I led drug and alcohol groups for a predominantly Hispanic high school. My first week there, I asked the 70 teenagers I was working with what they wanted to do after graduation. Sadly, only seven students reported that they wanted to get a college degree. As I laughed and cried with these kids throughout the school year, I became close to many of them. I had an "open door" policy with these kids, and I took advantage of the teachable moments it provided.

On the last day of my job, I again asked the students what they wanted to do after graduation. To my surprise, out of the 70 kids, 35 now wanted to attend college to pursue a degree in counseling psychology!

Let's not limit God with our thinking. A mentor can be found in practically any place. He or she might be a next-door neighbor, coach, teacher, youth pastor, co-worker, or another parent. The trick is to not overlook someone with potential. A mentor doesn't have to be a successful businessperson, celebrity, or star athlete. Accomplishments are nice, but they don't guarantee that the person will make a lasting impression on our teens. Our focus needs to stay on finding someone who possesses the character qualities we want to see developed in our children. But that person may be found in some place that's outside our comfort zone. So let's be ready! We never know when the right person will appear.

5. *Make contact* with the person.

Sometimes a mentor will appear without our ever lifting a finger. Some men and women feel called to be mentors and actively look for young people to influence. We shouldn't be passive about finding one, though. If we locate someone whom we believe God is leading us to approach, we can call him or her for an appointment.

When we talk with the person, we should explain that we've learned that a great way to help teens is to have someone outside the family spend time with them. Would he or she be open to something like that? We're not talking about a major commitment, and the person doesn't have to be a Bible scholar who will use lesson plans or original Greek manuscripts. Instead, we're looking for someone who will invest a little time in our teens' lives, who will lead by example more than by words. If the person isn't interested, we can ask if he or she knows others who would be.

A word of caution: We should avoid using the word *mentor* unless the other person uses it first. The idea may overwhelm him or her, because the thought of discipling someone can be intimidating. Perhaps we can talk about a specific problem we hope he or she can help resolve. Then the relationship may blossom into something much bigger. We also may not want to tell our teens that we're looking for someone to mentor them. Because of their need to separate and individuate, if they think the idea is coming from us, they may be resistant.

6. Set up a meeting so the teenager can *bond* with this person.

In chapter 7, we explained that shared experiences can bond people together. We can use that same wisdom here. One of the best ways to launch a mentoring relationship is to invite the person over for breakfast, dinner, or an outing. Perhaps the person can join the family on a day or weekend trip. The idea is to watch for chemistry and allow the relationship to blossom before anyone feels pressure to make something happen.

Before Terry Brown started to mentor Greg, he spent hours with our family. He ate meals with us, went to church with us, and accompanied us on family outings. These were great opportunities for Greg and Terry to bond.

If a good relationship develops between our teenager and the potential mentor, we can encourage the person to approach our child about meeting together privately.

7. Teach the teen to *ask questions.*

One of our favorite TV commercials showed a famous celebrity reading to a stadium full of young children. As this adult began to read *Jack and the Beanstalk,* a young girl blurted out, "Why did Jack buy the beans?"

The celebrity tried to answer the girl, but thousands of little hands went up all over the stadium, and little voices called out, "What kind of beans were they?" "How big were the beans?" and "What happened to Jack's cow? Did they eat her?"

The poor guy looked overwhelmed as he started answering questions about the story. Finally, he took one last query. A young boy screamed out, "When do we get snacks?" Instantly, thousands of little hands went up again, and the celebrity nearly fell off his chair.

As this commercial illustrated, children have a great ability to ask questions. They have a thirst for knowledge and are not afraid to ask who, why, how, where, when, and what. But as they grow older, they seem to lose the desire to question. Eventually, the only way to get teens to ask questions is by telling them, "The only stupid question is the one not asked."

If we want our teens to take full advantage of a mentoring relationship, we need to help them rediscover that childlike ability to ask questions. When we ask someone for help, we're essentially saying that we don't know everything. Most teenagers think they have everything figured out. But teens don't have all the answers. That's why *sophomoric* means "exhibiting great immaturity and lack of judgment." So we can help our teens by encouraging them to ask questions when they don't understand something.

More importantly, however, we need to *model* this by asking questions ourselves. Whether the help we need comes from a spouse, pastor, doctor, or mentor of our own, it will instill in a teenager's mind the truth that seeking help is not something only little kids do.

8. *Keep a watchful eye*—but don't intrude.

Like a mother deer who watches for danger, we don't ever want to assume that everything is fine with our teenagers and their mentors. We need to check periodically to see how things are going, to ask about the things our kids are learning. But we also need to make sure we're not trespassing on their time or relationship.

One mother we know demonstrated how to inspect her son's relationship with his mentor, Jim Shaughnessy, who's also a close friend of our family. Everyone enjoys being around Jim because he understands that a great friend finds out a person's goals and helps him or her achieve them. He has been that type of friend and mentor to his nephew Patrick, who was an excellent high-school football player. During one particular game, the coach—who could be cruel—pulled Patrick out of the lineup for no apparent reason. Instantly, Jim walked down on the field and confronted the coach. Fortunately, the superintendent was there and interceded before emotions escalated. Although Jim was embarrassed about acting out of anger, Patrick loved the fact that his uncle would protect him that way.

At the end of his senior year, the students and teachers selected Patrick as the student of the year. During the award assembly, the principal announced that not only did Patrick win the award, but he was also getting a football scholarship at a local university. Everyone cheered as he came forward to receive the honor. Patrick scanned the auditorium for his family. He found his parents but, unfortunately, not his Uncle Jim, who was away on business.

Later, during the celebration party, Patrick got a phone call that instantly lifted his mood. "Buddy man!" the familiar voice shouted in greeting. Patrick told Jim about the assembly, the award, and the scholarship. Jim voiced his pride and told Patrick he wasn't surprised because he had always believed in him. The last thing Jim said, however, caused Patrick to shed a few tears.

Jim stated that winning the award and scholarship was awesome, but that if he wanted to be remembered, he needed to do something special for his teachers. He encouraged Patrick to write each of them a letter, thanking them for investing in his life and acknowledging that he couldn't have earned the awards without their involvement.

Patrick thought this was a great idea and couldn't wait to write the letters. But then Jim went on to say that Patrick could even write his foot-ball coach and thank him. "Absolutely not," Patrick insisted. "He's been nothing but trouble for me. He's mean and grumpy, and I don't have anything to thank him for!"

Realizing how sensitive this was, Jim explained that he had been wrong to walk onto the field and confront the coach. He said that the next time he was in town, he was going to seek the coach's forgiveness.

Patrick was blown away. He couldn't believe his uncle cared about such an unlovable person.

Jim spent the next few minutes discussing some positive things the coach had done for Patrick. For the first time, Patrick realized that his coach had influenced his life in a good way. He got teary-eyed as his anger was replaced with gratitude.

After the phone call, Patrick's mother could see that her son was upset. So in a tender, nonthreatening manner, she asked about it. She knew Jim was capable of talking her son into mischief as well as good and wasn't going to assume Patrick was all right. Once she heard what Jim had encouraged her son to do, however, she stopped prying. She didn't want to interfere or damage the good foundation Jim was setting in Patrick's life. She merely inspected and then let God do the rest.

A few weeks later, the mom called Jim to explain what Patrick had done. She told Jim about a special note she and her husband had received from Patrick. In it, their son had thanked them for "investing in my life." It was the kind of gift every parent dreams of getting. She went on to tell Jim that Patrick had drafted several other letters as well, including one to his grumpy former football coach. "What you told my son worked," she said. "Thank you."

Patrick's experience demonstrates how a teenager can benefit from a mentoring relationship. In addition, Patrick's mother's reaction illustrates how we need to check on the relationship without interfering—without asking too many questions or inquiring too often. We must remember that our teens need to develop their own distinct identities and develop meaningful relationships outside the family. And since we have already turned the relationship over to the Lord, we can trust in Him that the time our teens spend with mentors is being well used.

In summary, a mentor can help our teenagers maintain their newly developed convictions. Mentors are people whom God brings into our teens' lives at various stages and for various purposes. They're committed to helping our teens grow and learn. "Mentors" can also be outside experiences. If you'd like to get a mentor involved in your teenager's life, we encourage you to take the eight steps outlined in this chapter.

WHEN TEENAGERS WALK AWAY FROM THE LIGHT

Failure is an event, never a person.
William Brown

This is a painful chapter for us to write because of some experiences we went through when Greg was a teenager. Greg is going to tell those stories from his point of view. Then, together, we will relate the things we did as he battled to rediscover the light of God from which he had walked away. We are grateful that, by His grace, we can explain how we survived Greg's teenage rebellion.

My (Greg's) experience of turning away from God spiritually reminds me of something that happened physically when I was 14 and attending Kanakuk Kamp, the Christian sports camp in Branson, Missouri. One thrilling adventure at camp was going caving, which meant exploring every inch of a large cave.

That summer, we found an unbelievable cave. It looked like the "Bat Cave" out of the movie *Batman*. It had small tunnels, a waterfall, deep crevasses, and cathedral ceilings. My friends and I thought we had died and gone to heaven! As we were exploring the cave, we decided to play a joke on our counselor, Dave.

About five of us broke away from the group and ran ahead. We hid behind a large rock and waited in ambush. As Dave neared, we could barely keep from laughing. When he reached the rock, we jumped out and screamed at the top of our lungs. The shock made Dave's knees buckle. I'll never forget how he looked as he crashed to the ground. We roared with laughter and accused him of being a wimp. As we walked back, however, Dave vowed that he would have his revenge. I should have believed him!

When we returned to the group, we decided to rappel into a cavern. Each boy begged to be the first one down, and Dave picked me. I should have realized something was up. After I strapped myself into a harness, they lowered me into the dark cavern, with my buddies providing a small amount of light. I must have descended 100 feet before reaching the bottom. I couldn't see as I unhooked the harness. I called for more light, but suddenly, everyone walked off.

I grabbed my flashlight and switched it on, and immediately I realized I was in big trouble. Dave had removed the batteries.

Standing there in total darkness, I could only imagine what was beyond my reach. I extended my hands but felt nothing. I had no idea if I was on the edge of a cliff or next to a room full of bats. I sat down, hoping someone would turn on a light. I quickly began to regret every horror movie I'd ever seen. I could have sworn I heard movement and loud breathing. I started hating Dave because his joke was better than mine. I pictured his wicked smile as he had walked away.

After several long minutes, my friends returned. When they finally shined their lights at me, I couldn't believe what was straight ahead. "Rocks!" I shouted in relief. "I'm surrounded by rocks!" The entire time, I had been standing in a big hole. I wasn't in a massive cavern with a bottomless pit. If I'd been able to extend my arms another 10 feet, I would have felt the rocks. Dave had played the perfect joke on me. I never realized how safe the cavern was. Without the light, my imagination got the best of me.

When teenagers walk away from the Lord, it's as if they're in a pitch-black cavern. They can't see. The Scriptures put it this way: "The eye is the lamp of your body; when your eye is clear, your whole body also is full of light; but when it is bad, your body also is full of darkness."[1]

As my caving experience also illustrated, teens who walk away from God cannot find safety. They're blinded by the darkness and unable to locate the way out. I should know; I lived that way for several years.

A Cave of Spiritual Darkness

"This can't be happening," I (Greg) begged silently that day in college. The full impact of our actions was just beginning to sink in, and I was feeling sick.

"Are you sure that we . . . you know . . . did it?" I asked my girlfriend. But the answer was obvious. We were going to have to face the truth that we had just experienced premarital sex. After all the years of keeping myself pure for my wedding night, I couldn't believe we had let ourselves go this far. Two hours before, we had been on our knees, praying for God to give us strength in this area. How could this have happened?

"We've just lost our virginity!" I wanted to shout. "What are we going to do?"

I'd heard many stories about friends who had premarital sex. I had always judged them harshly and thought them foolish. Ignorant. Unlucky. But now, I was the fool, the person others would shake their heads at and think, *Poor, stupid guy! Didn't he realize it only takes a few seconds to lose it?*

"Greg!" Her harsh tone brought me back to reality. "What are we going to do?"

"What?" was all I could manage. I was in total shock. I had no idea how to respond because I'd never thought this could happen to me.

What are we going to do? It seemed like such a simple question for such a complicated situation. As I stared at my girlfriend, I desperately wanted to undo what we'd done together. Ironically, we were both against having premarital sex—at least in theory. How had this happened? "Pride goes before a fall" was the scripture that now burned inside my head. I painfully recalled Dad quoting it at different times. I suddenly began to wish this whole thing were a terrible nightmare. But it wasn't.

My girlfriend and I spent the rest of the day talking about our dilemma. The questions we asked seemed to get more difficult as the conversation continued. "What if we get pregnant?" "Should we get married?" "How will we support a baby?" "What will others think?" Finally: "What will our parents think?" That was when it really hit me. Parents! I immediately flashed back to the times I had heard my parents say, "Greg, if you ever do something like have sex and get a girl pregnant, your father will have to quit the ministry."

Will have to quit. The words stung as if I were being attacked by a thousand hornets. My parents had made that proclamation out of a fear that I might do something foolish someday without thinking through the consequences. Little did they realize how right they would be. All the work my father was doing to help others would now end because of me. I felt I'd wrecked everyone's life—my girlfriend's and her family's and mine and my family's. But most of all, I thought about my dad. With my face buried in my hands, I pictured the millions of hurting people he helped.

I *couldn't* ruin his ministry to them. I *wouldn't*. So I decided I had to keep my terrible secret hidden.

In just a few hours, two lives had been turned completely upside down. Sadly, it would take many years for me to recover from my mistake. I had never realized such a short time could alter one's life forever. It was as if a massive tornado had blown through the center of my existence and destroyed everything in its path.

Several months later, my girlfriend and I broke up. We tried to make the relationship work, but the shameful history we now shared was impossible to overcome. We were a continuous reminder to each other of the sin we'd committed. It was more than either of us could bear.

I was able to keep my secret from my parents for several years. But in doing so, I descended steadily into a deep cavern of spiritual darkness. I began to hate God, my parents, and myself. The anger I felt caused me to turn away from God and my family. Because I didn't want anyone to know about my pain, I had to pretend everything was fine, so my parents never understood why I started to lie, cheat, and get into other kinds of trouble (including continued sexual activity). I also began to withdraw emotionally and physically, and I grew more argumentative. As a result, my parents had to take several steps to deal with my hurtful behavior. Those are the steps we'll present in this chapter.

My experience with sexual sin was a hard lesson in the reality that a belief must be grounded in a deep personal conviction or it may not hold up when tested. But our ever-gracious God can use even our worst choices to teach us wonderful lessons. Much of what's best about the man I am today is a direct result of having gone through that pain.

A few years after that sexual experience, I could no longer keep the guilt locked away inside. I was literally going crazy from the pain I'd been trying to endure alone. I decided I simply had to confess my sin to Dad. I'll let him describe what happened.

One day while we were talking in the living room, Greg said something that hit me (Gary) like an atomic bomb. "Dad," he began carefully, "may I share something that has really been bothering me?"

As a parent, you never want to hear an opening sentence like that, but I hesitantly responded, "Okay . . . sure."

"You're probably not going to believe what I'm about to say," Greg continued.

Now I started to get alarmed. *What could it be?* I wondered. Nevertheless, I told him to "try me."

And then the bomb exploded.

"A couple of years ago," Greg choked out, "I don't know how to say this . . . I had sex with my girlfriend."

A sense of relief swept over my body. *Greg is such a comedian,* I thought. "That's a good one," I said with a laugh. "You come up with the wildest jokes." But I found myself laughing alone. As tears welled up in his eyes, I stared in disbelief. "Are you telling me the truth?" I asked softly, not really wanting to hear his reply.

"Yes."

Greg and I sat there for several long minutes, just staring at each other. My heart sank. Finally I asked, "What are we going to do?" Greg lowered his head and began to cry as if a massive hole had been punched in the dam that had held back years of emotion. I gently placed my arm around his shoulder, and we sat there together, crying.

Nothing more was said for what seemed like an eternity. He asked me not to tell anyone until we figured out what to do next. He was especially concerned about his mom; we both knew this would crush her. But then Greg said something else that rocked me to the core: "I'm sorry you'll have to leave the ministry. I'm very sorry."

My heart sank even deeper. "Son," I said, choking back more tears, "is that why you waited so long to tell me? Did you think I'd quit my ministry because you had sex with a girl? How could you think something like that?"

"But you and Mom . . ." he said, looking confused. "You told me you'd have to if I ever had premarital sex."

I stared at Greg and, with all my might, tried to remember if I'd ever said something like that. I honestly don't think I had. But somehow Greg had received that message loud and clear, and it had cost him years of pain and agony. My heart ached for him.

As I held my son, I assured him that my love for him was as strong as ever. "I don't have to leave the ministry," I said. "I love you so much that if it were necessary, I'd gladly do it just to show how much I love you. I will never give up on you as long as we live." I even thought out loud about some of the things I could do if I had to discontinue my present work. But inside I was sick, fearful of what everyone would say. *What would people think if they knew my son had premarital sex?* I thought. *Would this discredit my ministry?* I would have to wait to find out.

Again my mind flashed to Norma. How would she handle this? What about Kari and Michael? They both looked up to Greg with such respect. How would all this play itself out in time? After several long hours, Greg and I agreed not to tell anyone else until we could come up with a plan.

Besides, I knew we both needed to seek wise advice before doing anything. We'll explain just what happened a little later.

Our desire for this chapter is twofold: First, we want to explain how we coped with Greg's rebellion. Second, we want to discuss how our family helped Greg find his way back to God's light. Through that painful experience, we learned 10 principles that can help parents survive a son or daughter's rebellion. If that's your experience now, we pray these ideas will help your family as well.

10 Ways to Help Teenagers Turn from Rebellion

1. Turn to *God* for support.

For parents, nothing is more painful than when our teens become prodigals—when they walk away from God's will. We may experience depression, sadness, anger, and fear for their well-being. The first thing we need to do is to turn to God for support. We are not alone, and He understands our emotions. He knows how it feels to have His children turn away from the light. Just look at the list of disobedient people in Scripture: Adam and Eve ate the forbidden fruit; Cain killed his brother, Abel (the first teens); Jonah ran from God; Peter denied Jesus three times; the apostle Paul killed the early Christians. The list could go on and on. In a number of places, God even likened His chosen people, the nation of Israel, to wayward kids. For example, He said through the prophet Isaiah, "Hear, O heavens! Listen, O earth! For the Lord has spoken: 'I reared children and brought them up, but they have rebelled against me.'"[2]

Yes, God understands what it's like to have loved ones turn away. So when our teens abandon our beliefs, we can turn to Him for wisdom, comfort, and strength. That is when He can best show us His love.

After Greg and I (Gary) separated that night Greg revealed his secret, I got down on my knees and prayed to God for His help in dealing with this situation. I was also able to thank Him for the valuable lessons He was teaching Greg through this experience. As we've said many times, trials in our lives usually produce many good things. So I prayed that God would discipline Greg in such a way that He would eventually receive glory.

The Bible says, "Do not regard lightly the discipline of the Lord . . . for those whom the Lord loves He disciplines."[3] And it reveals why discipline is so valuable: "All discipline for the moment seems not to be joyful, but sorrowful; yet to those who have been trained by it, afterwards it yields the peaceful fruit of righteousness."[4] What a great promise! As God's discipline trains us, we can reap a harvest of righteousness and peace. That's why we need to resist asking God to spare our teens from the painful consequences of disobedience. Instead, we should pray that they will learn from the experience.

It's hard to watch a child go through the rough times of rebellion. But we always remember the words of our friend Dr. Charles Swindoll, a renowned Bible teacher, when I (Gary) asked how he had become so loving and gracious. After he thought about it for a while, he responded with one word: "Pain." He explained that God had used all the agonizing pain he had experienced to build a spirit of love within him. I've seen it in him, so I know it's true. And that same love has been formed in my son Greg.

2. Allow them to *choose* their own path.

If our teenagers decide to follow the wrong path, we must understand two important things. First, we can't make wise decisions for them. If we try, we might actually drive them further away.

The biblical parable of the wayward son, with its wise and loving father, illustrates what we have to do, hard as it may be: "There was a man who had two sons. The younger one said to his father, 'Father, give me my share of the estate.' So he divided his property between them. Not long after that, the younger son got together all he had, set off for a distant country and there squandered his wealth in wild living."[5]

As we see in this account, the father could not stop his son from taking the wrong path. Instead the father had to watch his child make poor decisions and suffer the consequences. The dad could only wait patiently, with open arms, for the day his prodigal returned.

The second thing to remember is that though our teens choose their own path, we can make sure their choice does not crush the entire family. We still need to maintain order. Teenagers who walk away from the light should not be given complete freedom as they speed down the wrong road.

God understands what it's like to have loved ones turn away.

Just how we respond depends to a great extent on the age of the child and the situation. If a 13-year-old walks away from the light, we can't control his mind, but we can control his home environment. The family contract, described in chapter 6, is an ideal discipline method for this type of situation.

On the other hand, we may not be able to control much at all with an

18-year-old who is leaving for college. That's a completely different situation, and we might have to address it with "tough love."

3. Give them *tough love* when necessary.

When my (Gary's) son Michael was in the 10th grade, he got a D in Spanish class. Unfortunately for him, we had just amended our family contract to require retaking a class if you earned less than a C. That meant he would have to repeat Spanish during the upcoming fall semester. Michael was livid about the idea. He hated trying to learn Spanish, and to make matters worse, he would then have to take gym class at a different time from his friends. He was convinced he could get out of this "ridiculous" punishment if he only applied the right amount of pressure. *After all,* he reasoned, *Mom is a pushover.*

He would soon eat those words.

Over the summer, Michael took every opportunity to argue with Norma that the rule was stupid. "I'll never use Spanish in real life," he insisted. "So why make me retake it? It's a complete waste of time!" He even encouraged her to call his school counselor. "She'll explain why I don't need this class," he tried to rationalize.

It seemed as if each time they talked, Michael got more insistent and Norma grew more frustrated. She kept telling him she was going to follow through with our decision. "And don't even try speaking with your father!" she warned wisely. "My word is final." She knew that after a millisecond, Michael would have me convinced that retaking Spanish was the worst thing he could do.

After a few rounds of such verbal sparring, many parents would have given in and let their child off the hook. But Norma, convinced that Michael had not given Spanish class a 100 percent effort, was not about to relent. Instead, she applied tough love and made him retake the class. Michael finished the second course with a C+, proving that his mom had been right all along.

Tough love can be invaluable when our children don't follow the limits and rules we've established for the home. A couple named Phyllis and David York learned this through their own experience with a rebellious daughter and founded the Toughlove group to offer support and solutions to parents of out-of-control teenagers. Their main principle is straightforward: Understanding and forgiveness are wonderful expressions of parental love, but often they're not enough. David York made this comment in their book *Toughlove Solutions:* "I started out being this nice parent. 'Let me listen, let me be this daddy to you guys.' And what really needs to happen is to grab these kids and say, 'You really can't do that. You've got to follow the rules here, and if you don't we're going to call the police and have you locked up!'"[6]

Instead of whining and remaining passive, tough love encourages parents to set firm rules. The Scriptures say, "He who withholds his rod hates his son, but he who loves him disciplines him diligently."[7] That reference to the "rod" means any kind of discipline, but especially correction that's hard and painful for both parent and child. Tough love isn't easy, but it will help us to experience peace and happiness some day. As the Bible says, "Correct your son, and he will give you comfort; he will also delight your soul."[8]

When we establish tough love, the message the rebellious teenager receives is: *You can choose your own path, but we will not allow sinful behavior at home.* In making that stand, we provide security. As we explained in the family constitution chapter, rules actually create freedom and allow a teenager to feel safe. The same is true of tough love.

Applying tough love means setting up rules our rebellious teens must live by if they're going to remain at home. Those rules spell out what the family finds acceptable in areas like these:

- honor
- curfew
- honesty
- school attendance
- behavior
- chores
- use of drugs, alcohol, or tobacco
- allowance
- car privileges
- dating
- dress code

After we determine what rules are necessary, we put them into action with a family contract.

We need to keep in mind, however, that although limits are important, we need to choose our battles carefully. Some rules are essential and must be enforced, but rules dealing with less-urgent issues may have to be set aside for the time being—especially if the relationship with the wayward teen is volatile right now. In that case, the last thing we need is to get into further conflict over a "nitpicky" rule. So we need to make a list of the crucial rules and limits and explain to our prodigal teens that abiding by them is not an option.

As we emphasize the need for toughness, however, we must always keep in mind that it's tough *love*. Our teenagers can see through the veneer of toughness without love. That kind of parenting can actually make things worse. We try to keep the Bible's description of love in mind in all discipline: "Love is patient, love is kind."[9] And if we're tempted to feel judgmental, we do well to remember this scriptural warning: "Do not judge, or you too will be judged. For in the same way you judge others, you will be judged, and with the measure you use, it will be measured to you."[10]

Finally, because using tough love can be difficult and painful for the entire family, we need to seek support and encouragement from friends, church, a pastor, teachers, or a counselor.

4. Seek *support from friends.*

An English publication offered a prize for the best definition of a friend, and of the thousands of entries received, this was the winner: "A friend is the one who comes in when the whole world has gone out."[11]

What a precious insight! Many parents of rebellious teenagers feel the world has abandoned them. The years of pain and suffering they endure can be incredibly lonely. On the other hand, it can be extremely comforting to have friends who will stand by our side. We need to find those friends, the kind King Solomon wrote about: "A friend loves at all times, and a brother is born for adversity."[12]

When Greg revealed his secret about having had sex, I (Gary) knew our pastor would be such a friend to me. The next morning after Greg's confession, I met with the pastor for several hours. He was a great encouragement, and he also provided wise counsel that answered a key question: Did I, in fact, need to leave my public ministry? Since Greg was not in present and continuous rebellion and had repented of his sin, the pastor said, he didn't think I should give up my work.

You can imagine the anxiety I felt going into that meeting. Yet I knew from experience that I could count on our pastor to be a true friend. Likewise, we can find solid support from friends who have had experiences similar to what we're going through. Seeking such help in our trials is real wisdom.

5. Take care of our own *health and relationships.*

Since a period of teenage rebellion is highly stressful and emotional for parents, we need to make sure we take care of our own health by eating right and getting the necessary amounts of exercise and sleep. Many studies have shown that exercise reduces stress and depression, and it even releases a chemical that brings us pleasure and greater insight while we're going through difficult times. In addition, it's important to spend time relaxing and enjoying activities like hobbies that can take our minds away from our problems and revitalize us mentally and emotionally.

Most importantly, we need to work on our marriage and other relationships. Nothing can tear a marriage or family apart like a rebellious teenager. It's good to check in weekly with our mate and family on how things are going and talk about specific things we can do to make this time more bearable. We can also work to keep everyone connected to a good church or other support group, and perhaps even to a Christian counselor who will provide encouragement and a fresh perspective.

6. Assume only *the appropriate part of the blame.*

When I (Greg) got caught looking at a pornographic magazine as a teenager, my parents didn't turn against each other and point fingers. They knew I had made a personal choice to sin. They did ask each other if they had been clear with me about the dangers of pornography. They also talked about what they could do to help answer my questions about sex. But they did *not* blame themselves for my actions, as so many parents would be tempted to do.

In his book *Your Prodigal Child,* Dr. James Kennedy talks about the importance of this mind-set:

> No one can say that parents' actions do not influence their children's behavior, but it is just that—influence. It is not a cause and effect situation, as a match set to a dry thicket causes a forest fire. We do make mistakes and sin against God, but we have a choice in such a situation, just as our children do. We can confess our guilt and seek the forgiveness of God and our children or we can try to hide our sin. Yet, whether we repent or not, we need to recognize our sins cannot force our children into a life of sin.[13]

As we've said, we can't make our teenagers believe or not believe in something. We can, however, ask ourselves what we could have done differently. We can also ask God to reveal our shortcomings in the situation. Perhaps we need to take responsibility for some part of the problem and seek forgiveness.

One additional, related point is that while we need to continue to forgive our rebellious teenagers, they're also responsible to forgive us. This is a clear message throughout the Scriptures.[14] If they refuse, we must avoid assuming an inferior or lowered spiritual position relative to them—another big temptation for parents. We may want to get someone to hold us accountable for keeping a healthy perspective on who's responsible for what. It's not God's desire for us to be stuck in shame if our children refuse to forgive. We do our part, but then we allow Him to work in their lives. If we shoulder all the responsibility, we can actually hinder what God is trying to teach them.

7. Seek involvement from a *mentor*.

In the last chapter, we discussed how a mentor can play a major part in helping teens turn their beliefs into convictions. A mentor can also help when teens walk away from the light. Our teens might be so angry and resistant to our influence as parents that a person like Greg's mentor, Terry, could be their only way back. We can pray diligently that God will bring such people into our children's lives.

8. *Never abandon* the relationship.

When our teens do something wrong, it's easy to make them feel worthless, as if we've given up on the relationship. But the leaders of Kanakuk Kamp provided a good example of tenacious, loving discipline when I (Greg) was 18 years old and working there as a counselor. That summer, I was going through my "secret" rebellion against God and was not a model counselor. I especially resisted a few camp rules I considered "rigid," like the one that said counselors were forbidden to use the phones for personal calls until their scheduled nights off.

One particular night, I was missing my girlfriend, Rachel, so I rationalized that I needed to talk with her immediately. I figured the best way would be to row a canoe across the lake and hike to the local convenience store. Later that night, I convinced a couple of friends to join me, explaining that it would be perfect because no other camp staff would be out that late. Unfortunately, I overlooked one important detail.

It took us 30 minutes to reach the convenience store. When we walked in, the clerk noticed we were camp counselors. After we exchanged pleasantries, I was finally free to use the phone.

In the midst of explaining to Rachel the great lengths I'd gone to in order to talk with her, I suddenly saw something terrifying. Walking through the door was the camp director, Jack. I had forgotten that Jack always brought the night watchman a snack from the convenience store! My friends glared at me as we realized this "small" oversight.

We tried to hide, but it was no use. When Jack found us crouching behind a row of potato chips, he said with surprising calmness, "I'll talk to you guys when you get back to camp."

I was sick to my stomach as we rowed back. And to make matters worse, I had left Rachel hanging on the phone, probably thinking I'd been killed in a robbery. When we returned to camp, the entire leadership staff was waiting. As we walked toward our boss, I expected someone to yell, "Dead men walking!" Needless to say, it wasn't a pretty sight. I quickly admitted I was wrong and that whatever the punishment, I would willingly accept it.

The meeting, however, actually turned out to be a wonderful experience. Jack not only talked with me about my mistake, but he also praised me for some positive things I had been doing. The leadership staff concluded by thanking me for admitting the excursion was my idea and for being open to their reproof. Although I was stripped of my remaining nights off (tough love), I felt good about the way things had turned out—especially since Jack had kept the focus not on what I had done wrong but on our relationship.

Whatever rebellious actions our teens are taking, we need to keep showing them love. Just like Jack, our goal is to *love the sinner and hate the sin.* As the apostle Paul said, "Abhor what is evil; cling to what is good."[15] If we keep loving them as Jesus loves us even in our sinfulness, we never know when they might return to the light.

That's exactly what Norma and I (Gary) did when Greg was in spiritual darkness. Although we disagreed with his behavior, we never shut the door on our relationship, and he eventually found his way back to God and our family.

9. *Talk* with their *siblings.*

Any time a teenager walks away from the light, it affects the entire family. Not only do the parents suffer, but the siblings can be confused and hurt as well. That's why we need to talk things through with our other children. We must explain the truth of what's going on and how the family can still love the prodigal. We don't have to go into the details of the wayward child's behavior unless they're already known.

For instance, when Greg was rebelling against God, his younger brother, Michael, knew something was wrong. He didn't know the specifics, but he could tell Greg was different. Norma and I (Gary) explained that Greg needed to make his own choices in some areas. We talked about how Greg still loved us but needed time away. We never disclosed the details of what Greg was doing. Instead, we encouraged

Michael to ask Greg for himself if he wanted that information.

That's how we set up a boundary around a teenager's personal pain. We keep in mind that it's his story and let him tell the world when he's ready. As a matter of fact, this book is the first time Greg's story has been told publicly because he wasn't ready for others to know until now.

A great way to reach out to a prodigal teen is to make a list of all the ways we can show that the family still cares and wants a relationship. This can be a good opportunity to model godly love and forgiveness to our other children!

10. Above all else—continue to *forgive*.

"A wise man will make haste to forgive, because he knows the true value of time, and will not suffer it to pass away in unnecessary pain."[16] That could have been our motto as Norma and I (Gary) dealt with Greg after his confession. The meeting in which he revealed his secret to Norma was one of the most painful I've ever experienced. Nonetheless, we had to begin the healing process by forgiving Greg. Besides, who were we to judge or harbor anger? We had certainly made our share of mistakes as well.

In a well-known scripture, one of Jesus' disciples asked, "Lord, how often shall my brother sin against me and I forgive him? Up to seven times?"[17] Jesus' answer was that we should forgive as often as it's needed. But that doesn't mean we have to ignore our feelings of pain and anger. It's okay to be disappointed or angry at our teens for a time. Anger becomes damaging only when we don't deal with it.[18] We can pray and admit those feelings to God. He can turn them into the foundation of a new relationship with our children. Stuffing the feelings, on the other hand, will only increase our pain in the end.

> *Whatever rebellious actions our teens are taking, we need to keep showing them love.*

Another way to prepare ourselves to forgive is by increasing our understanding of the situation. Norma and I (Gary) really tried to get a grasp on Greg's current condition. What type of pain was he running from? How much anger was he carrying? What led him to fall in the area of sex? As we discussed these questions, it became much easier to empathize with his situation and forgive him. We also realized that our hurt feeling could be a reflection of our own level of maturity. What was God trying to teach us about ourselves?

As Norma and I learned through our experience with Greg, true forgiveness begins when we release the person from condemnation. In a sense, we're pardoning our teenager. Then forgiveness continues as we release the teen from all our expectations of perfection. This deep cleans a wounded soul instead of just wiping off its surface. And treasure hunting can be the antibiotic ointment that finishes healing the wound.

As the hurt subsides, we can start looking for ways to help our teenager. This will take the healing process even further. When we can reach out to those who have injured us, we're moving in the direction of godly love. Listed below are several ways we can help ourselves reach this point:

1. Write a love letter expressing what happened and how we would like the teen to respond to us in the future.

2. Talk with someone who has been through a similar situation.

3. Join a support group.

4. Meet with a counselor.

5. Read at least one good book on forgiveness. (We've recommended several in the notes section at the end of this book.)[19]

Remember That There Is No Guarantee

Although my (Greg's) situation worked out for the best and I was able to find my way back to God, some parents may follow the suggestions in this chapter and still not see their children return to His fold. Those moms and dads may well feel frustrated and disappointed. Ophelia R. Browning expressed those same feelings in the poem *Unanswered Yet:*

Unanswered yet, the prayer your lips have pleaded
In agony of heart these many years?
Does faith begin to fail? Is hope departing?
And think you all in vain those fallen tears?
You shall have your desire, sometime, somewhere.

Unanswered yet? Though when you first presented
This one petition at the Father's throne,
It seemed you could not wait the time of asking,
So urgent was your heart to make it known.
Tho' years have passed you, sometime, somewhere.

Unanswered yet? Nay, do not say ungranted,
Perhaps your part is not yet fully done.
The work began when first your prayer was uttered...
And God will finish what He has begun.
If you will keep the incense burning there,
His glory you shall see, sometime, somewhere.

Unanswered yet? Faith cannot be unanswered!
Her feet are firmly planted on the Rock.
Amid the wildest storms she stands undaunted
Nor quails before the loudest thunder shock.
She KNOWS omnipotence has heard her prayer
And cries, It shall be done! Sometime, somewhere.

The reality is that the 10 steps we've described do not guarantee our prodigals will return to the light. We can't make that choice for them. But we can provide the right environment for them to return.

I (Gary) recently had an experience that showed the *negative* impact an environment can have. I had joined Weight Watchers with some friends. We all had some winter pounds to shed, and we felt we needed the structured accountability. During our first meeting, we sat in a semicircle to hear a lecture. As the instructor began, I noticed a gigantic candy machine in front of the group. I felt like raising my hand and making a motion to have it removed before our next meeting. I thought this was a strange way to encourage weight loss: Put everyone's favorite candy in front of them and then lecture on self-control!

As the meeting went on, our instructor showed us several different kinds of junk food and explained how these would *not* help us lose weight. At the end of the meeting, my mouth was full of saliva from seeing all the food. I felt like Pavlov's dog that drooled when hearing the bell!

Afterward, my friends and I laughed about the experience. We couldn't believe the environment in which we had been placed. I didn't want to lose weight anymore; I wanted to go out and eat boxes of the junk food we'd seen!

If our teens walk away from the Lord, we need to make sure our homes are in order, with nothing in them that will cause further stumbling. Scripture warns, "Do not cause anyone to stumble."[20] We can ask ourselves, "Will this environment help lead our teens toward the Lord or further away?" In addition, one of the best things we can do is to *show* them the way. Again, our actions are far more powerful than what we say. As we walk consistently toward the Lord ourselves, our prodigals will have a light to lead them back home. And when they do return, we'll be able to utter the same words Jesus used: "Rejoice with me, for I have found my sheep which was lost!"[21]

13

LEAVING HOME IN HONOR

It has been said that there are only two lasting bequests that we
can leave our offspring—one is roots, the other wings.
Dr. John Santrock

As our older adolescents prepare to say "bon voyage," to go away to college or some other career pursuit, it's vital that they leave home in honor. But this means a transition must occur in our relationship with them, and that's often difficult. The need and the challenge are both illustrated in something Norma and I (Gary) went through with Greg.

At one point when he was in high school, he became dissatisfied with our church and told us, "I've been going to church all my life—why do I have to keep going?" We firmly believed he should still attend. As a compromise, we gave him the choice of finding another church. But the bottom line was that we could force him to obey our will.

When Greg went off to college, however, our ability to dictate his choices disappeared for all practical purposes. Our relationship had to change (a process that had been going on for several years, actually) from parental control to friendship. All we could do was encourage him from a distance. Instead of trying to manipulate him with guilt, Norma became a "prayer warrior." She said something one day that expressed the essence of our job when a teen leaves home: "In high school, I did more parenting. In college, I do more praying."

Difficult as it was to watch Greg make his own decision, Norma released him in the area of attending church. In answer to her prayers, it wasn't too long before Greg became active in his own church. But the key was for us to change our parenting from direct control to praying and encouraging.

World renowned author and Georgetown University professor Dr. Deborah Tannan says that everyone in the world has two great emotional needs that are often in conflict. One is the need to be *connected* to others in relationship, and the other is the need to be an *individual* who is not controlled by others.[1] Older adolescents preparing to leave home feel this struggle intensely with regard to us as their parents. They will always need to feel connected through things like visits at Christmas, but they also have a deep and growing need to be individuals free from our control. That allows them to function on their own in a responsible way, to become healthy, mature adults.

Mom and Dad have to become more like *friends* instead of benevolent dictators. This can be difficult because, for at least 18 years, we've been setting all the rules. Then, almost overnight, we're required to alter that focus entirely to friendship. In this chapter, we'll try to help by providing several tools for cutting the cord and allowing our teens to spread their wings and take flight. Specifically, we'll show how to:

- maintain an open-door policy.

- give our teenagers the keys to success in whatever they do.

- provide our teens with a blessing as they leave home.

Maintain an Open-Door Policy

We've all seen pictures of the mother bird who gently nudges her babies out of the nest. We smile as we watch the young birds crash to the ground while trying to learn the art of flying. Well, sometimes as parents we must provide our children with a gentle nudge out the door. But whenever and however they leave, our goal should be to maintain an open-door policy with them.

We can't simply push our teenagers into the world and expect that they will never need our encouragement or guidance. Instead, we can stay available. We can continue to listen and support them with our ears and words. We can offer a shoulder to cry on or wisdom when the road of life looks bleak or confusing. In other words, we can be a friend.

This *doesn't* mean we bail them out of difficult situations or become overly involved in their lives. We need balance in this new relationship, avoiding the extremes of enmeshment (overinvolvement) and disconnection (no involvement). Enmeshment is talking to an adult teen every day on the phone, providing a wake-up call each morning for a college student, or continuing to do a 20-something's laundry and cooking all his or her meals. On the other hand, disconnection is having little or no contact with an adult child, offering no encouragement or wisdom, or rarely asking deep questions about his life. The ideal place to be is somewhere in the middle of those extremes, still having meaningful interaction but with the *boundaries* proper to a parent/adult child relationship.[2]

One example of how Norma and I (Gary) set boundaries when our teenagers left home was that while we agreed to pay for their college education, they had to maintain a certain grade point average. And if they failed a course, they had to pay to retake it.

Another way we provided some "out the door" separation was to give them a certain amount of spending money while they were students and allow them to establish their own budget. If they spent it unwisely, they had to live with the consequences.

One time Greg went shopping at one of those huge discount warehouses. He had been looking for a new dress shirt, and here he found the motherload. Just his luck, this store was having a sale on his favorite brand! The style was exactly what he wanted, and they had it in five different colors. Impulsively, Greg bought five new dress shirts. In a matter of seconds, he had spent his entire budget for the month, even at the discount price. There were still 29 days in the month, but at least he'd look good starving to death!

"Maybe they can bury you in one of your new shirts," I said with a laugh when he told me about his dilemma.

"But Dad," he begged, "just give me an advance and I'll be able to hold out until next month."

Hard as it was to say no, Norma and I believed he needed to learn a lesson. As a result, Greg had to get a temporary job for the rest of the month. But at least he had nice shirts to wear!

In short, an open-door policy means we're encouraging our older teens to move into independent, responsible adulthood, but we're still available to help in ways consistent with that goal.

Giving Teenagers the Keys to Success in Whatever They Do

Part of preparing to send our children into adulthood is instilling in them three simple truths that will give them success in whatever they do. Here they are in order of importance:

1. Honor God, others, and themselves.

2. Decide how they'll serve others in genuine honor and love.

3. Understand and believe that they can do whatever they want in life with knowledge and skills. They must first gain the necessary knowledge in their chosen area of service and then practice applying that knowledge until they become skilled.

These three principles were drilled into each of the Smalley kids from early childhood. We practiced saying these things as we drove to the store, lay in a sleeping bag by a stream, or sat at a ball game. To this day, you could ask any one of them, "What's the most important thing in life?" and they'd say, "The I'm Third principle: Honor God, others, and ourselves." Next, you could ask, "What does it take to be successful in honoring others?" and the kids would say, "Knowledge and skills." Now that they're all into their own professions, they can testify to the power of these simple truths.

During late adolescence, many teens wonder about their future. It can be a time of great anxiety. Some decide early about education, dating, and a career. Others wait until the last minute. Meanwhile, parents wonder if they can be helpful with these decisions. The answer is *yes*. Although we can't make the choices for our kids, we can teach them the art of making wise decisions using the five M's (see the next section).

Research verifies the importance of helping our sons and daughters in this area. As we pointed out earlier, several studies found that when a teen has no goals or plans for the future, he is at greater risk for involvement with premarital sex. Likewise, teens who don't intend to go to college are more likely to have sex, get lower grades, and give in to peer pressure than those who are college-bound.[3] So by helping our teens figure out their futures, we can also help them resist negative peer pressure and improve their grades.

Because teenagers have a strong need for independence and to forge their own identity, however, many will resist their parents' attempts to help with this difficult process. Instead of forcing the issue, parents must learn to be available when the opportunity presents itself. These times are when our teens ask questions like:

• Where will I go to college?

• What type of friends should I make?

• How should I spend my social time?

- What will I do with my life?

- How much time should I spend with my family? My siblings?

- How can I make money, and what will I do with the money I earn?

- Whom will I date, and what do I expect from marriage?

- What do I believe?

Questions like these provide parents with occasions to teach their teenagers the five M's that follow. Together, they constitute the best way we know of for making decisions that incorporate honor. (Remember, however, that we don't want to give our teens all the answers.)

The Five M's

Using the five M's, Norma and I (Gary) taught our children to *honor* God and others, *serve* God and others, and become successful. I wrote about this approach years ago in a book called *Joy That Lasts,* but not in the context of parenting teens and sending them into the world with confidence and excited faith. Here are the five M's:

1. Who is going to be their *master?*

We all serve someone or something. We serve ourselves, our job, our lusts, our ideas, our God, or something else. The choice is ours. Some choices lead to greater fulfillment, and others lead to enslavement or dissatisfaction. We can't blame anyone or anything else for our choices. We might try to, but the buck really stops with each of us. The first M, then, is for our teens to decide who is going to be the master of their lives.

We were able to say as the Smalley kids were growing up, "Those of us in this home will serve God." We all agreed at different times to follow His leading. We wanted to honor Him above all else. Nothing or no one meant more. As the psalmist said, "Bless the Lord, O my soul; and all that is within me, bless His holy name."[4] The word *blessing* means to "bend the knee before someone who is of highest worth." When we thought of blessing God, we imagined bending our whole life—our thoughts, feelings, body, and everything else that makes up who we are—before the Lord.

Consistent with a desire to honor God, teens often ask, "What is God's will for my life?" But that may not be the best question to ask, and asking the wrong question can lead to unfortunate mistakes, as one lady illustrated when she was looking for a vacation campground. She was an old-fashioned lady, always delicate in her language. She and her husband were planning a week's vacation in Florida, so she wrote to a particular campground for a reservation.

She wanted to make sure the campground was fully equipped but didn't know how to ask about toilet facilities. She just couldn't bring herself to write the word *toilet* in her letter. After much deliberation, she finally came up with the old term "bathroom commode." But when she wrote that down, she still thought she was being too forward, so she started all over and this time referred to the bathroom commode merely as the "B.C." "Does the campground have its own B.C.?" the proper lady inquired.

Although we can't make the choices for our kids, we can teach them the art of making wise decisions.

Well, the campground owner wasn't old-fashioned at all, and when he got the letter, he couldn't figure out what the woman meant by a B.C. After worrying about it for a while, he showed the letter to several campers, but they couldn't imagine what the lady meant either. The campground owner finally came to the conclusion that the lady must be asking about the local Baptist church, so he sat down and wrote the following reply:

Dear Madam:

I regret very much the delay in answering your letter, but I now take the pleasure of informing you that a B.C. is located nine miles north of the campground and is capable of seating 250 people at one time.

I admit it is quite a distance away if you are in the habit of going regularly, but no doubt you will be pleased to know that a great number of people take their lunches along and make a day of it.

They usually arrive early and stay late.

The last time my wife and I went was six years ago, and it was so crowded we had to stand up the whole time we were there. It may interest you to know that right now there is a supper planned to raise money to buy more seats. They're going to hold it in the basement of the B.C.

I would like to say it pains me very much not to be able to go more regularly, but it surely is no lack of desire on my part.

As we grow older, it seems to be more of an effort, particularly in cold weather. If you decide to come down to the campground, perhaps I could go with you the first time you go, sit with you, and introduce you to all the other folks.

Remember, this is a friendly community.

We can only imagine the look of horror on the poor woman's face when she received the letter. But the problem began when she asked the wrong question. And when we ask the wrong question of God, the outcome may be a little more serious than confusion about toilet facilities. In their excellent book *Experiencing God*, Henry Blackaby and Claude King comment on asking the wrong question about God's will:

> What is God's will for my life?—is not the right question. I think the right question is, What is God's will? Once I know God's will, then I can adjust my life to Him. In other words, what is it that God is purposing where I am? Once I know what God is doing, then I know what I need to do. The focus needs to be on God, not my life![5]

What is God's will? A lawyer once asked Jesus that same question. Jesus replied that God's highest will, the greatest commandment, was to "love the Lord your God with all your heart, and with all your soul, and with all your mind." Then He added the second greatest commandment: "You shall love your neighbor as yourself."[6] That covers all the bases; everything else required by God flows from these two dictates. Obedience to the first fills our lives; obedience to the second allows us to overflow with motivation, creativity, and excitement about life. Seeing people motivated, healed, and blessed by our love for them increases our self-value, and that starts the overflow in our lives.

Every decision our teenagers make, therefore, needs to begin with *loving the Lord* and *serving others*. When that's their desire, they have truly made God the master of their lives.

The second M is where teens and adults find their strongest motivation to spring out of bed every day and serve others.

2. What *mission* does the Master want them to accomplish?

Why are so many people so *un*motivated and *un*excited about their jobs or schools? It's usually because this second M isn't as clear in their minds as it needs to be. Helping teens find their mission in life greatly increases their energy level for work.

A life's mission is what God wants us to carry out in order to honor others with our service to them. What do they need that we would love to do for them? What could get us to jump out of bed, excited to be serving others?

I (Greg) spent a great deal of time praying and carefully assessing my interests, skills, and dreams to discover what my life's mission might be. I reasoned that my top interest was to be a lawyer, and I figured I could serve others by helping them resolve their more serious arguments. My dad must have told me a thousand times that I'd make a great lawyer because I was a good negotiator. I had been able to calmly assist in solving many of our own family disputes. I even worked for the Branson, Missouri, prosecuting attorney's office for two summers while attending college.

But something happened to completely change my mission. Before college graduation, I had applied to several law schools. I was determined to keep trying even if I were rejected at each of them. If necessary, I would retake the Law School Aptitude Test or even go to a foreign law school. I was confident, however, that one of the best schools in the U.S. would accept me. Finally, my first letter arrived in the mail. I was shaking as I tore it open, thinking, *This could be it. I'm finally going to law school!*

"Mr. Smalley, we regret to inform you . . ." the letter started. I grew sick to my stomach. After all my college work and the countless hours of filling out the application—one small, disappointing paragraph. I threw the letter away in disgust. But wait—I still had six other possibilities. Surely one of them would accept me! But no. "Mr. Smalley, we regret to inform you . . ." I read six more times. I got so good at recognizing a rejection letter that I could tell simply by the weight of the envelope. I began to wonder why the schools couldn't just say what they really meant: "Dear Mr. Smalley, you're an egg-sucking dog, and we don't like you! How dare you apply to our fine institution? Don't call us, we'll call you!"

Feeling dejected, I nonetheless believed that this was merely a setback and that I would eventually get into a law school. But Dad had a different idea.

I (Gary) had noticed that Greg was spending all his free time helping teenagers at church and counseling them with their parents. He would come home late at night and keep me up for hours telling me how exciting it was to see these teens change and how pleased the parents were about the time he was spending with their kids. Night after night, I'd hear how fulfilled he felt by working with these teens. So I decided to take a gamble late one day when he was in an exceptionally talkative mood. Challenging his mission, I asked, "Greg, have you ever thought of becoming a counselor?"

"Don't try to control my future, Dad," Greg growled. "I've always wanted to be a lawyer, and that's what I'm going to do. Please don't get into it with me tonight."

I was silent for a few seconds, and then I decided to help him face reality. "Son," I said in a soft voice, "you're spending all your free time with kids at church. You're counseling, and you keep telling me how much you love it. Honestly, how much have you really even thought about law school?"

I had simply pointed out the obvious. Once again, however, Greg flared up. After a few more questions, what had started out to be a friendly talk turned into a three-hour argument. It was one of the most intense discussions I've ever been in. I got so confused at one point that *I* almost became convinced to enter law school. But I hung in there and never stopped pointing out what Greg seemed to be happiest doing.

Several weeks later, after Greg met with some other people, he finally came to me and said, "You know, Dad, you're right. I do love helping kids become better individuals, and I love working with their parents. I never thought of it before, but maybe I should look more carefully into counseling."

It's important to point out here that Greg's basic mission had not changed. He still wanted to help people solve their biggest and most important problems. What was shifting was his *method,* the way in which he would accomplish his mission.

Three months later, after a long meeting with his good friend Dr. Gary Oliver, Greg was enrolled in a master's degree program in counseling at Denver Seminary. After graduating, he went on to Rosemead School of Psychology at Biola University in Southern California to earn his doctorate in clinical psychology. He not only loves counseling, but he's also good at it. In fact, he's now one of my mentors.

It's scary, isn't it, how influential we can be in the lives of our teens. We need to be careful what we say to them, because it can change the course of their future. My attitude was that I would support whatever Greg did. I just wanted him to recognize what I saw as his deep interests.

How can young people serve others as an expression of true honor and love? There are literally thousands of possibilities. They could, for example:

- Help them with their physical pain.

- Help them find shelter, like a house they will enjoy.

- Sell products that protect their eyes, ears, etc.

- Protect them from world enemies.

- Build places for them to live or work, like homes or offices.

- Make products that ease their load in some way.

- Produce or sell food to feed them.

- Design or create products that get them where they want to go.

- Sell products to maintain their homes or businesses.

- Bring them enjoyment and encouragement by being an actor or speaker.

- Help them figure out how to love and honor each other more. (This last one is my [Gary's] personal method.)

When teens identify their own way of serving others, they'll also find a higher degree of motivation in life, a greater desire to start learning the knowledge necessary to serve skillfully.

It's important, however, that we don't confuse the "what" question and the "how" question. The two must be answered separately and in order. The "what" (mission) is an overarching theme or broad area like "helping people who are sick." The "how" (method) is any one of hundreds of ways to get our mission accomplished, like being a nurse, doctor, physical therapist, or dentist.

One of the best ways for teens or anyone else to discover their mission is to seek the counsel of friends. A mentor can really help in this area. When I (Gary) was trying to determine my life's mission, I met with several of my closest friends, my family, my pastor, and a few professionals. I kept asking what they saw me doing in life. I especially remember asking a close friend, Jim Stewart, what he thought I should do, and he sealed the decision for me. He said, "I'm looking for someone who desperately wants to help families and couples to stay in love and have more satisfaction in all their relationships. If you feel like God wants you to do this, I'll help support you and Norma in getting started." My heart leaped inside, and the rest is history.

After our teens have chosen their Master and acquired peace about what He wants them to do in serving others, we go to the third M, figuring out how they will accomplish their mission.

3. What *method* will they use to accomplish their mission?

Now we get much more specific. Here is also where our teens choose the type of schooling or specific training they need. For example, if their mission is to help people who are suffering physically, they need to choose a vocation that does that. Here are some additional ideas about matching a mission to a method:

MISSION (what I'll do in life)	METHOD (how I'll do it)
Relieve people of physical pain	Doctor
	Dentist
	Nurse
	Physical therapist
	Hospital administrator
	Pharmacist
	Relief worker
Feed those who are hungry	Missionary
	Restaurant worker
	Grocery store worker
	World hunger relief
Provide shelter for people	Building contractor
	Remodeler
	Interior decorator
	Motel operator
	Builder of inexpensive homes for the poor
Help people spiritually	Missionary
	Missionary pilot
	Preacher
	Chaplain
	Crusade team member
	Film producer
	Evangelist
Help hurting families	Seminar leader
	Pastor
	Mentor for couples
	Psychologist
	Social worker
	Counselor in a hospital
	Author

This list could go on and on, but we trust you get the idea.

Many teens have no real purpose in school. Some attend only because they have to, others because it's the thing to do, and still others because it's fun. But schools were created to help kids get ready for their adult lives in every way. And when our teens know what they want to do with their lives and how they plan to do it, they'll want the knowledge it takes to be successful.

A person's method and even basic mission can change several times over the course of a lifetime, and that's okay. But we always want to have a mission and a method clearly in mind, sticking to them until we become skilled at serving others. We've found that satisfaction in life is directly proportional to how well we serve. We've also learned that when we become good at serving and keep our focus on serving, we're rewarded financially.

4. How will they best *maintain* their mission?

Once our teens have recognized their mission and are actively pursuing some possible methods, they'll begin to see which are most effective and concentrate on those. They also need to learn not to hold too tightly to a particular method because it's only that—a way to reach a goal. As soon as they see their method is no longer as effective as it once was, they should start looking for better methods. It's a tragedy to watch people stay with a method that no longer works just because they're used to it or it's comfortable.

For example, when I (Gary) first started writing books as one method of helping others to keep their love alive and growing, I used typewriters. We usually had about seven typists and four editors. Now we use one computer with the ability to edit, spell check, and find grammatical errors. When I learned that many people would rather watch a video than read a book, we went to the effort and expense to put my seminar on tape. And when some experts suggested we could help even more people through television, I agreed to try offering our materials in that medium even though I found the prospect intimidating at first.

5. Will they find a *mate* who agrees with their mission?

When our teens know their Master, mission, and method, they're much better prepared to decide the type of person with whom they should spend the rest of their life.

As I (Gary) seriously prayed for a wife, I sought a person who wanted to go in the same direction as I felt called of God. I certainly loved Norma—she was my best friend—but I still asked about her own calling to see if we were going in a similar direction. We agreed we fit together like a hand in a glove, and that has turned out to be exactly the case. She has always been involved in my ministries, and she's the CEO of our current ministry. She has not only been a tremendous help through the years, but she has also been my encouragement and special sounding board in most decisions.

In the same way, our teens need to include compatibility with their life's mission and method as one of their key factors in choosing a marriage partner. A good "fit" in this area can be an incredible blessing, a bad "fit," a lifelong source of tension and dissatisfaction.

The Key To Accomplishing the Five M's

To use the five M's effectively in discerning and carrying out God's will, our teens need a character quality illustrated by a boy who happened to be a farmer's nephew. The farmer, wanting to teach his nephew to be responsible, sent him a box of chickens. After reading the cover note, the boy ripped open the box and sent the chickens scattering in all directions. The next day he wrote his uncle, "I chased them all through the neighborhood, but I only got back 11."

A few days later, the uncle phoned and told his nephew, "Talk about persistence! I only sent six!"

When we remain *persistent*, anything can happen. This is the secret to obtaining God's will after it has been discovered. When I (Greg) concluded that God wanted me to become a counselor, I applied to many schools. Although I finally earned my doctorate, I first got rejected by seven graduate programs! It was like the law-school experience all over again. I couldn't understand it. But I firmly believed that God would open a door, so I continued to apply. The good news is that within a month of my first rejection letter, I was accepted by the school from which I eventually graduated.

Let's encourage our teenagers, then, to remain persistent if they fail initially in pursuit of their mission and method. We can tell our own stories of failure. We also recommend the book *Storms of Perfection*, which recounts the stories of hundreds of successful people who all failed miserably in the beginning. Many of those people failed several times before they finally achieved their goals. Persistence can pay off in great ways!

When It's Time to Say "Bon Voyage"

One of the most difficult experiences parents must face is the day that a child leaves the nest. I (Gary) will never forget the day Greg left for college. My emotions felt as if they were on a roller coaster. On the one hand, I was excited for him to have the opportunity to experience college life. I knew he would have a great time. He would finally get to live out the life for which we had prepared him. On the other hand, I was sad about the thought of "losing" one of my best friends.

The night before Greg left, Norma and I gave him a farewell party. We invited over many of his high-school and church friends. Toward the end of the evening, we gathered everyone around the living room and asked each person to say something meaningful to Greg. This was our way of blessing him before we sent him into the world.

The words said that night went well beyond our expectations. Some people recalled humorous incidents they had been through with him, while others told how Greg had influenced their lives. We loved the look on Greg's face as he received the many blessings from his friends and family. It was definitely a night none of us will ever forget.

The "blessing ceremony," as we have come to call that night, was so successful that we've repeated it at other major events. For example, when our three children got married, we had a blessing ceremony at each rehearsal dinner, again with great results. So we encourage all parents to do the same for their teenagers before they leave home. It doesn't have to be a big production. Nor does it have to involve other people. We could just write a letter or have a special family dinner to bless the one who is leaving.

When we remain persistent, anything can happen. This is the secret to obtaining God's will after it has been discovered.

In case you're not familiar with the blessing concept (covered in detail in the book *The Blessing*, by Gary Smalley and Dr. John Trent), let us summarize it here. First, in any way we can find to express it, we need to let our teens know they are highly valuable to us and we are thrilled to have them as our children. We can identify several things about them that make us proud and communicate that in different ways. Norma and I (Gary) wrote a letter to each of our kids telling them exactly why we were proud of them. We gave parties when they left, during which we presented plaques expressing our appreciation of them. Then we wrote letters after they were gone to reinforce our deep joy about who they were and what they could become if they so chose.

We've gone so far as to say that whatever they want to do in the future, we'll always be there for them. We'll support them in any way we can and cheer them on to victory or share their defeats. We don't want even a hint of any question in their minds about how we feel about them. It's our privilege as their parents to give them this extremely important gift of the blessing.

Something that happened to me (Greg) when I was working at a mental hospital illustrates the power of a second type of blessing. During a group meeting, I introduced myself and then fielded questions from the patients. One question was whether I had any children. With pride, I showed a picture of my then-two-year-old daughter, Taylor. Several hours later, I had one of the most meaningful interactions I've ever had with a patient.

Her name was Michele, and she wasn't your typical teenager. Terrible scars covered her arms from where she'd repeatedly tried to kill herself. She had no parents and had been in and out of group homes and hospitals for the past several years. When I first met her, she was under heavy medication and could barely talk. Nevertheless, she was determined to speak with me. "I heard you have a daughter," she announced, "so I want to give you some parenting advice!"

As someone with two master's degrees and a doctorate in psychology, my first thought was, *What could this hurting teenager possibly teach me about parenting?* But I quickly learned that she would become one of my greatest teachers. Our encounter lasted only a few seconds—long enough for her to hand me a small note. Here is the parenting advice I received that day:

> Hi, my name is Michele, and this is what I have to say. Ever since I was a little girl, I spent time with my father on Fridays. Fridays were not just another day of the week for me. It was a special time with my father. We would go places, and it made me feel happy inside to know that my father liked being with me. Sometimes we couldn't go out—but my father always apologized and made it up to me later. Being with my father was very special. He died a few years ago. I truly believe that I would not be in the hospital if he were alive today. When we went out, we talked about my problems and he listened to me. I just want to say if you are a father—have a "Friday" with your daughter.
>
> Michele

Sadly, Michele would never again get to experience a "Friday" with anyone. Several weeks after giving me that note, she took her own life. But she left a small legacy behind—words I'll cherish forever.

As Michele said, regular time spent with our children as they prepare to leave the nest can be a tremendous blessing to them. We might call her "Fridays" a family ritual, which is any activity that can draw people closer together. Researchers Wolin and Bennett have identified three kinds of rituals: family celebrations, family traditions, and patterned interactions.

Family celebrations include holidays and other occasions practiced by a particular culture, such as weddings, religious holidays, Jewish bar mitzvahs, and Thanksgiving. Family traditions are less culture-specific and more peculiar to a given family. Birthdays, anniversaries, and family reunions are examples of these.

The third type of family ritual is patterned interactions. These are the most frequently enacted but perhaps the least planned. They include dinnertime, bedtime routines, and weekend leisure activities.[7] According to Wolin and Bennett, families that have few or no rituals suffer more from the pathologies of our day, such as alcohol and drug abuse, depression, binge eating, and family violence. On the other hand, participating in family rituals reinforces family identity, fosters communication, provides a sense of belonging, and is a way to transmit the family's values, attitudes, and goals. Finally, rituals help members learn crucial family rules.[8]

We parents can use all three kinds of family rituals to bless our teenagers, both while they're still at home and as they prepare to leave the nest. Such experiences will bond us to one another for a lifetime.

As we come to the end of this book, we would like to ask: What are the levels of honor and anger in your home today? What's the state of your relationship with your teenager? What are you prepared to do in the next week and the next month to insure that when the time comes, your child will leave home in honor?

Put another way, what kind of "memory book" are you writing together as a family? Could you and your spouse and children spend an evening of sharing and laughter saying, "Remember when . . ."? Does your book contain any stories that get better with the telling? Do the pages have vivid color pictures of crazy dilemmas, rainy nights in a tent, midnight church services, picnics at the park, or bedtime stories? Or is it filled with gray stories of frustration, bitterness, and disappointment? Whichever way it reads, your family story can only be written once!

Notes

Chapter One

1. "Be angry, and yet do not sin; do not let the sun go down on your anger, and do not give the devil an opportunity" (Ephesians 4:26-27). For an in-depth understanding of anger, see Dr. Gary Oliver and Norm Wright's excellent book entitled *When Anger Hits Home*.
2. J. Barker, *Paradigms* (New York: Harperbusiness, 1993).
3. J. B. Kupersmidt, M. R. Burchinal, S. S. Leff, and C.J. Patterson, "A Longitudinal Study of Perceived Support and Conflict with Parents from Middle Childhood Through Early Adolescence" (paper presented at the meeting of the Society for Research on Adolescence, Washington, D.C., March 1992).
4. M. Elias, "Couples In Pre-Kid, No-Kid Marriages Happiest," *USA Today*, 12 August 1997, sec. D, p. 1.
5. J. H. Block, J. Block, and P. F. Gjerde, "The Personality of Children Prior to Divorce," *Child Development* 57 (1986): 827-40.
6. B. Burman, R. S. John, and G. Margolin, "Effects of Marital and Parent-Child Relations on Children's Adjustment," *Journal of Family Psychology* 1 (1987): 91-108.
7. Matthew 22:37-40.
8. James 1:2-3.

Chapter Two

1. *The Denver Post.*
2. Matthew 22:37-39.
3. Psalm 127:3.
4. Matthew 6:21.
5. D. Kalmuss, "The Intergenerational Transmission of Marital Aggression," *Journal of Marriage and the Family* 46 (1984): 11-19.
6. K. D. Craig, "Social Modeling Influences: Pain in Context," in *The Psychology of Pain*, ed. R. A. Sternbach (New York: Raven Press, 1986), 67-95.
7. M. Elias, "Kids Tend to Take After Oft-Divorced Parents," *USA Today*, 11 August 1997, sec. D, p. 1.

Chapter Three

1. John Santrock, *Adolescence* (Dubuque, Iowa: Times Mirror Higher Education Group, Inc., 1996), 178.
2. Gary Oliver, *Real Men Have Feelings, Too* (Chicago: Moody Press, 1993), 100.
3. Ephesians 6:4.
4. Gary Smalley, "Hidden Keys to Loving Relationships" (seminar manual, 1988), 32.
5. Proverbs 15:1.
6. Gary Smalley, *The Key to Your Child's Heart* (Waco, Tex.: Word Books, 1984), 27-28.
7. James 1:20.
8. This is a clear message throughout the Scriptures. See, for example, Matthew 6:14-15; John 20:23; and Colossians 3:13.

Chapter Four

1. H. Markman, S. Stanley, and S. L. Blumberg, *Fighting for Your Marriage* (San Francisco: Jossey-Bass, 1994), 28.
2. These studies found that this type of communication produced very positive results concerning parent and adolescent conflict: S. L. Foster, R. J. Prinz, and K. D. O'Leary, "Impact of Problem-Solving Communication Training and Generalization Procedures on Family Conflict," *Child and Family Behavior Therapy* 5 (1986): 1-23; A. L. Robin, "A Controlled Evaluation of Problem-Solving Communication Training with Parent-Adolescent Conflict," *Behavior Therapy* 12 (1981): 593-609; S. Stern, "A Group

Cognitive-Behavioral Approach to the Management and Resolution of Parent-Adolescent Conflict" (Ph.D. diss., University of Chicago, 1984).

Chapter Five

1. D. Curran, *Traits of a Healthy Family* (New York: Winston Press, 1983), 23, 26-27.
2. John Santrock, *Adolescence* (Dubuque, Iowa: Times Mirror Higher Education Group, Inc., 1996), 564.
3. L. Steinberg and A. Levine, *You and Your Adolescent* (New York: Harper Perennial, 1990).
4. Proverbs 19:2.
5. Proverbs 13:10.
6. Proverbs 17:17.
7. Proverbs 29:17.
8. Proverbs 12:1.
9. Proverbs 13:18.
10. Proverbs 15:32.
11. Hebrews 12:11, NIV.
12. Ecclesiastes 4:9, 12.

Chapter Six

1. For a discussion regarding mission statements, refer to chapter 13 or to Stephen Covey's book *Seven Habits of Highly Effective Families*.
2. This article repeatedly saved our necks in two important ways: First, it made us more aware of honoring each other so we wouldn't offend each other. Second, when we noticed anyone hurting or avoiding others by being silent, we would ask if there was anything wrong. Time after time, the offended person would say, "Nothing is wrong." But because we were all extra sensitive toward each other, we could tell when someone was hurt, frustrated, or feeling unsafe. We would pursue the one hurting, and inevitably the person would admit his hurt, and we could clear up the offense. This article kept us free from anger and therefore more open to each other and to God.
3. R. B. Stuart, "Behavioral Contracting Within the Families of Delinquents," *Journal of Behavioral Therapy and Experimental Psychiatry* 2 (1971): 3.
4. John Santrock, *Adolescence* (Dubuque, Iowa: Times Mirror Higher Education Group, Inc., 1996), 179.

5. National Association of Secondary School Principals and Sylvan Learning Centers, "Voices from the Classroom."
6. V. A. Basalel and N. H. Azrin, "The Reduction of Parent-Youth Problems by Reciprocity Counseling," *Behaviour Research and Therapy* 19 (1981): 297-301.
7. W. DeRisi and G. Butz, *Writing Behavioral Contracts: A Case Simulation Practice Manual* (Champaign, Ill.: Research Press, 1975).
8. Ibid.
9. Ibid.
10. R. B. Stuart et al., "An Experiment in Social Engineering in Serving the Families of Predelinquents," *Journal of Abnormal Child Psychology* 4 (1976): 243-61.
11. D. Baumrind, "Effective Parenting During the Early Adolescent Transition," in *Advances in Family Research*, vol. 2, eds. P. A. Cowan and E. M. Hetherington (Hillsdale, N.J.: Lawrence, Erlbaum, and Associates, 1991).
12. John Santrock, *Adolescence*, 179.
13. E. H. Erickson, *Identity: Youth and Crisis* (New York: W. W. Norton, 1968); J. J. Padgham and D. A. Blyth, "Dating During Adolescence," in *Encyclopedia of Adolescence*, vol. 1, eds. R. M. Lerner, A. C. Peterson, and J. Brooks-Gunn (New York: Garland, 1991); E. L. Paul and K. M. White, "The Development of Intimate Relationships in Late Adolescence," *Adolescence* 25 (1990): 375-400; B. Roscoe, M. S. Dian, and R. H. Brooks, "Early, Middle, and Late Adolescents' Views on Dating and Factors Influencing Partner's Selection," *Adolescence* 22 (1987): 59-68; J. K. Skipper and G. Nass, "Dating Behavior: A Framework for Analysis and an Illustration," *Journal of Marriage and the Family* 28 (1966): 412-20.
14. T. H. Ollendick and J. A. Cerny, *Clinical Behavioral Therapy with Children* (New York: Plenum Press, 1981), 150.

Chapter Seven

1. G. Armsden and M. R. Greeberg, "The Inventory of Parent and Peer Attachment: Individual Differences and Their Relationship to Psychological Well-Being in Adolescence," *Journal of Youth and Adolescence* 16 (1987): 427-54.
2. J. P. Allen and K. L. Bell, "Attachment and Communication with Parents and Peers in Adolescence" (paper presented at the meeting of the Society for Research in Child Development, Indianapolis, Ind., March 1995).

3. John Santrock, *Adolescence* (Dubuque, Iowa: Times Mirror Higher Education Group, Inc., 1996), 87.

4. Ibid.

5. B. M. Newman and P. R. Newman, *Development Through Life: A Psychosocial Approach* (Pacific Grove, Calif.: Brooks/Cole Publishing Co., 1975), 323.

6. Ibid.

7. John Santrock, *Adolescence*, 87.

8. M. S. Faust, "Somatic Development of Adolescent Girls," *Monographs of the Society for Research in Child Development* 42 (1977): 1; R. M. Malina, "Growth Spurt, Adolescent, II," in *Encyclopedia of Adolescence*, vol. 1, eds. R. M. Lerner, A. C. Petersen, and J. Brooks-Gunn (New York: Garland Publishing, 1991); J. M. Tanner, "Growth Spurt, Adolescent, I," in *Encyclopedia of Adolescence*, vol. 1.

9. John Santrock, *Adolescence*, 91.

10. Ibid., 92.

11. D. N. Ruble and J. Brooks-Gunn, "The Experience of Menarche," *Child Development* 53 (1982): 1557-66; E. B. Grief and K. J. Ulman, "The Psychological Impact of Menarche on Early Adolescent Females: A Review of the Literature," *Child Development* 53 (1982): 1413-30.

12. John Santrock, *Adolescence*, 96.

13. Eastwood Atwater, *Adolescence* (Englewood Cliffs, N.J.: Prentice Hall, 1996), 198.

14. Ibid., 201-2.

15. H. Sebald, "Adolescents' Peer Orientation: Changes in the Support System During the Past Three Decades," *Adolescence* (winter 1989): 936-46.

16. Dolores Curran, *Traits of a Healthy Family* (New York: Winston Press, 1983), 143.

Chapter Eight

1. Romans 5:3-5.

2. Romans 6:1.

3. Dr. William Worden (one of Greg's professors at Rosemead School of Psychology, Biola University) is an expert in grief. He has an excellent book *Grief Counseling & Grief Therapy: A Handbook for the Mental Health Practitioner* that we highly recommend when going through the grief process.

4. Proverbs 17:17.

5. See John 3:16.
6. 1 Peter 5:7.

Chapter Nine

1. C. A. Darling, D. J. Kallen, and J. E. VanDusen, "Sex in Transition, 1900-1984," *Journal of Youth and Adolescence* 13 (1984): 385-99.
2. Centers for Disease Control, *The CDC Survey of Adolescent Sexual Activity* (Atlanta: Centers for Disease Control, January 1992).
3. R. D. Day, "The Transition to First Intercourse among Racially and Culturally Diverse Youth," *Journal of Marriage and the Family* (November 1992): 749-62.
4. J. D. Forrest and S. Singh, "The Sexual Behavior of American Women, 1982-1988," *Family Planning Perspectives* 22, no. 5 (1990): 206-15.
5. Josh McDowell and B. Hostetler, *Right from Wrong* (Dallas: Word Publishing, 1994), 159.
6. J. D. Forrest and S. Singh, "The Sexual Behavior of American Women, 1982-1988," 206-15.
7. A. Thornton and D. Camburn, "Religious Participation and Adolescent Sexual Behavior and Attitudes," *Journal of Marriage and the Family* 51 (August 1989): 651.
8. See 2 Timothy 2:22.
9. Ephesians 4:18-24.
10. H. D. Thornburg, "Sources of Sex Education among Early Adolescents," *Journal of Early Adolescence* 1 (1981): 174.
11. T. D. Fisher, "Family Communication and the Sexual Behavior and Attitudes of College Students," *Journal of Youth and Adolescence* 16 (1987): 481-96; also see N. L. Leland and R. P. Barth, "Characteristics of Adolescents Who Have Attempted to Avoid HIV and Who Have Communicated with Parents about Sex," *Journal of Adolescent Research* 8, no. 1 (1993): 58-76.
12. M. Coleman, L. H. Ganong, and P. Ellis, "Family Structure and Dating Behaviors of Adolescence," *Adolescence* (fall 1985): 537-43.
13. "The Younger, the Sooner," *Youthworker* (spring 1987): 122ff.
14. P. L. East, "The Younger Sisters of Childbearing Adolescents: Their Sexual and Childbearing Attitudes, Expectations, and Behaviors" (paper presented at the meeting of the Society for Research on Adolescence, San Diego, February 1994).
15. See 1 Kings 14:22; Psalm 77:9; Proverbs 30:33; Ecclesiastes 7:9; Isaiah 60:10; Amos 1:11; and Proverbs 29:22.

16. P. H. Dreyer, "Sexuality During Adolescence," in *Handbook of Developmental Psychology,* ed. B. B. Wolman (Englewood Cliffs, N.J.: Prentice Hall, Inc., 1982).

17. Eastwood Atwater, *Adolescence* (Englewood Cliffs, N.J.: Prentice Hall, Inc., 1996), 388.

18. M. Coleman, L. H. Ganong, and P. Ellis, "Family Structure and Dating Behaviors of Adolescence," 537-43.

19. R. Jessor et al., "Time of First Intercourse: A Prospective Study," *Journal of Personality and Social Psychology* 44 (1983): 608-20.

20. N. Gibbs, "How Should We Teach Our Children about Sex?" *Time,* May 24, 1993, 60-66.

21. R. T. Michael et al., *Sex in America* (Boston: Little, Brown, 1994).

22. E. Douvan and Adelson, *The Adolescent Experience* (New York: Wiley, 1966).

23. B. Roscoe, M. S. Dian, and R. H. Brooks, "Early, Middle, and Late Adolescents' Views on Dating and Factors Influencing Partner's Selection," *Adolescence* 22 (1987).

24. N. Gibbs, "How Should We Teach Our Children about Sex?" 60-66.

25. S. Gordon and J. F. Gilgun, "Adolescent Sexuality," in *Handbook of Adolescent Psychology,* eds. V. B. Van Hasselt and M. Hersen (New York: Pergamon, 1987).

26. N. Gibbs, "How Should We Teach Our Children about Sex?" 60-66.

27. P. Y. Miller and W. Simon, "Adolescent Sexual Behavior: Context and Change," *Social Problems* 22 (1974): 58-76.

28. E. Rosenbaum and D. B. Kandel, "Early Onset of Adolescent Sexual Behavior and Drug Involvement," *Journal of Marriage and the Family* 52 (1990): 783-98.

29. W. Furman, E. A. Wehner, and S. Underwood, "Sexual Behavior, Sexual Communication, and Relationship" (paper presented at the meeting of the Society for Research on Adolescence, San Diego, 1994).

30. G. R. Fox, "The Family's Role in Adolescent Sexual Behavior," in *Teenage Pregnancy in a Family Context,* ed. Theodora Ooms (Philadelphia: Temple University Press, 1981).

31. John Santrock, *Adolescence* (Dubuque, Iowa: Times Mirror Higher Education Group, Inc., 1996), 388.

32. C. Cassell, *Swept Away: Why Women Fear Their Own Sexuality* (New York: Simon & Schuster, 1984).

33. D. J. Flannery, D. C. Rowe, and B. L. Gulley, "Impact of Pubertal Status, Timing, and Age on Adolescent Sexual Experience and

Delinquency," *Journal of Adolescent Research* 8 (1993): 21-40.

34. J. Gargiulo et al., "Girls' Dating Behavior as a Function of Social Context and Maturation," *Developmental Psychology* 23 (1987): 730-37.
35. John Santrock, *Adolescence*, 396.
36. Jo Durden-Smith and Diane deSimone, *Sex and the Brain* (New York: Warner Books, 1983), 198.
37. James 1:14-15.
38. See Luke 18.
39. Philippians 4:6.
40. 1 Thessalonians 5:17.
41. Matthew 21:22.
42. See Matthew 7:7-11; Luke 11:9-12; John 14:14; John 16:23; and 1 John 3:22.

Chapter Ten

1. 1 Kings 11:4.
2. 1 Kings 14:21-22.
3. Donald Sloat, *The Dangers of Growing Up in a Christian Home* (Nashville: Thomas Nelson, 1986), 33.
4. Matthew 7:4, NIV.
5. Deuteronomy 6:7.
6. B. Spilka, "Cults, Adolescence, and Religion," in *Encyclopedia of Adolescence*, vol. 1, ed. R. M. Lerner, A. C. Petersen, and J. Brooks-Gunn (New York: Garland Publishing, 1991).
7. G. Gallup and D. Poling, *The Search for America's Faith* (New York: Abingdon, 1980).
8. Matthew 18:6.
9. Matthew 7:25, NIV.
10. 1 Peter 1:6-7.

Chapter Eleven

1. Al Janssen, ed., *Seven Promises of a Promise Keeper* (Colorado Springs, Colo.: Focus on the Family Publishing, 1994), 51.
2. 2 Timothy 2:2.
3. B. Narramore and V. C. Lewis, *Parenting Teens* (Wheaton, Ill.: Tyndale House Publishers, 1992), 152.
4. G. Gallup and D. Poling, *The Search for America's Faith* (New York: Abingdon, 1980).
5. Mark 11:24, NIV.

6. Howard Hendricks and William Hendricks, *As Iron Sharpens Iron* (Chicago: Moody Press, 1995), 63.
7. M. Weiner-Davis, *Divorce Busting* (New York: Fireside, 1992), 65-66.

Chapter Twelve

1. Luke 11:34.
2. Isaiah 1:2-3, NIV.
3. Hebrews 12:5-6.
4. Hebrews 12:11.
5. Luke 15:11-13, NIV.
6. David York and Phyllis York, *Toughlove Solutions* (Garden City, N.Y.: Doubleday & Co., 1984), 54.
7. Proverbs 13:24.
8. Proverbs 29:17.
9. 1 Corinthians 13:4.
10. Matthew 7:1-2, NIV.
11. Grace Methodist Church, "Grace Pulpit," Atlanta.
12. Proverbs 17:17.
13. D. James Kennedy, *Your Prodigal Child* (Nashville: Thomas Nelson, 1988).
14. See Matthew 6:14-15; John 20:23; and Colossians 3:13.
15. Romans 12:9.
16. Samuel Johnson, *The Rambler.*
17. Matthew 18:21.
18. Ephesians 4:26-27.
19. Because it's so traumatic when a teenager walks away from our beliefs and faith, we recommend the following excellent books that focus on helping parents deal with a rebellious teenager: *Leaving the Light On,* by Gary Smalley and Dr. John Trent; *Joy That Lasts,* by Gary Smalley; *The Gift of the Blessing,* by Gary Smalley and Dr. John Trent; *Your Prodigal Child,* by D. James Kennedy; *Parenting Isn't for Cowards,* by Dr. James Dobson; *Toughlove Solutions,* by David and Phyllis York; *When Your Kids Aren't Kids Anymore,* by Jerry and Mary White; and *Keeping the Doors Open,* by Peter Lord.
20. 1 Corinthians 10:32, NIV.
21. Luke 15:6.

Chapter Thirteen

1. Dr. Deborah Tannan, *You Just Don't Understand* (New York: Ballantine, 1990).

2. An excellent resource for more detail on healthy family bound-aries—how to honor one another in ways that allow each of us to remain individuals—is the book *Boundaries*, by Dr. John Townsend and Dr. Henry Cloud. It's worth reading once a year.

3. P. Y. Miller and W. Simon, "Adolescent Sexual Behavior: Context and Change," *Social Problems* 22 (1974): 58-76.

4. Psalm 103:1.

5. Henry Blackaby and Claude King, *Experiencing God* (Nashville: Broadman & Holman, 1994), 14.

6. Matthew 22:37-38.

7. S. J. Wolin and L. A. Bennett, "Family Rituals," *Family Process* 23 (1984): 401-20.

8. Ibid.

Other Faith and Family Strengtheners
From Focus on the Family ®

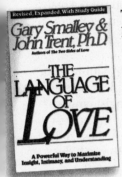

The Language of Love

Do you say one thing, yet mean another? Are you often misunderstood? You *can* bring understanding and intimacy to all of your relationships. And this book by relationship "experts" Gary Smalley and John Trent shows you how "emotional word pictures" will convey what you truly mean in an unmistakable way. Paperback.

The Two Sides of Love

Do you long for deeper affection from the people you care about most? Do you wonder what it takes to make commitments *really* last? Discover the key to balancing love's "hard" and "soft" sides in this book from Gary Smalley and John Trent. You'll soon find you're forging closer, stronger relationships with the ones you love. Paperback.

LifeTraining

Help your teens (and the rest of the family!) establish a strong, lasting faith in God. This unique devotional from popular author, speaker, and camp director Joe White equips parents and kids with tools to strengthen their spiritual foundation. There's even a section devoted entirely to memorization and 100 Bible verses no Christian should leave home without! Hardcover.

• • •

Look for these special books in your Christian bookstore or request a copy by calling 1-800-A-FAMILY (1-800-232-6459). Friends in Canada may write Focus on the Family, P.O. Box 9800, Stn. Terminal, Vancouver, B.C. V6B 4G3 or call 1-800-661-9800.

Visit our Web site (www.family.org) to learn more about the ministry or find out if there is a Focus on the Family office in your country.

Welcome to the Family!

Whether you received this book as a gift, borrowed it from a friend, or purchased it yourself, we're glad you read it! It's just one of the many helpful, insightful, and encouraging resources produced by Focus on the Family.

In fact, that's what Focus on the Family is all about—providing inspiration, information, and biblically based advice to people in all stages of life. Started in 1977 by Dr. James Dobson, a psychologist who was concerned by the pressures facing the American family, the now international organization exists for one purpose, and one purpose only: to encourage and strengthen individuals and families through the life-changing message of Jesus Christ.

For more information about the ministry, or if we can be of help to your family, simply write to Focus on the Family, Colorado Springs, CO 80995 or call 1-800-A-FAMILY (1-800-232-6459). Friends in Canada may write Focus on the Family, P.O. Box 9800, Stn. Terminal, Vancouver, B.C. V6B 4G3 or call 1-800-661-9800. You may also visit our Web site—www.family.org—to learn more about the ministry or to find out if there is a Focus on the Family office in your country.

•   •   •

"Love Is a Decision"

Whether you're married or single, a parent or grandparent, there's never been a more perfect opportunity to learn to strengthen *all* your relationships than the "Love Is a Decision" seminar!

Featuring best-selling author and president of Today's Family Gary Smalley and his two sons, Greg and Michael, this exciting, two-day conference reveals ways to divorce-proof your marriage, resolve conflict, and nurture loving, lasting relationships.

For more information, contact Today's Family, 1482 Lakeshore Drive, Branson, MO 65616. Or call 1-800-84-TODAY (1-800-848-6329).